MW00964639

Additional Praise for *Social Media Strategies for Professionals and Their Firms*

"Passion plus depth of knowledge combined with excellent writing is destined to produce a great read. Michelle combines all of these attributes in *Social Media Strategies for Professionals and Their Firms*. Michelle understands the importance of how social media is changing the way knowledge workers communicate and collaborate. Bridging the gap between social media and our knowledge economy, the advice contained in this book will enable professional firms to utilize these dynamic new technologies to leverage their intellectual capital, thereby creating new levels of effectiveness and wealth for their stakeholders. An inspiring and essential read for any professional firm leader."
—Ronald J. Baker
Founder, VeraSage Institute (verasage.com), Author, *Implementing Value Pricing: A Radical Business Model for Professional Firms*

"A candid approach to addressing professional service firms' social media pain points (e.g. ROI, Policy) combined with a critical strategic view and loads of practical nuts and bolts explanations on how to get 'out there.' *Social Media Strategies for Professionals and Their Firms* is a must-read for every partner and marketing director—even social media 'veterans' will find fresh ideas. Brilliant advice, brilliantly delivered."
—Debra Helwig
Marketing Communications Manager, IGAF Worldwide
Author, "Service Minded" (http://debrahelwig.wordpress.com)

"Michelle Golden has crisply demonstrated why firms must have a participative social media strategy. The ROI (Return On Ideas) upon reading this excellent book begins the moment you put it down and engage your customers, your prospects, your team members, and your life as you reap the benefits of Ms. Golden's wisdom."
—Daniel D. Morris, CPA
Senior Partner, Morris + D'Angelo, Not Just Another CPA Firm®
Silicon Valley, California

"Today's professionals constantly hear that they 'have to be' part of the bewildering and always-changing social media landscape; but rarely does anyone tell them how or why. Michelle's book answers those two critical questions. This comprehensive, one-stop resource clears away the clutter and gives readers practical, principled, reliable guidance towards a mastery of social media and the benefits it can provide."
—Jordan Furlong
Partner, Edge International
Publisher, law21.ca

"Michelle Golden's writing has resonated with professional service audiences for many years. While many marketers 'talk the talk,' Michelle speaks from experience as a pioneer actively engaged online as the Web evolved from a static medium to an interactive one. She first advocated the business advantages of a great Web site, then blogging, and now *Social Media Strategies for Professionals and Their Firms* is here to help professionals navigate their participation on social networks. I am very excited about this book's release, and have no doubt lawyers and accountants alike will find it to be a valuable resource."
—Steve Matthews
Principal, Stem Legal Web Enterprises Inc. (stemlegal.com)

Social Media Strategies for Professionals and Their Firms

The Guide to Establishing Credibility and Accelerating Relationships

MICHELLE GOLDEN

WILEY

John Wiley & Sons, Inc.

Published by John Wiley & Sons, Inc., Hoboken, New Jersey.

Published simultaneously in Canada.

For general information on our other products and services or for technical support, please contact our Customer Care Department within the United States at (800) 762-2974, outside the United States at (317) 572-3993 or fax (317) 572-4002.

Wiley also publishes its books in a variety of electronic formats. Some content that appears in print may not be available in electronic books. For more information about Wiley products, visit our web site at www.wiley.com.

Library of Congress Cataloging-in-Publication Data:

Golden, Michelle.
   Social media strategies for professionals and their firms : the guide to establishing credibility and accelerating relationships/Michelle Golden.
      p. cm.
   Includes index.
   ISBN 978-0-470-63310-6 (hardback); 978-0-470-93389-3 (ebk); 978-0-470-93390-9 (ebk); 978-0-470-93391-6 (ebk)
   1. Internet marketing.   2. Social media–Economic aspects.   3. Electronic commerce.   4. Success in business.   I. Title.
   HF5415.1265.G63 2010
   658.8'72–dc22

                                                                    2010028561

Printed in the United States of America.

10 9 8 7 6 5 4 3 2 1

For my children: Jared, Alex, Peter, and Gwen,
I love you more than words can say.

Contents

Foreword

What a remarkable phenomenon. It took centuries to go from the invention of the printing press to today's *New York Times*. It took less than a decade for what we now call the social media to destroy—or seriously damage—the concept of print or hard copy communication. Print publications, the long traditional purveyors of both news and advertising, are now urgently seeking a new relevance, as newspapers and magazines seem to be disappearing before our very eyes.

It took less time than that to substantially alter the nature of professional services marketing—to change marketing communication from the marketer assaulting the prospective clientele, to making marketing a dialogue between buyer and seller. This despite both the innovative process of the internet and social media and their complexities.

Part of the phenomenon is that so much of the social media began on college campuses, as ways for young people to communicate with one another in a social context, and then went on to become significant business tools that have been adopted by the very same professionals who said—as the once-managing partner of Price Waterhouse once put it not that long ago—"We will advertise over my dead body." He did not live to see the emergence of social media, which would have undoubtedly upset him.

An old expression that seems, in this new environment, to have taken on new significance, is "learning curve," which is relevant in the new social media. As new media become more ubiquitous, and as their use as marketing devices become more complex, and as the uses of the media incite stronger competitiveness, the learning curve becomes longer and a bit harder. In this new media, rapid evolution plays a large part, as each day brings new innovation. The Internet each day brings new tips and advice and instructions—much of it shallow and made obsolete by the next day's innovation. It's an interesting irony that many of the guidebooks on social media still come from printing presses. And as with so much instructional literature, they tend to deal with the mechanics, and too often, miss the rationale of the techniques of social media. To the older marketer or lawyer or accountant, this can be more frustrating than instructional.

And so the blessing of this book. It's insightful—a history, a philosophy, a context, and an intelligent and sustaining analysis of the process behind Facebook, Twitter, LinkedIn, the blog, and the Internet itself. Oh, yes—and the how-to. It's a total immersion in this new world of dialogue marketing, and marketing by interaction with the prospective clientele—of talking with the prospect rather than merely talking at the prospect. It is thoughtful, and for the non-techie, totally comprehensible.

Michelle Golden could very well have written this book from her own vast experience, yet she is smart enough to draw upon the observations of others, since this is a very large subject, with a wide range of points of view. (Significantly, the extensive lists of chapter-by-chapter endnotes are mostly dated in this decade.) The result is marvelously comprehensive. It is total immersion at its best.

No, it's not a dull graduate thesis. It's a vibrant tour of a new landscape—a new environment. You enter with an explanation of the development and evolution of social media, then go through a discussion of communication strategy and its relation to new media, then to a discussion of social media and business purpose, then to its mechanics, then to its role in marketing and its strategy, and finally to the basics of its environment. You come out in the end knowledgeable, and likely, wiser, about social media. It becomes a useful tool in your marketing structure. You are armed, and need bring only the imagination to use social media competitively.

One other thing about this book. It's timely. It will not go quickly stale, as so many contemporary how-to books do in this rapidly changing environment. May I be permitted to say that Michelle Golden has done a brilliant, magnificent job?

Bruce W. Marcus, Editor
The Marcus Letter On Professional Services Marketing

Introduction

At the core, I'm a practical person with a big-picture goal of increasing the profitability of professional firms, and that's how I broach the subject of *Social Media Strategies for Professionals and Their Firms*. It's equally relevant for any size firm, from a sole practitioner to the largest professional firms in the world.

This book discusses practice growth for professionals who provide advice, counsel, and ideas to others. These valuable offerings are labeled by practitioners themselves as mere "services," when what they *really* are is the conveyance of knowledge accumulated from years of practical (and impractical) experience, on top of years of education. Sure, you're doing someone a service, but your actual offering is knowledge and its skillful application—like a surgeon knowing exactly where to cut and, just as importantly, where not to.

Traditional corporate marketing techniques—interruption and passive advertising—simply do not do you and your "knowledge offering" justice. Most advertising and public relations campaigns, as well as sponsorships, brochures, and brochure-ware Web sites (Web 1.0) merely bark "we're here" messages. They accomplish little with regard to illustrating to audiences the true differentiator of *your* knowledge: that it comes from *you*. But another method does.

How will a prospective buyer of the benefits of your knowledge know, or at least reasonably estimate, that *your* deliverable, and the style in which you deliver it, is what they want or need?

Demonstrating your credibility and unique nature are key. Way back in the era before *Bates v. State Bar of Arizona*[1] (and the subsequent lifting of ethical restrictions for lawyers and accountants to advertise) this was achieved the old-fashioned way: via personal interaction and conversations.

In a surprisingly enduring article written by Bruce Marcus[2] shortly after *Bates*, he describes the root of marketing: ". . . every professional must recognize that in every relationship with a client or prospective client, in every contact, in every activity, there is an element of practice development."

These interactions were, and still are, "relationship marketing" in its purest form. These conversations tend to be one prospect or customer at a time, so conducting many is quite time consuming. Plus, earning the chance to even have this sort of personal conversation sometimes takes substantial patience and effort, especially to move a discussion from broad topics to the other person's needs, and then to your knowledge or expertise.

After 1977's changes to ethics restrictions, firms began to dip their toes in some traditional corporate-type marketing activities in hopes of doing some of this conversing en masse. But professionals were relatively slow to adopt traditional marketing tactics, and did so with notable resistance. Marketing personnel and consultants struggled to help firms become comfortable with formal corporate messaging. Important point: professionals weren't immediately comfortable with corporate-speak or brochure-type lingo (aka fluff or gobbledygook)—their instincts were actually right on.

Even ten years after *Bates*, an article in *Minnesota Lawyer*[3] magazine implored lawyers to understand that brochures, though a departure from the (pre-*Bates*) "'old school' approach to client development" were "sales tools" that "if done well, summarize the essence of your firm." Firms were urged to use brochures and, later, their offspring, brochure-ware (Web 1.0) Web sites, in their business development efforts. The real problem is that these no longer work, if they ever really did at all.

And now that firms are finally on board with formal corporate messaging, we strategic marketing advisors must deliver the unwelcome news that most traditional forms of marketing are proving ineffective, particularly formal corporate messaging. The marketer's job now is to persuade their firms to abandon this approach to marketing and, indeed, return to relationship marketing. The welcome news is that technology now enables us to conduct relationship marketing on a much larger scale via the use of online Web applications frequently referred to as social networking tools in a "space" referred to vaguely as social media. In this space, the one-to-one conversations that are still so important in marketing can happen between you and multiple other people, *simultaneously.*

When you shift your thinking about what you think "marketing" should be from generic corporate-speak broadcasting to providing focused evidence of your credibility while simultaneously sharing glimpses of your personality—your humanness—you find you're able to achieve an entirely different result from your marketing efforts. Practitioners are experiencing results that include building deeper relationships more quickly, with less face time. Approaches are now less random and more strategic because social media tools are more conducive to specialty-based marketing than general marketing. Practitioners are able to gain credibility among certain targeted groups of people through sharing relevant information—the most effective strategies are often, but not always, built around content delivery.

More importantly, social media can reduce your time, energy, and expense in achieving your marketing objectives—and can more consistently leverage marketing across all levels of your firm so you and your practice aren't so distinctly separated into "rainmakers" and "nonrainmakers."

This book explores different purposes behind using the social Web to supplement your business development efforts and, perhaps, to even become the core of your marketing strategies. Depending on the nature of the practice and the personalities of the individual practitioners, there is potential for a professional firm's marketing efforts to center around content that is housed online and disseminated via the social Web.

The goal of *Social Media Strategies for Professionals and their Firms* is to provide several specific ways for professionals to have a *more effective online presence,* whether it's your entire marketing platform or simply a component of it. You will understand how to integrate the social Web into broad firm- or niche-level marketing plans, weaving social media into more traditional forms of marketing. You'll also come away with an understanding of which of today's tools suit your purpose and style best, as well as what it takes to succeed with each medium.

I've set out to provide you with a strong understanding of the advantages social media bring to your firm's marketing efforts and to the business development role of the individual practitioner. If you weren't already keen to enter the realm of social media, it's my greatest professional hope that this book will inspire you to give it a try.

How to Use This Book

Ultimately, this book is intended to provide specific, quick-start "how to" information in the HOW and TIPS sections for those busy individuals eager to jump in. And to help you be as *effective* as possible in your social media use, I provide a WHY section, rich with detailed strategic ideas and guidance.

Whichever group you fall into, quickstarter or planner, the initial WHAT section is recommended for all readers because it contains valuable social media fundamentals for professionals and their firms.

Feel free to flip around in the book—reading from front to back isn't necessary. You'll find abundant cross-referencing to other chapters to help you find supplemental information on related topics.

Social media tools change constantly—faster than any prior marketing tools in existence—thus writing a book about something sure to expire soon was daunting, to say the least. My approach therefore was to focus on purpose and strategy. When it comes to the "how" section, I do go into some descriptions of how to use the tools to the extent needed to convey "why" I'm making a particular recommendation. But even if the location of a feature in LinkedIn or Twitter changes, for instance, by the time you read this, the intent discussed herein should still be applicable.

Further, since some details referenced in this book are certain to change before the book even prints, a delightful aspect of social media is that it enables the rapid sharing of supplemental information. An ongoing resource for new information, tips, and ideas regarding social media as well as practice management and marketing are found on my blog at goldenpractices.com.

I'd love to hear from you to discuss any aspect of this book, or questions you might have. I can be reached at michelle@goldenpractices.com, on twitter (@michellegolden), LinkedIn at www.linkedin.com/in/michelle-golden, or my Facebook company page: www.facebook.com/GoldenPractices.

I hope to "see" you around on the social Web.

Acknowledgments

I wouldn't do what I do or know what I know without the honor and experience of working and talking with brilliant people every single day. Because I speak professionally and work privately with a number of professional firms and their associations, it is inevitable that some of the examples cited and people mentioned within this book are friends and customers. I tell you this in the interest of full disclosure and to provide context behind my acknowledgments.

My first thanks go to the brilliant Mr. Bruce Marcus for writing my very thoughtful (and humbling) foreword. Bruce, you are a true thought-leader in professional services—far beyond marketing, as it *must* be for marketing to succeed. Further, you are a remarkable example of the wisdom of keeping an open mind and challenging the why behind the what. And I am beyond delighted that you offered, on LinkedIn no less, to review this book when I mentioned writing it. Having read some of your past book reviews, this was a little scary, I'm not going to lie. Thus, that you found the book worthy of contributing a foreward means more to me than you'll ever know. Thank you so very much.

I am grateful for the opportunity to write this book and for that I owe an enormous thank you to David Pugh, then acquiring editor, and now associate publisher of John Wiley & Sons. And my appreciation goes to Meg Freeborn, my developmental editor, who improved this book in many ways. Thank you both, and, David, I'm so glad you discovered my blog—this book's existence proves that social media works!

Success with blogging and other social media would never have happened without the support, friendship, and link-love(!) of these fellow bloggers and writers: Stephanie West Allen, Allan Boress, Bill Carlino, Tracy Coenen, Liz Gold, Charles Green, Jim Hassett, Debra Helwig, Arnie Herz, Matt Homann, Dennis Howlett, Dan Hull, Dianna Huff, Tom Kane, Rita Keller, Dennis Kennedy, Patrick Lamb, Suzanne Lowe, Patrick McKenna,

David Maister, Bruce Marcus, Steve Matthews, Mark Merenda, Tom Mighell, Rob Millard, Kevin O'Keefe, Barbara Walters Price, Gerry Riskin, Mike Sansone, David Meerman Scott, Jay Shepherd, Allison Shields, Thom Singer, Rick Telberg, Joel Ungar, Howard Wolosky, and the wonderful folks behind the Stark County Law Library Weblog. My heartfelt appreciation goes to the thousands of blog readers, blog authors, Twitterers, and Facebookers who read my content, expand upon it, share it, and allow me do the same with your content. This book would not exist without you.

I am grateful for wonderful customers and friends in the professions— in addition to those named above—from whom I continue to learn so much about the practical application and value of social media and business networks—both my own and theirs: Jim Baalmann, Lisa Benson, Ruth Binger, Heidi Brundage, Gale Crosley, Becky DaVee, Scott Heintzelman, Jennifer Hertzig, Tom Hood, Mark Koziel, Chris Laughton, Karen Love, Eric Majchrzak, Erin McClafferty, Kevin Mead, Rob Nance, William Newman, Paul Neiffer, Michael Platt, Mitch Reno, Jim Rodgers, Andrew Rose, Rebecca Ryan, Bill Sheridan, Sean Smith, René Stranghoner, Joel Ungar, Tracy Crevar Warren, Howard Wilkinson and crew, and numerous admirable colleagues from Association for Accounting Marketing's Discussion List and the original (free) LawMarketing ListServ.

A special thanks to Sue Sassmann, whose radiant smile and incredibly positive attitude made each day in the office a joy as she worked so well beside me for several years—it was an honor to work with you.

Also, a heartfelt thank you to my International Association of Facilitators (IAF) friends, who inspire and sustain me: John Butcher, Dominic Fewer, Cameron Fraser, Taralee Hammond, Lynne Roth, and Christopher Whitnall. Dom and Taralee, truly, without our long talk in Vancouver, this book would not be.

Many, many thanks to my VeraSage Institute colleagues: Scott Abbott, Ron Baker, Justin Barnett, Peter Byers, Daryl Golemb, Brendon Harrex, Paul Kennedy, Ed Kless, Chris Marston, Tim McKey, Dan Morris, Tim Williams, and Yan Zhu, for teaching and giving in ways that definitely can't be measured, for the best things truly cannot. A special acknowledgement is necessary for my late fellow Fellow, Paul O'Byrne, whose rich friendship, "humour," and incredible passion for life have truly changed mine. I love you and miss you, Paul.

What would a writer be without the support and encouragement to think harder and push to a level deeper than she ever thought possible? I owe an enormous debt of gratitude to this handful of very special people. I can always count on my wise and refreshingly outspoken friend and mentor, Melinda Guillemette, to tell me the truth even when it's hard to hear—I value this, and you, immensely! Mark Bailey and his lovely wife, Janice, inspire and support me with their generosity of spirit (and home) as they nurture my pursuit of intellectual stimulation and emotional satisfaction. My beloved friend, Debra Helwig, a gifted writer, consummate professional and devoted mommy, moves me to work hard at becoming a stronger writer _and_ a better person. Plus, she has that gift I've only seen in Southern women—the ability to tell you you're a nonsensical mess in such a way that it feels like high praise. And my dynamic young friend Stacy Soefer, in her passionate support, motivates me to work harder, teach more, and pause often to laugh and enjoy life—we should all have a younger mentor, too! And how I admire my brilliant, driven friend Ron Baker who challenges me constantly in oh-so-many ways. He insists that my arguments and logic be sound, and teaches me that there is both honor and value in losing an argument—that acquiescing having learned something new is a thing of great beauty. Thank you, dear friends—you mean the world to me.

And most of all, thank you to my family. Mom and Lou, thank you for teaching me to love thinking, reading, and writing. And also for always praising my creativity and writing so that I could believe in my ability to communicate—I'm positive I wouldn't enjoy writing and speaking so much if I hadn't carried forward such good feelings about it from my childhood. Dad and Roseman, thank you for your amazing love and support each and every day. You are powerful role models in word and deed; I'm so proud to be your daughter. Grandma Flo, you are tops! I hope to be even half the grandparent you are. Thank you for your influence in your love of words and your love of family—I cherish you.

To my children, Jared, Alex, Peter, and Gwen, thank you for your patience and understanding with my work schedule and travel over the years, and especially during the months this book was unfolding—missed games, events, and a mentally half-present mom is unbearably tough—you've been troupers. To my daughter-in-law, Melissa, soon-to-be mother of a precious grandchild, thank you for adding, so beautifully, to our family. And to my husband, Nick, my enormous gratitude for your encouragement over the years and your support on the homefront.

PART I

WHAT

What Firms Need to Know
about Social Media

CHAPTER 1

Defining and Understanding "Social Media"

Social media are a continually changing set of tools (and their users) that facilitate online relationships and information sharing. It's also important to understand what it is *not*: "social media" is not a strategy. Social media are plural and, individually or collectively, they are *not strategies*. Further, social media applications, in and of themselves, are neither *initiatives* nor *tactics*.

Strategy is "a course of action, including the specification of resources required, to achieve a specific objective."[1] Strategies are achieved through one or more initiatives that involve various tactical steps that use specific resources. Social media tools are the resources. How, exactly, you elect to use a specific tool (compare a social media application to a telephone) within an initiative comprises your tactical approach. Measuring a tool's effectiveness can only be accomplished at the initiative level, not the tool level. A lot of people get hung up on return on investment (ROI) calculations to justify their social media efforts. However, asking "What is the ROI of social media?" is a lot like asking "What is the ROI of your phone?" The obvious response regarding either tool is, "that depends entirely on what I'm using it for."

"Interacting with clients on LinkedIn" or "friending potential hires on Facebook" are not adequately defined tactical approaches. That is like saying, "Call clients on the phone." Why? To achieve what? A plan must be much more specific than this in order to be effective in business development with measurable outcomes.

The pressure for firms to get on board with a social media presence is mounting. From multiple sources, professionals are advised that their firms "must be there" lest they miss out. Firms and their marketers report they feel rushed to dive in to implement a "Facebook strategy" or "LinkedIn strategy." While I applaud the attention now given to social media, I caution against approaching the mere use of Facebook, LinkedIn, or any other tool, as the objective rather than being clear, in advance, about what you are ultimately seeking to accomplish with its use. Explore Part II: WHY for concrete ideas and tactical approaches that might fit as integrated components of your firm's broader strategies and marketing initiatives.

If it seems like semantics when I insist on separating *tool* from *strategy* in defining social media, think of its importance this way: It is falsely reassuring for firms to think they have a strategy when they merely have a vague reference to tools that could be used any number of ways—effectively or ineffectively. You would no more label social media a "strategy" than you would label the local Rotary Club or Chamber of Commerce a strategy.

Which information gets shared and how it's shared will vary by tool; with whom relationships are developed, and for what purpose, will vary by goal. These four aspects drive your social media strategy.

How Misconceptions Led to Misuse

The social media tools covered in this book, with the exception of LinkedIn, were *not* developed for the purpose of marketing. They were developed for communicating.

It didn't take long for corporations and marketers to smell opportunity and start flooding these communication channels with their broadcast messaging. But broadcast messages offend the online community. Heed this. Learn what the marketers from top brand managers to newbie do-it-yourselfers are learning: To succeed in social media, respect the aversion of "the community" to advertising, PR spin, and blatant self-promotion. Adopt the approach the online community respects: usefulness, authenticity, altruism, and validation by outside parties.

Social media are not *just* the tools or mediums, for they could not exist without their users—not a nameless, faceless TV or radio audience, but real people with whom ongoing relationships are possible. The relationship aspect is the "social" part and the communication vehicle is the "media" part. This doesn't seem much different than a telephone—a tool, and group to call—except that with social media, a level of complexity surrounds the ongoing visibility of the conversation, the open access to it, and the appropriate tone of use.

The tools in this book are used most effectively to support strategies where you've already concluded there are distinct benefits to online relationship development, whether or not you intend to share content (such as with blogging) as well. For professionals and firms, adding a content element exponentially increases the value of social media efforts because your expertise is knowledge based.

Interestingly and unfortunately, many professional firms take the opposite approach: content sharing *without* relationship development. This suboptimal approach is evident in the many blogs by authors who only post to their blogs—they don't read other blogs or comment on them—they don't participate in the community. True content marketing is when content and relationships go hand-in-hand.

I believe it's due in part to misunderstandings about the definition of social media—not understanding that relationship part—that firms mistakenly implement social media tools as a vehicle for one-way content delivery (aka "broadcasting") versus two-way channels that enable relationships to grow. This is severely underutilizing these tools and, worse, using social media "one way" sends negative messages suggesting the firm and its people are (a) inaccessible, (b) uninterested in relationships, or (c) unaware of social media behaviors—or all three. In other words, the firm doesn't get it.

I hesitated to present these negative message consequences of social media misuse because firms might refrain from using social media if they fear they could look bad by doing it wrong. But on further thought, I don't believe this is the primary hindrance to social media use for firms. I think firms' larger concerns are fear of risk exposure and time wasting, because these are the concerns that emerge almost immediately when firms begin discussing social media use. For this reason, I tackle risks and concerns early in the book.

By their very nature, social media tools are built on a foundation of openness, authenticity, sharing, and spontaneity. As such, using social media tools effectively in a corporate setting requires a certain level of trust and the ability to adopt similar values. The subjects of values and trust are also discussed deeply in this section because they are foundational and, while "trusting your people" sounds like an obvious and easy thing, professional firms tend to have rather controlling environments that don't reflect trust. This can be a significant barrier to success in social media.

Advantages of an Effective Online Presence

This book helps you create a more powerful online presence for yourself or your firm. For practicing professionals seeking to develop more or better business, an *effective* electronic presence is one that:

- Makes you easily findable
- Presents you as a unique, interesting person with character and personality
- Demonstrates your "expertise" or "specialization" (words for internal use only if verboten by your profession's ethics boards)
- Illustrates that you are a thinker and, hopefully, a reader
- Reflects your accessibility
- Conveys a consistent picture of you from site to site

Additionally, social media can enhance your presence at the firm level such as with a social media newsroom managed by non-practitioners, but this is secondary to practitioners' direct involvement with social media—it doesn't help you with the social part, directly building relationships with people who hire you or refer you.

Social media is not a panacea. It is definitely not a magic bullet of marketing. But it may prove to be every bit as effective, if not more so, than any marketing your firm has done to date. Social media will not solve operational problems but could possibly help bring some to light. If you know something is *very* broken, I would put off embarking in social media until you fix it.

If your firm has some significant service issues, just having the communication channel available will not be enough to correct the problems; nurturing the relationship back to health is still required. Similar to issues raised through a client survey, it would be unwise to ignore reports or hints of problems. However, creating the additional channels through which people can tell you of problems is powerful. When issues surface, address them without blame avoidance and with a spirit of gratitude for the opportunities to correct the problem before client defection occurs. I've witnessed several instances in firms where a dented and repaired client relationship became stronger than the un-bruised one.

Service recovery expert, marketing professor, and co-founder of the Center for Services Marketing & Management, Stephen Brown, confirms this phenomenon saying that their studies show that "customers who've experienced a strong recovery can sometimes become more loyal than those who haven't experienced any service failures."[2] He explains that world-class firms want customers to complain when service failures have occurred so they have the opportunity to recover well. Not only does this potentially increase loyalty, it helps stave off negative word-of-mouth.

Types of Social Media

The four social media tools that are featured in this book: LinkedIn, Twitter, Facebook, and blogs, are chosen because they are presently the tools most suited to professionals. Social media tools fall into two categories: firm-sponsored (i.e., owned/managed) or individual (i.e., private) publications known as blogs (i.e., "Web logs," which are Web sites of a certain type), and third-party forums such as Twitter, Facebook, and LinkedIn.

There is more flexibility, albeit more complexity, in using a firm or individual blog than in using third-party forums. The thing to remember about a firm-sponsored publication is that the URL (i.e., Web address) of that publication is either within your firm's Web site or is directly attached to it. This gives your firm a lot of search marketing juice. A lot.

The strategy is a primary driver behind which tool to use. Your final choice should factor in several things: your comfort level with each tool, the amount of time you are willing and able to invest in marketing, where your desired contacts are already congregating, and each respective tool's ability to support or align with your short- or long-term goals.

No matter what else you do, every practicing professional should have a thorough LinkedIn profile. Additionally, though not an interactive social platform per se, every professional should also set up a Google profile. It takes just a few minutes and can make you much more findable through search, especially if your name is common or contains a regular word (as does mine with "golden").

I strongly recommend starting with an active LinkedIn presence because it is purely business oriented, you need a good, solid profile anyway, and, finally, when your use of the tool is thorough, as I recommend in Chapter 8, it affords you the opportunity to "play" with variations of the features also found in Twitter, Facebook, and blogs. It's an ideal entry point.

What Social Media Help Achieve

Through engaging other people in conversations online or by self-publishing, or both, social media tools can help you personally, or your firm, in five key areas:

1. Reputation and credibility building (via self-publishing):
   - **Personal:** Demonstrate knowledge, leading to expert or thought-leader status.
   - **Personal:** Attract attention, leading to speaking, writing, and media mention (as expert) opportunities.
   - **Personal and firm:** Accomplish organic "pull" marketing via excellent, relevant content.
2. Prospect identification and conversion (via engagement):
   - **Personal:** Convey demeanor and demonstrate accessibility.

- **Firm and personal:** Locate and qualify prospects via research identifying prospect health, mutual acquaintances, and listening to them (getting to know them) in social space before interacting.
3. Networking (via engagement):
   - **Personal:** Deepen current relationships with more frequent and better quality contact.
   - **Personal:** Form new relationships both with those who find you and those you seek out.
   - **Personal:** Connect people in your circle together for their mutual benefit.
   - **Personal:** Promote others to increase goodwill and pay it forward.
4. Recruiting (via engagement and self-publishing):
   - **Firm and personal:** Demonstrate uniqueness in the way that you participate in social media.
   - **Personal:** Reinforce specialty areas via self-publishing and thought leadership in those spaces.
   - **Personal and firm:** Illustrate culture and camaraderie by sharing photos and stories, and engaging team members and prospective employees in conversation.
5. Customer relations, service, and brand enhancement (via engagement):
   - **Personal:** Get to know the people you do business with better.
   - **Personal and firm:** Demonstrate accessibility individually and as a firm to increase loyalty and positive brand positioning.
   - **Firm and personal:** Listen—what's being said about you and your firm; engage—improve perceptions via positive interactions (i.e., represent well).

As you approach your planning (much more in Chapter 5), you'll first want to thoroughly understand what each tool can and cannot potentially accomplish for you. You'll then evaluate which particular social media tools coincide with your other current marketing, recruiting, and client service initiatives.

Next, anticipate what is involved in deploying your chosen social media. Considerations will be understanding your audiences, identifying resources, setting up your accounts or blogs, and planning for maintenance efforts. You must decide if the investments necessary to achieve success with the tools, *relative to your goals*, are worthwhile.

Firms that report poor results with any marketing endeavor, including but not limited to social media, have, more often than not, either picked the wrong tools or deployed them ineffectively. A test for this is whether the firm can satisfactorily answer the questions, "Why are you using that particular tool?" and "What, specifically, are you seeking to achieve?" With thoughtful goals, a focus on reaching and interacting with the right people, and proper use, this should not happen.

Tool comparison charts (Tables 3.1 and 3.2) featured in Chapter 3 illustrate the potential benefits and concerns of LinkedIn, Twitter, Facebook and blogging, side by side, so you can see the relative potential for each tool's use in a variety of situations. Two common "objectives" that are fulfilled using these social media tools are credibility—through sharing content, learning, and conversing—and networking: getting to know people better and connecting them to others they'll benefit from meeting.

Credibility Through Content and Conversation

Self-publishing is a way of sharing content that involves either writing your own original content (including outsourced content) or publishing an aggregation of others' work, with or without contextual commentary. The former offers you the greatest potential benefit, while the latter is still valuable enough to undertake if the alternative is to not publish at all. Producing content does take effort, but it's not as labor intensive as you might think, especially because you probably already produce valuable content on a frequent basis. I'm not talking about writing formal journal articles with citations here, just little tidbits, ideas, and tips. Do you send emails? Answer questions? Content for the Web is best served in the same small portions because that is what people can readily consume.

When you offer content, you seek to convey your qualifications and credibility by demonstrating:

- **Cumulative knowledge:** Based on past experiences and/or formal education
- **Exceptional service skills:** Including clear communication, accessibility, responsiveness, promises upheld, positive attitude
- **Critical thinking ability:** Ability to connect two or more ideas together, draw conclusions, take a stance, explain it well

By targeting your content to the right readers, the objective is to attract people to read your online publications. Proof that you are hitting the mark with your content is that after a while (it doesn't happen immediately) readers either converse with you by commenting publicly or sending you private correspondence, or they will refer to your published content. Referring to it means either linking to you from their Web sites or blogs, posting links on Twitter, LinkedIn, Facebook, or other networking sites, or, finally, by bookmarking it with tags using a bookmarking tool like StumbleUpon, Reddit, Del.icio.us, or Digg.

Networking: Get to Know People, Connect Them

Networking has long been regarded as a chief aspect of business development for professionals. In a world where technology has increased our workload through accessibility and speed (no more "check's in the mail"), we all find it challenging to manage our time. Networking is highly effective and yet takes a low priority for most professionals. Networking is much easier for busy professionals to undertake on a frequent basis when it occurs online.

Touching base, getting to know one another better, promoting others' work and activities among your valuable connections, and connecting others together, can happen in minutes a day from anywhere. These essential relationship-deepening activities can take place while you sit at your desk, making the most of a few minutes here and there, or while you're at home, in your PJs, snuggled up beside your toddler. As we all juggle busy lives, networking events that eat up precious multihour blocks, yet reach only a small audience, are decreasing in appeal when contrasted with far more effective and flexible online networking options. This isn't to say that online communication will or should entirely replace face-to-face interactions. But online interactions can dramatically accelerate relationship development in between face-to-face meetings.

Think, also, about the large percentage of people for whom face-to-face networking is downright painful—many people avoid it. "Too busy" is the most common excuse, but discomfort is probably the most common reason. Forcing people to network is not the answer—misery shows. Few people truly love meet-and-greets. Some, like me, put on a happy face but count the minutes until they're over; others are visibly uncomfortable throughout. Online networking affords even the shiest professionals an opportunity to make a positive, memorable impression. Getting and staying in front of key people in meaningful ways has never been easier.

Considering that social media interaction eliminates travel time and replaces physical attendance at some events, virtual social time also provides more concentrated interaction time. These combined time-savings allow for more frequent interactions with the people it makes the most strategic sense for you to get to know better. Through these more frequent exchanges, you can get to know people at a much deeper level, far more quickly than when you are limited to face-to-face interactions.

Think of the credible colleague you meet at a business conference and know you'd be wise to keep in touch with. Traditional "continued touches" might be a handwritten "it was nice to meet you" note along with adding the person to the firm's newsletter mailing list. Next year, when you see him at the conference, he might know a little bit more about you or your firm from those newsletters, but what more do you know about him? About his business or his interests? Yet when you add a LinkedIn or Facebook connection to the above efforts, if you've used the tools correctly, by the next year you'll not only know a lot more about him, but you will have interacted in the interim. As a result, at the next annual conference, you will sit down as friends who know some of each other's accomplishments, personal hobbies or interests and degree of interest in them, and perhaps even some of those valuable personal details that bring people closer together. Through this sort of contact, the relationship is dramatically accelerated; this happens all the time through social media.

Also, consider the necessity of staying visible to referral sources without being too intrusive. Brief, casual, pleasant exchanges afforded through these tools serve as gentle reminders of your existence and relevance. The greater number of these interactions with prospects, clients, and other referral sources, the greater your potential for success with them.

Social media seems to have the most opportunity to change "rainmaking" behavior results for a firm's professionals in two ways. One is that it provides a less intimidating way for more introverted professionals to interact with others and showcase their expertise. Another that resonates greatly with professionals who are parents of young children or have other, significant time commitments outside of work is the flexibility to "socialize" on their own schedule, while on the road, or in the comfort of their home. What we're witnessing is a greater level of relationship development and "presence" than we'd otherwise see from both of these types of professionals. From some professionals who fit these scenarios using social media well, I've seen sales results exceeding the originations of some highly successful "traditional-style" rainmakers. Further, because of the social media activities, the entire firm benefits from an elevated Web presence.

Establish Credibility While You Network

While it isn't requisite, combining your networking with the occasional sharing of your own content is extremely valuable. If creating content is out of the question for you, there is plenty of great content out there that authors would be delighted to have you share with your contacts. This is a big part of what social media tools are about. The key to effective content sharing is relevance—sharing the right information with the right people.

New media also make it very easy and instantaneous to disseminate credibility-reinforcing content. Messages and conversations shared have staying power, unlike a spoken conversation, so others can explore them and learn from them, too. Documents and conversations that are Web based and searchable serve to market you 24/7/365. While you sleep and vacation, people can be impressed by you and what you know. They can access your stored intellectual capital when they want it, and not just when you send it out to them. In this "Google It" era of Web-based research by all demographic groups, this is enormously beneficial to your practice.

How We Got Here

The speed at which the Internet has changed our lives is stunning. Organic growth took a data tool and morphed it into a conversation tool, which in turn created communities. Yet the time it has taken for business to understand all this and adapt to it has not been commensurately fast. In fact, for a long time, the business community and the Internet community had "I don't need you and I don't respect you" attitudes toward one another.

This sentiment was well described more than ten years ago by Christopher Locke in a prophetic book, *The Cluetrain Manifesto*[3]:

> *A maxim often heard online is that the Internet routes around obstacles, meaning it ignores them. In its early phase, the Net ignored business; Internet audiences simply weren't interested. And the feeling was mutual. Business ignored the Net for a long time, not seeing it as what it thought a media market should look like, which is to say television. This mutual ignorance served as the incubator for a global revolution that today threatens the foundations of business as usual.*

If we don't understand something, we tend to dislike it or ignore it, don't we? At least until we cannot ignore it any longer because it interferes with us or our beliefs. Or because someone convinces us we can and should capitalize on it.

Where businesses have missed the boat in hawking their wares and services on the Web, as you'll see below, was in trying to use traditional marketing techniques online. Businesses simply did not adapt and innovate quickly enough. Many continue to apply the old sales and advertising models to this new environment. But new media calls for some rather noncorporate approaches—essential for success in online marketing.

Web Marketing's Evolution from Impersonal to Personal

Almost two decades ago, AOL, Yahoo!, and others introduced us to their advertisers' flashy (and rather tacky) banner ads, later followed by more subdued pay-per-click (PPC) advertising. What we were witnessing were traditional print, TV, and radio advertising approaches migrating to the Web. These still exist but have been refined through sophisticated targeting opportunities for which we largely have Google to thank. Some professionals are finding excellent results with PPC ads.

But something else emerged—something far better that could never be achieved through print, television, and radio: all one-way "broadcast" devices that operate on the advertisers' schedules and terms, not those of the viewers. People slowly began to harness the Web to successfully develop two-way relationships and demonstrate their credibility. These results correlate beautifully with what professionals must ultimately do to enrich and grow their businesses in person or otherwise.

Consider the timeline in Figure 1.1. While the "data" capture (work) aspect of the Web was under way, programmers needed a place to collaborate. And as programmers are prone to do when taking breaks from work, they play, and the games began. Online profiles and short-term or long-term correspondence via "forums" were first explored by gamers and geeks, but gradually expanded into the mainstream. Because users could express opinions with equal access, formal or informal cliques and classes formed in order to separate some users from others. Where mechanisms were available, people voted or ranked some users as more reliable, credible, or active than others. Expert reviewers, super-users, and power sellers emerged on discussion forums, business forums like eBay, and commercial sites where there were built-in social media elements such as Amazon and Epinions.

Even where mechanisms to rank were unavailable, trust and credibility were recognized through word-of-mouth. Users ultimately decide whom to trust, and once they trust someone, they look at whomever else that person trusts and, soon, a "trusted circle" develops. The most credible or trusted users gain loyal followings. And, as with most societies, formal or informal rules emerge, and troublemakers become outcasts or are banished. Cultural anthropologists of the future will no doubt look back on the emergence of the social Web as a complete subculture of great importance—one that is especially interesting because it includes every culture (with Internet access) around the globe.

In retrospect, it shouldn't be surprising that an enormous societal change has occurred—one that affects all our businesses. The Web ceased to be effective for traditional broadcast advertising with its hype and spin. Some speculate that this is because traditional ads lack desired interaction and engagement inherent in social media. I believe it resulted more from the blog community—large enough by the mid-2000s to be very influential— sharing a common disdain for corporate fluff and BS. There is a very low tolerance for exaggerated claims, sanitized PR messages, and puffery (aka corporate-speak and empty buzzwords) on the social Web. Basically, the social Web—comprising people of *all* ages—has rejected the corporate advertising approach thrust upon us since at least the 1940s.

Fellow content advocate, David Meerman Scott, has strong opinions about *gobbledygook,* describing the overabundance of jargon-laden

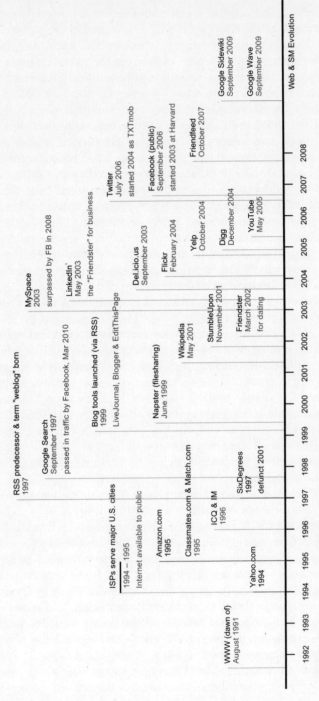

FIGURE 1.1 Evolution of the Web and Social Media

Source: © 2010 Golden Practices Inc.

phrases—an offense he says is committed most by business-to-business (B2B) technology companies—and I'd say consultants, accountants, and lawyers are right behind them.[4] Scott published *The Gobbledygook Manifesto* e-book in 2006. He says these jargon-using writers either "don't understand how their products solve customer problems, or are too lazy to write for buyers."[5]

As a review of professional firm Web sites illustrates, they resort instead to using language like "tailored services" and "creative solutions" while they discuss their "broad range of services," "risk-based approaches," and "world-class knowledge and experience." The closest that many firms get to addressing their readers is in acknowledging "today's complex business environment" and promising to "work closely with clients" in order to "achieve success for our clients."

This is not valuable or compelling language. It makes us glaze over in part because it needs translation, and in part because we are being blatantly sold *at*, not talked *to*. We need to provide much more specificity and meaning in our verbiage. You will find guidance on this in Chapter 12.

As you determine how and where your firm might participate in social media, I cannot reinforce enough that social media forums are not the place to broadcast advertise in the traditional (now old-fashioned) or vague corporate-speak way. When you think about the roles trust and credibility played in the growth of Web communities, it makes complete sense that the values that reign supreme in the communities today are authenticity, transparency, humanizing, sharing information, and even respectfully disagreeing.

The New Way We Buy

The way most of us consume information has dramatically changed. It's not just news that we seek as in the newspaper days, it's also background information that helps us justify our purchases, reassuring us that we are making the right decisions. When we buy a car or a book, a stroller, or a chain saw, more often than not, we first research options and reviews. This isn't an entirely new concept—methods that predate the Internet include *Consumer Reports* magazine. Before that, people largely relied on word-of-mouth—we asked friends and family.

Now, even buyers of services perform their research online, whether for business or personal needs. Many of us, but especially those under age 35 who've grown up with the Web, wouldn't consider making a major purchase or business commitment without first investigating the seller's background and offerings along with their public feedback. Which do you think a researcher values more: the seller's claims or the buyer's experience reports? Well, both are potentially unreliable, right? Unless the buyer sharing his or her experience is more credible than an average stranger. Perhaps one or more buyers are persons of influence. Or perhaps the seller doesn't merely have statements on a Web site about being knowledgeable and specialized; what if there is an archive of material that discusses concepts, trends, and practical examples about dealing with the topic at hand?

We still have to use our judgment and we have to use filters, particularly BS filters, in order to discern the quality of the sellers' and buyers' information, yet we have something to go on. But what if all we can find about a professional is a brochure-ware Web site? And what if there is no public feedback whatsoever? This doesn't bode well when compared to another professional or firm with both exceptionally demonstrative content and validating public feedback.

For professionals, this is where illustrating your knowledge and capabilities come very much into play, especially online. Brochure Web sites are beyond dead in a world where people seek content that is actually useful information.

Law and accounting firms are just about the worst offenders when it comes to failing to evolve from first-generation or brochure Web sites. Regardless of some attractive redesigns, on most of today's law and accounting firm Web sites, the content is nearly identical to what those firms stated on their very first Web sites (circa 1995). Think back. Where exactly did that text come from? Yes—It came directly from the we-we-we, all-about-us, gobbledygook-filled brochures that the firms used back in the 1980s. If you sit down and really try to read this content, it's painful to get through and it's entirely unhelpful because it doesn't actually say much of anything at all. Further, the words are mostly the same words that other firms are using to describe themselves and their services. Finally, when we describe "ourselves and our services," what significant piece are we missing? Oh yeah. The reader.

Today's Web thrives on content that is diverse and complex and meaningful. Web sites with dull, staid brochure-type verbiage stand out in a bad sort of way. Our attention-deficit-behaving society simply demands that we find relevance and substance when surfing online, or we quickly move on. All of us are, in effect, crying out: "Don't waste my time."

The remedy is to house intellectual capital relevant to your areas of practice online, connected with, or in lieu of, your basic Web site. Blogs—by their nature and structure—deliver this. The "traditional" brochure Web site can even be replaced with a strong blog and a few informational pages, especially for smaller firms. Blogs are just Web sites wherein the "pages" are built a certain way that is conducive to garnering search results when the content is on target with what a reader is hoping to find.

Social Media versus Other Marketing Approaches

Professionals worry about how "vastly different" Web marketing channels are than the other, more familiar territories. But, I'll illustrate how, generally, the same laws of attraction and selection apply. We'll look at some differences and similarities between old and new.

How They're Different

There are a few characteristics that make "social media" different from other types of marketing:

Tone: Unlike the marketing we have all experienced since the 1940s—very much about hype at the expense of honesty—social media marketing is very much about being authentic and even fallible.

Conversation: Online now means "two-way" conversations in which the company or professional listens and buyers participate. Sometimes the buyer is the *only* contributor—but the company should never be the only contributor.

Validation: Buyer (or consumer) reviews and opinions are at least as influential, if not more so, than the claims of the seller, and the features or benefits the seller purports to have. Traditional positioning approaches actually erode trust and credibility.

Reach: Using social media tools, a firm can achieve far greater reach, with more dramatic results, in far less time—and at significantly less cost—than with almost any other communication mechanism.

Control: There is no longer a need to wait, hoping the media will pick up a story, while you pray that the context and the quotes are accurate. It's now possible to go live, to a global audience, with whatever story you want—the entire message completely in your control. Best of all, if your story merits media attention, journalists (national, local, and trade media) can find you without you having to pitch them.

The fifth, control, is probably the biggest single change for marketers in the new media era. With the low cost and ease of access, self-publishing, particularly blogging, has turned mass media upside down.

While many traditional publishers *still* refuse to acknowledge the role of blogs in legitimate news and reporting, an impressively early (May 2005) and transparent acknowledgement came from *BusinessWeek* magazine about the changing landscape of journalism[6] brought on by digital media:

[Blogs] represent power . . . . In the age of mass media, publications like ours print the news. Sources try to get quoted, but the decision is ours . . . . Now instead of just speaking through us, they can blog . . . if they master [it, and] get other bloggers to link to them, they reach a huge audience.

Because of the time and cost to produce and deliver newspapers and other print media, long-standing news vehicles were initially undermined by television's evening news. Then cable news surpassed the daily produced news programs with their ability to share both breaking and produced stories all day long, occasionally in real time. Now, even cable news isn't real time enough for many of us because we can seek very specific news (think of it as an equivalent to specialties such as weather, sports, and elections news) on demand.

The Internet empowers, literally, the entire world population to watchdog and report what we see. It may not always be accurately or professionally reported, but we, as readers, use our judgment to filter and discern the validity—and then as facts unfold, we can still look to mainstream media to vet the information and sort truths from rumors.

So how does this impact you as a professional and change things for your firm?

Firms have an entirely new set of tools for the toolkit, but clearly, they aren't tools you and your firm are used to. They do require learning a new language if you want to use them successfully for business development. The "language" used in marketing for the past 30-plus years simply isn't understood online at this point in time. Visualize a population of people staring at you as you babble words they can't comprehend. The new language is authenticity—it's time to relax and be "real" on the Web. It's not even that scary. In fact, it's pretty liberating.

The "voice" has changed entirely. Everything is brought down a notch or two as far as formality is concerned. This doesn't mean you have to start using text lingo (U2, B4, LOL, etc.) but you should be aware of it. Most imperative, authenticity and transparency are requisite to achieve credibility. In Robert Scoble's Corporate Weblog Manifesto, Item Number One is: "Tell the truth. The whole truth. Nothing but the truth. If your competitor has a product that's better than yours, link to it. You might as well. We'll find it anyway."[7] And this is the spirit of social media.

Social media are *only* a place for your firm (at the corporate level) to be if you can stomach this major change in approach to presenting your firm. If you cannot, it's a waste of your time and energy to invest in a firm-level social media presence. Instead, encourage individuals to establish strong LinkedIn profiles, set up their Google profile, and leave social media use to your people at the individual level.

But if you choose to adopt them at the firm level, social media tools can reduce your firm's time, energy, and expense in achieving your practice development objectives. The tools enable you to more consistently leverage marketing across all levels of your firm so that you aren't so distinctly separated into "rainmakers" and "nonrainmakers." As a means to the end—social media tools get people to *the point of personal interaction* faster because strong relationships are developed more quickly than when forced to wait to be together in the same physical place or for a "good enough" reason to call or write.

How They're Similar

Before the social Web, professionals would ultimately seek to meet or interact with the business buyer, person-to-person, for a shot at forming a good relationship. The same overall goal exists now, but now you "meet" in different, more convenient places, and introductions come from surprising, never-before-imagined sources.

The greatest success through social networking occurs when we *actively advance* a relationship *from digital to personal.*

These online relationships are not the end goal. Personal contact is. Personal may mean by telephone, if not face-to-face; these days, virtual may not be ideal, but it can certainly suffice. I have clients I wouldn't recognize on the street, and I'm sure that people within your organization could say the same. This isn't altogether new, though it's been the case since the advent of the telephone as a business tool. The Web is just another tool that facilitates the more casual "meetings" and interactions that lead to the personal contact.

Overall, new media strategies are nearly identical to traditional marketing strategies—for better and for worse. What I mean by this is that the opportunity for ROI is comparable to that of traditional marketing. Social media are not the be-all, end-all; they are not a panacea. The same way that traditional marketing efforts can reap zero ROI, so too can social media.

Like traditional marketing efforts, with clear purpose, defined goals, and steady implementation, efforts involving social media tools can be highly effective and time saving. And without forethought and planning, results of using social media are unpredictable at best, and can prove downright *ineffective*—the same being true of more familiar forms of marketing such as hosting events, seminars, golf outings, cocktail receptions, participation in organizations and associations, writing, speaking, mailing campaigns, and so on.

Have you ever invested your (or your firm's) energy, time, and funds in any of these efforts, yet felt disappointed with the results? Have you ever felt frustration knowing other firms have had terrific success with these activities? The degree of success is directly proportional to the amount and quality of planning, execution, and follow-up. Social media are no different.

Creating a LinkedIn profile and doing nothing at all with it is comparable to attending your local Chamber meeting and sitting with the same pal month after month—it's passive participation. If you've had a LinkedIn profile and wonder why no one seems to have called from it, you are probably at the passive level of involvement—just like a wallflower at the Chamber meeting. The LinkedIn profile alone isn't going to generate results. Just like anything else, results come from maximizing the effort, taking it from passive to proactive as a recognized resource or with consistent outreach.

Table 1.1 helps explain the varying degrees of success, or lack thereof, we see with both traditional, familiar tactics and their new media equivalents.

Firms worry about abuse of social media tools. More specifically, firm owners worry about excessive use by each other or employees without a return on investment. But the types of activities mentioned in Table 1.1 show that social media participation, just like traditional marketing activities, is much more effective at an individual level than at a firm level. A strong individual presence online boosts the practitioner's firm in the same way that a rock star's success elevates the record label that signed her. Two strong individuals associated with the same firm make the firm appear even better. Three or more rock stars and your firm obtains something comparable to premier recording label status.

By no means am I saying that only partners should be active. On the contrary, social media participation should be encouraged and supported at all levels of the firm. Not only is it the most highly leverageable marketing activity type there is, it just happens to be both very affordable and very powerful. It also comes more naturally to the nonsenior crowd and fits the busy, juggling lifestyles most of us have these days.

Despite being highly leverageable, delegating the job of social media participation to a generic representative of the firm, especially a nonpractitioner, is suboptimal. A "firm" presence is less personal and far less interesting than the presence of practitioners as individual humans. The "in-person" equivalent of this would be sending a mascot (random employee) dressed in your logo to an association event rather than your knowledgeable practitioners. Your firm is represented there, which is usually better than no presence, but it is not nearly as effective or memorable as a human who can engage others in meaningful conversation.

Like various clubs or associations, LinkedIn, Facebook, Twitter, and blog communities are like separate places to hang out, each offering distinctly different atmospheres and amenities. Choosing where to hang out

TABLE 1.1 Comparing Familiar and New Media Marketing Methods by Activity Level

Level of Activity	Description	Familiar Methods	New Media Methods
PASSIVE ("come to me")	This is the most common level of marketing activity at firms of all sizes. Familiar Methods column items are often aided by marketing personnel, and items in the New Media Methods column are usually done directly by the practitioner. Unleveraged means incomplete or lacking systematized follow-up.	Most advertising Static Web sites Directory listings Sponsorships, unleveraged Seminars, unleveraged Mail (postal or email of any kind with no personal follow-up)	Linked In, unleveraged (such as having only a partial profile, few contacts, and/or little interaction) Facebook, unleveraged Twitter, unleveraged Blogs (includes reading others, but not commenting, or authoring one's own blog posts, but not actively reading or interacting with any others)
PARTICIPATORY (being present)	Merely showing up is suboptimal. Heavier involvement and visibility, with sincere interest and goals such as planned contacts for each meeting, are ways to maximize these activities.	Local general business organizations Local trade organizations Peer organizations Local charities/ community National (Int'l) equivalent of all the above	Become active in the online communities of peer organizations and local trade, charity, and community organizations Blogs, leveraged well Twitter, leveraged well LinkedIn or Plaxo, leveraged well Facebook, leveraged well

(Continued)

TABLE 1.1 (*Continued*)

Level of Activity	Description	Familiar Methods	New Media Methods
RESOURCE (publishing, sharing)	These credibility-building activities are excellent for any type of professional at any stage in his/her career. These actions directly involve the practitioner and lead to your being the "resident expert" (even if we cannot use the word *expert* publicly).	Peer publications Trade publications Talk radio, TV, feature columns, other expert features Media coverage External recognition (honors, awards, contributions to one's profession) Free advice of any kind (phone, lunch, articles, newsletters)	Become active in the online communities of trade and peer publications as well as media forums and comments Self-publish (Web) Articles Blogs E-newsletters News releases
OUTREACH (proactive)	These attention-getting activities help keep the professional or the firm front of mind and can usually be performed by someone other than the practitioner (marketing department or outsourced resource).	Postal or email *with* good follow-up Invitations of any kind Telephone contact (before they call you) Lunches, breakfasts, dinner meetings Seminars Free advice, shared generously	Blog (share your mind, your ideas, your advice) Tweet (help others, occasionally point to your own content) Facebook, event invitations LinkedIn Create viral buzz Set up events and groups to continue the dialogue after an event

and establish your presence is every bit as personal (if somewhat less important) than choosing which church, synagogue, temple, or mosque you are comfortable attending.

Not all new media tools are equal. This book discusses the tools and their nuances, so you can evaluate their correlation with your overall purpose. Building a strong online presence is neither expensive nor difficult. Feeling simultaneously empowered and overwhelmed with the possibilities as you discover them, however, is probable.

Catching Up and Moving Forward

Research of professional firms' Internet use shows the two top reasons firms haven't evolved quickly with regard to their online presence. First is the belief that their primary desired audience (Baby Boomers and high-wealth individuals) aren't on the Internet much, and second is a consciously adopted "wait and see" attitude toward technology.

The "wait and see" approach is quite understandable since most professional firms—and businesses in general—were on the forefront of technology in the late 1980s and early 1990s, adopting the exciting new tools availed to us. From document management systems to financial software and database management, the new tools to make businesses dramatically more efficient were impossible to resist. The pace continued until the heavy, and very costly, "be ready" push in preparation for Y2K. Then many businesses subsequently decided to depart from "immediate adoption" of new technology due to the increasing pace of change, high cost to keep up with each emerging technology, and its even more rapid obsolescence.

The pace of technological change overwhelms most of us. But when it comes to Web-based communications, CPAs seem to have taken a longer bye than their legal and other business counterparts. Today, law firm blogs number in the several thousands; accounting firm blogs are fewer than 200. Lawyers were also much faster on the uptake of LinkedIn, Facebook, and Twitter. But quite a few accountants and other professionals are active on Twitter, Facebook, and LinkedIn. This is good news.

Regarding social media, especially blogs, nonlawyers can be comforted by the fact that lawyers pioneering this channel have hashed through a lot of the "risk" questions and concerns, especially pertaining to liability, content rights, and ethical restrictions. The lawyers on the forefront of social media emerged in 2001 and 2002 and absolutely paved the way for other professionals. Some of the earliest legal bloggers were: Walter Olson (Overlawyered), Rick Klau (tins), Eugene Volokh (The Volokh Conspiracy), Ernie Svenson (Ernie the Attorney), Carolyn Elefant (My Shingle), Glenn Reynolds (Instapundit), Sabrina Pacifici (beSpacific), Denise Howell (Bag and Baggage), and Marty Schwimmer (The Trademark Blog).[8] Most of these pioneers are still at it; I encourage you to ask them if they feel it is worthwhile.

We also have the entire legal blogging community to thank, at least partly, for elevating the credibility of blogs. I believe this has a great deal to do with the number of law professors who blog. Back in 2006, there was much discussion about blogs encroaching on the law journal space—perhaps even replacing them. Would law journals become obsolete? This discussion escalated once blog content began being cited in court judgments. As of August 2006, eight different blogs had been cited 32 times in 27 cases.[9] This was groundbreaking for the credibility of blogs in the professional community. Legal blogs have not replaced law journals, but they have definitely made their mark.

The Growth of Accounting and Legal Blogs

Looking back at professional firm blog growth, in 2003, after just two years, there were at least 62 legal blogs. By 2010, there are several thousand legal blogs and tens of thousands of lawyers who write for blogs (or *blawgs,* a term some lawyers love and others eschew for its elitist nature),[10] and 48 percent of the AmLaw 200 law firms are blogging, with these 96 firms operating 297 blogs, or an average of three blogs per firm.[11]

By contrast, there were only 12 accounting blogs in 2006 when there were more than 1,000 legal blogs. Just over a year later, in June 2007, there were 23 accounting blogs—not yet double; however, between 2,000 and 3,000 legal blogs existed.[12] July 2008 brought us to 51 accounting blogs, June 2009 to 95, and April 2010 to 154. There has not exactly been impressive growth on the accounting side.

Granted, on the accounting side, my count captures only customer- or prospect-focused (practice development purpose) blogs, not blogs that are aimed at a peer audience (often former CPA turned consultant). If we were to add those, the number would increase, but it would not double. On the legal side, many of the blogs seem to be written *by* lawyers, *for* lawyers—so you could cut the number in half if you wished, and there is still no comparison. Plus, I would argue that lawyers refer work to one another far more often than accountants do, so sharing their practice expertise and service philosophies with other lawyers still has more potential to serve a business development purpose.

Returning to a Culture of Adaptability

Social media have been around longer than a decade—it's time to catch up. The great news is that catching up doesn't take long once you get "out there" with a strong online presence. But in order to retain that strong presence online, it's going to require many firms to readopt a culture of rapid adaptability that we felt disinclined to have for the past decade or so. This is because social Web technologies evolve constantly. New options merit prompt evaluation since leveraging them quickly could be of significant competitive advantage.

Open-mindedness, flexibility, and adaptability are crucial traits for firms who will successfully adopt and leverage the Web-based communication tools in their practices.

Professional service firm marketing is beginning a significant shift— expect it to be dramatically different in five to ten more years as online marketing increases in importance. Going forward, much of a firm's marketing function and role will be to better understand buyers' needs and publish relevant content, particularly online. Content inspired by buyers' needs provides information that addresses their "buying cycles" instead of our old-fashioned content that has been created to support the firm's "selling cycle." More publishing will be online and social media will continue to play a huge role in disseminating worthy content.

As you can imagine, in light of these changes, the strategies and policies you adopt with your social media initiatives will always be better when they are not software or application specific, but are purpose driven according to the long-term needs of the firm.

CHAPTER 2

Social Media Policies and Guidelines: Rules of Engagement

It's entirely understandable that many professionals are reluctant to embrace social media, either individually or on behalf of their firms. The reasons most often cited range from concerns about abuse or misuse by employees, to information technology (IT) security threats and bandwidth consumption concerns, to dread about adding yet another "thing" to the already overflowing plates of busy professionals.

As much as companies have tried over the last decade to stifle employee access of third-party email sites and certain other Web sites, it's simply impossible to restrict the entire Internet. Why bother to lock out Hotmail/Yahoo! when people have email and text on their smart phones? The lockout era is over. It's counterproductive to block most Web sites, too. Most discouraging for the leery employer that bans the media, smart people who like a challenge (there tend to be quite a few in professional knowledge firms) will dedicate some of their work time and energy to finding a way to circumvent the ban. Remember, as a teenager, the thrill of stretching or breaking a rule just to see if you could pull it off?

Disallowing LinkedIn, Facebook, blogs, and Twitter (yes, some firms still block some or all of these) is cutting off the firm's nose to spite its face. These are valuable tools for those who wish to use them for business.

Don't let the continuing influx of draconian policy advice scare the daylights out of you. An article appeared in an accounting trade publication in March 2010, featuring guest expert Nancy Flynn of the ePolicy Institute.[1]

The article warns against what employees might say when they use the Web and email—concern about employees making disparaging remarks about the firm. This is not a specific communication tool problem! The problem is rooted in having an unhappy employee who will find a forum to air his or her displeasure. Another worry Flynn cites is the inappropriate sharing of client information. This can happen if employees are either unaware of what is acceptable or they don't care. Either education or termination is the solution. Flynn's advice, however, includes limiting personal mobile phone use during company hours, as well as social media and personal email use during company hours or on company devices, and banning various URLs, particularly those of social media sites.

Concern about people not getting their work done is the real issue behind the bans, anyway, right? Today's reality is that it's pointless to worry about the way people spend their time, but rather hold people accountable for the end result: Either they are cutting the mustard with performance or they aren't. Don't spend a lot of energy worrying about who is using what forum, and instead, if issues arise at the individual level with regard to performance, then address problems one-on-one with that individual.

More often than not, fears directed toward social media are misplaced. Be careful not to turn to policy-setting where concerns about judgment and lack of necessary education are the core of the problem.

Policy Depth and Tone

How rigid does your social media or communications policy need to be? It's a tough question.

First, social media are different than other things for which you probably have policies. By their very nature, social media value, and are built upon, a foundation of openness, authenticity, sharing, and spontaneity. As such, using social media effectively in a corporate setting requires a certain level of trust. This is simply a fact.

Some firms, given their current management style and culture, do not, in truth, have a high enough trust level to support broad social media practices. This can change. And even with a moderate trust level, there are some tools and approaches that can succeed. But which tools are used, how, by whom, and to what degree of success, are intrinsically tied to the level of trust and autonomy in your organization.

Good leaders trust that others will do what's right and are in turn trusted by those around them to do the same.

—Peter Drucker

Interestingly, higher-trust firms sometimes deploy policies that come across as low trust. Policies set tone. What you do is more impactful than what you say. If you say, "We trust your judgment" and then disseminate a 15-page document containing rules for social media use on behalf of the firm, you've effectively countered your "we trust you" statement.

Which is true? Probably the truth is: "We trust some, or most, of you." Build policies geared for those whom you *do* trust. Well-crafted guildelines will also protect you if you need to take disciplinary action. But when you create a policy that is a set of rules addressing the lowest denominator, you offend the trustworthy people and repeat offenders tend to act as though they believe policies don't apply to them, anyway. Put bluntly, heavy-handed control does not go over well with professionals who have chosen such judgment-oriented professions as accounting and law. The people in your firm with the best judgment are your most valuable, least expendable team members; therefore, they are the ones you least want to insult.

Learning from Dress Code Policies

To illustrate the last point, consider the firm's dress code. Rather than having a single statement articulating the firm's formality of attire (professional, casual, etc), most firms have extremely detailed policies that, in truth, exist because a relatively low percentage of employees commit fashion faux pas. The style-challenged or judgment-impaired team member may improve with conversation to heighten awareness and perhaps a little education to improve fashion skill. Or the situation may simply be irreparable. For instance, lack of respect is simply inexcusable and symptomatic of a larger attitude problem.

Instead of the difficult one-on-one conversations (in all fairness, confronting employees about such things isn't pleasant, nor is it a strong suit of professionals), many, many hours can go into investigating what other firms do, debating and documenting what constitutes appropriate attire, training for all, and sometimes "experts" are even brought in to discuss and model good and poor examples of dress.

The employees with the better judgment weren't a problem to begin with, yet they are now micromanaged, which they neither deserve nor appreciate. Moreover, their opinion of management may diminish because the true source of the problem (and most employees know exactly who this was intended to "correct") wasn't addressed directly enough to realize it was "them." Almost inevitably, after the policy implementation, some of those initial problem employees still sport their flip-flops or laundry-heap trousers and someone is designated to have a conversation with the offender—back to where the company could have just started.

My point is that simple guidelines, along with education—either in groups or one on one—are more than adequate for your best employees. More detailed requirements are potentially damaging to otherwise good relationships and are often ineffective against problem employees, anyway—a true waste of resources. If someone who works for you doesn't "get it" and he or she continues to violate your standards repeatedly, you don't need a policy, you need to correct a hiring mistake.

Abusing Social Media at Work

Yes, social media forums can be distracting. So are telephones and the Internet. All of these tools can be used for "goofing off." But they also empower us to get our jobs done exponentially faster than without them.

Unlike the days when firms could lock down the Internet to "control" productivity, restricting online access to social media tools does not prevent "playtime" on the company clock. It can be argued that it inspires our very smart people to spend their precious time circumventing our restrictions, instead of working. But more notably, with such affordable smartphones, people surf the Web, text friends and family, and access all the banned tools—anytime they want. Resistance truly is futile.

Hiring well is more crucial than ever. We have to be even more thoughtful and diligent in detecting signs of professionalism and good judgment in those we hire. And then continued training peppered with lots of trust is the only way to deal with this in a healthy manner.

Like parenting, we cannot rule with an iron fist and simultaneously expect to foster well-adjusted, self-sufficient individuals.

Assessing Your Firm's Risk Tolerance

How social media friendly is your firm right now? To help assess the level of rigidity you're likely to exhibit in your Communications and Social Media Use policies, take this quiz. The results can help predict your firm's likelihood of success in using social media tools to their fullest potential.

Answer the following questions on a scale of 1–5, with 5 being the highest.

1. How important is autonomy* among your firm's values and current practices?
2. How important is innovation among your firm's values and current practices?

3. To what degree does your culture demonstrate trust in, and respect of, employee judgment? (*Hint:* Look at some of your current policies.)

Add your answers to determine your total score.

Results

11–15: Social media usage can flourish in your firm because trust inspires people. A brief, mellow policy will be more than adequate and you won't have to worry about hampering people's enthusiasm with rigid, unfriendly policies.
Samples: Baker & Daniels, Mayo Clinic, and Headset Bros
www.bakerdstreamingvid.com/publications/Baker_Daniels
_Social-Media-Policy.pdf
http://sharing.mayoclinic.org/guidelines/for-mayo-clinic
-employees
www.headsetbros.com/Articles.asp?ID=135

6–10: Social media usage may be less than it could otherwise be. A tendency toward carefully worded, detailed policies serves to convey that the firm is wary or skeptical and somewhat concerned about being embarrassed by employees.
Samples: Jaffe template, Harvard Law, and Microsoft
www.jaffeassociates.com/pages/articles/view.php?article
_id=330
http://blogs.law.harvard.edu/terms-of-use
http://socialmediagovernance.com/MSFT_Social_Media
_Policy.pdf

1–5: Social media don't fit well with your current culture. Very specific, restrictive policies probably suit your firm best. Look closely at the underlying reasons for your concerns and try to understand the root cause so you can work on building a more knowledgeable, worker–friendly environment—one that fosters autonomy and trust.
(I'd rather not embarrass any organizations by listing them here, but these policies tend to exceed five pages, and include everything but the kitchen sink.)

*Autonomy: from the Greek word *autonomos* meaning self-ruling

Policy examples across many different sectors are compiled at Social Media Governance: http://socialmediagovernance.com/policies.php.

Beware of Policy Overkill

Before you create policy governing social media use, there's one more thing to consider and incorporate in your thinking. Remember when email was first introduced and only certain "special" people were allowed to have it because firms were worried about what people might say or send with the tool? And more recently, recall how people reacted when you rolled out your first Internet usage policies?

Policies can very easily de-motivate your team. Essentially, your social media policy depth and tone have heavy implications—they shape and define the firm's culture. You now have an opportunity to either strengthen your culture of trust or undermine it. This is no small thing.

A lot of bad information is circulating right now, both in trade publications and among firms who are sharing "sample policies" with one another. Because of the potential magnitude of imposing an ill-fitting policy on your team, be particularly wary about rolling out another organization's policy with your firm's name stamped on it. A one-size-fits-all policy could actually damage your employee/management relationship.

Further, several of the policies and procedures that I've seen circulating around right now contain requirements and restrictions that impede some of the most successful applications of new media tools, undermining the very point of these communications efforts. It's unfortunate that these documents are spreading faster than chicken pox in a preschool.

Five Factors Contributing to Discomfort

In late 2008, I facilitated a session of 40 managing partners who came together to discuss policies covering emerging communication tools including social media, texting, and instant messaging. Details of the session's goals and approach are found in an article I wrote for *Practical Accountant*.[2] In small group discussions, each table of managing partners separately explored two questions: one intended to provoke discussion about the depth of management's knowledge of these communications tools, and the second to explore why firm owners (not necessarily just the ones in the room) are so uncomfortable with them.

The group identified several factors contributing to the lack of comfort in their firms surrounding social media use, and, when sorted and grouped, the results fell into five categories:

1. **Fear of the unknown:** Lack of knowledge and understanding
2. **Professionalism:** What image does it send when the tools are used?
3. **Perceptions of waste:** Inefficiencies and unproductive time; business versus personal

4. **People skills:** Are they hindered or underdeveloped when people communicate less personally?
5. **Legal concerns:** Liabilities and risk mitigation.

The first three, it was agreed, are solved through education and creating clear expectations that suit your firm's culture. For this, I recommend engaging your team members to do the teaching and collaboration on expectation setting. These concerns and solution approaches are discussed in greater depth later in the chapter (see "A Facilitative Approach to Policy Development").

The fourth item, people skills, might require some awareness training and some preventative strategies as well. More interestingly, this is already considered to be an issue with the introduction of email into daily business use over the last decade and a half. Our collective experiences with the diminishing communications skills observed since email's introduction is probably behind this concern.

To the fifth point, legalities will always be an issue. Audit trail, risk mitigation, and processes to ensure quality control are realities those in the professions must address. Be sure that any lawyers you turn to for social media–related policy guidance aren't fearful about social media—consult lawyers who are very knowledgeable of, and have personal experience using, these new media. Research to see what social media activities they undertake. Start with a Google search—if you don't find them listed on the first page of Google when you search the names, find another advisor.

The group's overall takeaway: once their beliefs about communications technologies were evaluated and put into perspective they realized their policy behaviors were counterproductive and, in many cases, unfounded and reactionary.

Bear in mind that blogging and engaging others in social media is a worthy and valuable undertaking that creates high visibility for your firm. If you lay down too many restrictive "laws," you can kill or hamper the spirit of the effort. If it isn't "fun" for people to engage, they either won't do it or they'll do it poorly. You are seeking to inspire balance of responsibility and freedom or autonomy, much the way you do in your day-to-day work as a professional.

Liability and Risk Mitigation

With publicly disseminated content, whether a Web site, blog, tweet, print, or spoken word, according to the Electronic Frontier Foundation (EFF), we face the same general liability issues and we receive the same freedom of speech and press protections.[3] The EFF advises that the laws applying to blogs are "broadly applicable" to other types of online publishing. The main legal liability issues include:

- Defamation
- Intellectual property (copyright/trademark)
- Trade secret
- Right of publicity
- Publication of private facts
- Intrusion into seclusion

Regarding jurisdiction, the EFF states: ". . . the Constitution and federal laws, such as copyright law or Section 230, apply nationwide," but other laws such as "defamation, reporter shield laws, and privacy laws are defined by each state (within constitutional boundaries)." Other countries have less strong protections and need to be studied at the local level.

The liability concerns most frequently voiced by professionals surround:

- **Comment concerns:** Specifically third-party comments on firm-sponsored sites
- **Content concerns:** Being liable for inappropriate statements, in trouble with standards boards for statements construed as promising particular results or outcomes (most problematic for lawyers and registered investment advisors), and securing your intellectual capital
- **IT and security concerns:** Worry over losing or damaging irreplaceable data belonging to others, or unintentionally spreading malicious code

The Web and social media do pose security concerns, yet the jury is back and the verdict is in: the benefits of social media outweigh the risks of divulging sensitive information. Even the military has recognized this, and they rely on education and good judgment to manage security threats. If the U.S. military, with its enormous size and extremely high-stakes operations, can do this, a professional firm most certainly can.

In an article on social media benefits trumping fears, 26-year-old Spc. Michael Williams describes his practice of self-censorship to protect sensitive operations while stationed in the Middle East[4]:

> I know others want to know what I do or what I have done," he said. "I appreciate that . . . . However, it has been proven since recorded history began, that some things just should not be divulged." Similarly, Staff Sgt. Randall Cates says he watches out for himself and his colleagues, "Any type of media that can be accessed from the Internet

can be exploited by anyone seeking to do harm. I practice self-censorship every time I get on the Internet and encourage all my soldiers to do the same."

The military also appears to recognize that ignorance of social media is more dangerous than risks lingering upon understanding them:

"Researchers warn that if the government distances itself from Twitter and Facebook, Web 2.0 ignorance could pose its own security threat and hinder Department of Defense communication, efficiency and community-building efforts." And yet the article states, "There's no coordinated, department-wide policy for the DOD's use of social software tools internally, between agencies or with the public."

According to the article, the benefits of social media to the military are similar to those of professional firms: innovation, creativity, and meaningful conversation to build rapport and credibility with otherwise unreachable audiences. The bottom line is that they also recognize that "too much control could also be an obstacle." According to Dr. James Jay Carafano, a senior research fellow who studies national and homeland security issues at the conservative Heritage Foundation, "One of the benefits of social networking is the ability to innovate . . . and to be highly unstructured. If you start putting structure on that, you start eliminating some of the creativity and innovation."

Again, if the military can do it, a business can definitely do it. Education for all employees is key. And whether you have firm-level social media–related initiatives or not, education is necessary. Obviously, employees could mention the company in a profile not intended for work purposes, and it could come up in a Google search for your firm's name. These mishaps are preventable, as are most security holes.

Comment Concerns

It's wise to have a comment policy on any firm-sponsored sites, as well as somewhere on your company or personal Facebook pages and your LinkedIn profile, and perhaps on your background graphic in Twitter if you relay stories, ideas, or advice in these places.

As the owner or sponsor of a private site with a comment policy in place (read on for ideas about how to word your policy), commenters don't automatically maintain the right to post anything they wish. Your policy ought to include a statement indicating that all comments are moderated and that you retain the right to edit or remove comments at your sole discretion. In the interest of transparency and open conversation, you should also state what behaviors are not acceptable (that impact your "discretion") and would cause the removal or altering of comments.

The EFF advises that First Amendment rights do not allow "commenters to say whatever they want," and continues with exceptional advice in keeping with the spirit of the social Web: "Nevertheless, we encourage you to allow wide-open and robust debates in the comments on your blogs. Private action to edit or delete comments may be legal, but can also exclude important voices from a debate."

The court upheld a blogger's freedom from liability by third parties, according to Lawrence Savell, who says that in *Barrett v. Rosenthal*, "the Supreme Court of California ruled that, pursuant to the Communications Decency Act of 1996, 'plaintiffs who contend they were defamed in an Internet posting may only see recovery from the original source of the statement.'"[5]

As a practical matter, other than spam comments (people or bots using your comments feature to sell their products or services by linking to their sites that are unrelated to your topic) the instance of inflammatory or vulgar posts is extremely slim. I know of only a few received by my circle of blogging colleagues in more than five years that I've been blogging. This just isn't a common occurrence. But a stated policy will protect you in the event that it does happen.

Again, I am not a lawyer, so you should seek the counsel of an attorney who is knowledgeable in mass media law and the application of laws to the social Web, as well as being comfortable with using the Web to communicate, similar to the understanding of social Web nuances conveyed by the EFF.

Content Concerns

In the ten-plus years that professionals have been blogging, there is very little lawsuit activity. Professionals often want to know: "What happens if I share my opinions and, in doing so, say something that I shouldn't or unintentionally mislead someone with advice? Can I be sued?"

Kevin O'Keefe, an attorney, is president of Lexblog—a company that develops, hosts, and supports the majority of today's legal blogs. He was asked by a large, traditional law firm's general counsel about social media liability and ethics violation risk. O'Keefe reported that in six years, and with thousands of lawyers blogging on their platform, they "have not had any LexBlog lawyer authors who experienced ethical or liability problems."[6]

But O'Keefe also referenced a series of lawyers' social media "fails" that were highlighted in a 2009 *New York Times* article.[7,8] Four lawyers had exercised extremely poor judgment in their blog posts and on Facebook.

Two called judges names: "Evil, Unfair Witch," and "Judge Clueless"; another delayed trial, citing a death in the family, and the judge in his case busted him upon seeing his Facebook postings about drinking and motor-biking instead of grieving; and the fourth lawyer blogged about a case in which he was a juror.

As O'Keefe summarizes:

> *The lawyer acting as general counsel responded saying something to the effect of "We're not foolish enough to let that sort of thing happen. If that's the worst LexBlog has seen, it looks like a law firm may publish blogs without getting into ethical and liability difficulties."*
>
> *The lawyer then asked that I follow up our discussion with an email setting forth what I represented in the call. Rightly so, he wanted to have my representations with other research he may have done in his due diligence file.*
>
> *I'm not dismissing ethics and liability concerns when it comes to law blogs. But be practical when examining the issue.*
>
> *If you're smart, act prudently, educate yourself as to the ins and outs of blogging, develop standards of good blogging, and, if appropriate, have someone oversee your firm's blogging practices, the ethics and liability risks are minimal.*

When it comes to libel (print or web defamation), it is best defended with truth in fact. According to *The Blog Herald,* opinion can also be defended (without guarantee of success, of course) on the basis of personal view or opinion that is "fair comment on a matter of public interest."[9] The burden of proof falls to the plaintiff, who, if a public figure, "must also prove actual malice."

When you write content that contains opinion and advice, there are several things you can do for protection:

- Avoid absolutes (e.g., always, never, will, must), weaving in words like *may, might,* and *could* instead.
- Have appropriate disclaimers on your blog or other Web page that resemble what you would include in your print or email newsletter— that ideas in the content do not constitute specific professional advice, and the reader should consult an accredited professional to help assess his or her unique situation.
- Know and comply with ethics rules of your state, province, and other governing and professional standards bodies.

I'll talk more about disclaimers below, but a terrific example of a lawyer disclaimer is found on the blog of veteran legal blogger, Denise Howell.

She is an intellectual property (IP) and technology lawyer who started blogging in 2001 and is credited with coining the term *blawg*. To read her disclaimer, visit the "About" page of her blog at www.bagandbaggage.com/about/.

SECURITIES AND EXCHANGE COMMISSION (SEC) COMPLIANCE

Special situations exist for wealth managers who, under Rule 206(4) of the Investment Advisors Act of 1940, cannot display anything remotely resembling an endorsement from a client. While you cannot control (and aren't expected to control) what clients may write or post on their own domains, including Twitter, Facebook, or LinkedIn, you cannot host their comments or recommendations on your domains. There is little room for debate and no tolerance for breaches in a compliance audit.

The rule of thumb is that if you have the ability to remove or delete the endorsement, it is within your control and you would be expected by the SEC to do so.

As to social media participation in general, increasing numbers of investment advisors, asset managers, and fund companies are getting antsy sitting on the sidelines, waiting for compliance to figure out how to adapt to real-time communication, while social media grows and investors seem to expect advisors as well as fund companies to be listening and participating, just like the rest of the world. Incremental social media adoption is occurring with Vanguard launching YouTube and Facebook pages, and integrating social-media-esque content rating features on its Web site. Several companies have Twitter accounts, as do many advisors.

There are a handful of advisor blogs out there—doing quite well, I might add—and, yes, compliance does add a layer of hassle to getting your content live. You have to be even more committed to social media than those in less regulated professions. But it is possible to achieve if you are interested and dedicated.

SECURING YOUR INTELLECTUAL PROPERTY   Protecting your firm's IP is another concern of professionals in the knowledge fields. According to the Blog Herald, copyright term is currently the "lifetime of the author plus 70 years for works of personal authorship and 95 years for works of corporate authorship."[10] Further, the copyright symbol is not required to be displayed for a work to be protected, either yours or the work of someone whom you are citing. This is where *fair use*—a legally defined term with a lot of gray area—comes into play. Without going into details, if you unfailingly cite the source, repeat the bare minimum content urging a reader to go to the original author's page to see the full piece, and use the information with good intention and without appearing as though someone else's thoughts are yours, you'll be pretty safe. It's fair to expect the same of others. You actually *want* people to cite your work. It elevates your credibility and puts your name in front of a larger audience.

Sometimes people or automated "bots" will repost your content on their fake, spammy blogs called "splogs." They do this mostly to highly read and rated blogs, and they do it for the purpose of drawing search engine traffic because your content has good SEO, or search engine optimization. If you come upon such a site and can locate the creator (not usually easy to do), you can write a cease-and-desist letter. If that doesn't work, you can report the site to the Internet service provider (ISP) hosting the splog—and they will be required to remove it or the ISP can be held liable for the copyright infringement. I'll tell you from personal experience, however, that this is a pain, and the ISP puts the burden of proof on you, as the copyright holder, to prove the content belongs to you by filing a Digital Millenium Copyright Act notice. You aren't required to force removal when this happens, so it is up to you whether it is worth the time and energy to pursue. You'll have to weigh the cost/benefit of having your content elsewhere.

The social Web is about sharing content while respecting authors' rights, thus what has emerged is a terrific licensing mechanism, understood by the Web publishing community, called Creative Commons that works alongside copyright. The most frequently used Creative Commons license type is the Share Alike (sa) license, but other licenses are Attribution (by), Non-Commercial (nc), and No Derivative Works (nd). You can learn more about them at http://creativecommons.org/about/licenses/. License types are often combined (e.g., cc-by-sa), so you'll want to specify how people can refer to your work and understand what the terms mean so you know how to refer to the work of others.

IT and Security Concerns

Partners in law and accounting firms sometimes tell me their IT professionals urge them to restrict all access to social media sites. This, in some firms, even means eliminating the ability to view blogs. I couldn't help but think of this when I was in China last year and unable to view blogs, Twitter, and Facebook. Are we really emulating China in our firms? Really?

It seems "security" is a reason often cited for these restrictions, but I'm sure partners are further swayed by what is, in their minds, the "positive" benefit of keeping people off social media sites during business hours. I hope I am effective—within this book—in making the case for supporting business-related social media interactions. But let's discuss the security issues. Not being an IT expert myself, I asked IT and practice management consultant Jim Boomer, CIO of Boomer Consulting, Inc. what his advice is to firms who are blocking social media, or still considering doing so. Jim doesn't agree with locking down social media sites, suggesting it is an overreaction:

> *We've seen this trend before. Consider the similarities with the Internet and email when they first infiltrated the workplace. Users were click-happy and infecting networks left and right. IT's knee-jerk reaction was to block its usage. As time passed and the tremendous value of Internet access became apparent, companies started to ease up on the controls and focus more on training end-users on appropriate online behavior. I believe that, once again, as social media in the business matures and the value becomes unquestionable, IT will focus less on control and more on end-user training.*

Jim knows this, alone, won't satisfy IT professionals steadfast in their determination to avoid all possible risk. For this he recommends:

> *Software tools are available to help the enterprise manage security while still taking advantage of public facing social media sites. In addition, there's a trend of moving business data into secure social environments to increase ease of access to data and leverage the benefits offered by public tools such as LinkedIn and Facebook.*

With these IT and security concerns, education is absolutely key. Being Web sites themselves, social media do pose security concerns similar to those inherent in email and any other Internet use.

Like email, a concerning aspect of social media sites versus other Web sites is that there is an element of trust in clicking links that have come from names you recognize. For this reason, Kaspersky Lab, an Internet security vendor, says: "malicious code distributed by social networking sites is ten times more effective in terms of successful infection, than malware spread via email."[11] For a very long time, email spammers have capitalized on the tendency of people to trust their "friends" in order to obtain access to login credentials and contact lists and to launch malicious code that is possibly harmful and almost always a nuisance. As computer users, we've learned to be increasingly cautious about email schemes, and we need to do the same with social media.

To mitigate these risks, reinforce to employees the importance of remaining skeptical about suspicious links, especially when delivered in poorly worded messages and items not personally addressed. Jim Boomer stresses applying the same approaches to social media as to other web-based communications:

> *Training end-users to use the same common sense that they use when surfing the web or reading email is so important. If the question "should I click on this?" runs through your mind, default to no. If you don't feel 100% sure about something that is sent to you, regardless of the means it was sent, ask the sender if it was really from them before clicking on anything.*

Some social media tools are trying to help. On Facebook, when friends share links, the link usually displays a preview, so this helps validate its authenticity. When using Twitter or LinkedIn, users can rely on link preview application plugins (usually with browsers other than Internet Explorer such as Firefox, Safari, or Chrome) allowing them to hover over a link before clicking to preview it and help determine if it is legitimate. In Twitter, it is wise to refrain from clicking on any link received through the Direct Message feature unless you absolutely know it's safe because you were expecting the link from the sender.

Employees should also be taught to be extremely selective about third-party applications that ask for Facebook, Twitter, or LinkedIn login credentials—phishing scams rely on users' relatively casual willingness to share this information. The more a person intertwines the various social media tools through third-party applications that cross-post and so on, the more vulnerable he or she becomes. With the exception of LinkedIn's Twitter cross-posting service, it's best to avoid these applications.

And to help prevent hacking, educate employees about not using the same passwords across multiple sites. And do you know that "password" is the most common password? Don't use that. Conduct training sessions to heighten awareness about what scams (phishing, etc.) look like, what precautionary measures people can take for personal and corporate privacy, and good practices for protecting image and reputation.

Keep Policies Simple

You *could* have one policy for Twitter, another for blogs, and yet another for Facebook. And this would establish a requirement to create an entirely new policy for every new tool that emerges. Considering the speed of innovation with Web-based tools, you don't want to have to reconvene your policy makers to create and debate policy for every newly emerging tool, do you? At the pace of social media evolution, this may occur several times per year. Or, worse, you could refuse employees' access to the tools because you don't have time to make policies governing their use.

So let me ask, how do you do approach policy now? Do you have one policy for email, another for telephone conversations, another for articles, another for speaking at seminars, another for letters, another for memos, and yet another for texting?

Do you presently have a general communications policy? Consider saving yourself management time and hassle by operating with one solid general communications policy. Such a policy should sufficiently cover every type of employee communication from telephone calls and old-fashioned letters to blog comments, "tweets," and Facebook posts. This simplifies things for management and for team members, too. It's a lot easier for people to remember (and comply with) the firm's general communications standards than it is to reference separate policies around each and every tool.

A good communications policy that represents the values of the firm, and still leaves ample room for your professionals to exercise their judgment, is ideal. You are, after all, professionals.

Before Forming a New Policy

Before you start developing a new policy or revamping an old one, gather any of the following documents that you may already have:

- The firm's core values statement
- Any current policies governing the items below and other communication-related policies
- All disclaimers the firm uses for print and Web, including anything that covers:
  - Articles
  - Newsletters
  - Seminars
  - Print and email correspondence
  - Answering the phone
  - Conversations at business lunches
  - Giving "free" spontaneous advice

Review existing policies for alignment with your core values and for possible "overkill." Are there elements you would strike in light of what you've read so far? Are there elements you'd like to retain in a big-picture communications policy? If so, set these aside for possible inclusion as you read more about policy elements and suggestions.

A Facilitative Approach to Policy Development

I am a facilitator. As such, I want to share a secret. Involving the right people in the process of policy creation is the magical secret to success in policy adherence. It is also the vehicle through which your firm's leadership gets to *really* know how people feel about the tools and their applicability in the business environment. Through a facilitated conversation, management can actually get the team to outline the concerns the business should have and to propose solutions, which creates an entirely different attitude toward the firm's resulting policy. I cannot overemphasize how valuable this is to an organization.

The creation of social media policy is the perfect place to experiment with this better approach, especially after the morale-damaging ways in which most firms have laid out their email, Internet, and even dress code policies. Trust me on this. A facilitative approach empowers the "next generation" to contribute, and they will surprise you.

Elect to create a more fitting and culture-preserving (or even culture-improving) policy through a healthy and informed process.

Engaging Leadership

In the managing partner session I facilitated (mentioned in "Five Factors Contributing to Discomfort"), I could have simply lectured to the group on what their concerns ought to be and how to approach them. But instead, the leaders spent time deliberating on their own heartfelt concerns that I shared with you earlier. You and your partners may have some different concerns. If you want to avoid revisiting the same concerns in future partner meetings, be sure that everyone's concerns are aired and analyzed, validated, and resolved in order for them to be put to rest either through education or articulated guidelines.

Social media use is complex and pushes a lot of buttons for partners. It is worthwhile to get your partners in a room and provoke discussion to explore why your partners might be uncomfortable with the practices. Try asking: "What factors do you think contribute to our lack of comfort in using these forms of communication?"

Engaging Team Members

Remembering that a key cause of the managing partners' discomfort with new media was fear of the unknown, the resolution is found through education. A great source of education may be right under your noses—ask your resident experts: team members who use new media. Here is an approach to try:

- Invite them to educate your management team. "Teach us about [insert tool here] and give us specific ideas about specific business applications of [tool] for our firm."
- Ask them to anticipate concerns about the tool's use (gets them into owner mind-set).
- Charge them with creating "best practices" to address those concerns.
- Consider empowering them as a subgroup to evaluate future "emerging" technologies in a similar way.

Policy Elements and Samples

We've discussed how policies speak volumes about your culture. In a profession where judgment is requisite and highly valued, it's imperative that you honor the intellect and judgment of your firm's employees.

At one end of the spectrum, we have employment lawyer Jay Shepherd's two-word corporate blogging policy that can also conveniently double as a firm's communications policy.[12] The two words are "be professional." At the other end of the spectrum, we have "kitchen sink" policies. Being reasonably risk averse, accountants (and lawyers) tend to want to include at least a little something addressing every possible scenario.

The danger to your firm in reviewing a bunch of other policies—including several to which I've provided links—is that you will probably be tempted to identify every possible scenario and include at least a few sentences on each. In no time at all, you'll have a 20-page policy. And I've thoroughly covered the detriments of overkill policies throughout this chapter.

The majority of "social media" concerns are adequately addressed within policies that may already exist—the first three policy categories listed below. There are just a few remaining items, specific to social media tools that could be added in a fourth category.

1. Liability disclaimers
2. General communications and behavior
3. Internet and email policies
4. Specific social media tool policies

You may also wish to create a "purpose statement" regarding the firm's social media. A purpose statement is different from a "policy," but you may decide it fits under "guidelines." Many companies incorporate the two.

Remember, when it comes to social media, people need to feel *inspired*, not controlled or forced, or they will not participate effectively. A good example of a "purpose/policy" example that inspires more than it controls is www.rightnow.com/privacy-social.php.

Regarding the policy samples below, I provide my own disclaimer. I'm not an attorney. Again, for your social media needs, be sure to find an attorney who's more comfortable with (not more fearful of) social media than you or your firm. The policy recommendations herein are not guaranteed for completeness, accuracy, and legality. Seek the advice of informed legal counsel who are well skilled in social media–related communications as well as assistance from state and federal governmental resources, to make certain your legal interpretations and decisions are appropriate.

Liability Disclaimers

There are some basic legal disclaimers you'll want to include for public access on your firm-sponsored publications such as blogs, Web sites, wikis, or any other firm-owned and branded Web-based forum. In addition to the IRS Circular 230 Disclosure and your general privacy policy, it's customary to include disclaimers on the following topics:

- **Nonspecific advice:** "This information is of a general nature, not intended to be specific professional advice; seek the opinion of a professional to advise you in your unique situation."
- **Individual versus firm views:** "Authors' opinions are their own and do not represent the view of the company."
- **Third-party content:** "The firm is not responsible for the accuracy or appropriateness of third-party comments or articles, including those of guest authors and editorial contributions."
- **"Letters to the editor" (in blogs, print newsletters, or other forums where they are allowed):** "Comments, letters, and other submissions are moderated and may be edited or withheld at the sole discretion of the firm."

ADDITIONS TO THE EMPLOYEE MANUAL   Related not so much to firm liability but to each employee's personal liabilities and responsibilities, there are a couple of items of guidance and advice you may wish to add to your overall employee manual. Again, these pertain to Internet or social media use outside of the firm, but these communications vehicles have heightened the need for firms to disclaim liability for employee actions and make employees aware of possible consequences for their online behaviors.

You may wish to inform employees about their own personal liability regarding their written and verbal statements. Sample verbiage below comes from Susan Heathfield on About.com[13]:

Employee Personal Legal Liability

Recognize that you are legally liable for anything you write or present online or in print. Employees can be disciplined by the company for commentary, content, or images that are defamatory, pornographic, proprietary, harassing, libelous, or that can create a hostile work environment. You can also be sued by employees, competitors, and any individual or company that views your work as such.

Just this week, I learned of a scenario in which the presence of this statement would have been helpful. A firm's employee was bullying another employee on Facebook and it was brought to the human resources director's attention. Both Facebook accounts were private, so it wasn't technically a firm issue, but the situation was definitely creating a hostile work environment, and the firm, with this statement, would have had a basis on which to discipline the employee.

The employee manual is also a good place to include the following request in the event an employee starts his own blog:

If an employee authors a non-firm-sponsored blog or Web site, it should include a simple and visible disclaimer, such as "these are my personal views and not those of [FIRM], my employer."

Some firms ask employees to adhere to some guidelines in their nonfirm forums and communications. A nice, simple policy for use in such a situation follows. The concepts here are solid enough that this could also serve as the firm's "social media policy" if you prefer short and sweet.

Sample Policy for Employee-Originated Publications or Communications Outside of the Firm

Know and follow the firm's guidelines for conduct and communications. Be mindful of what you write. Remember that you have an audience. Do not use ethnic slurs, insults, or obscenity. Avoid writing about inflammatory topics solely to pique prurient interests. Always try to add to a discussion constructively and ultimately to add value. Do not let your ego get the better of you.

Apply the rules of good writing. Be accurate in your posts: others will look to them as a source of information and news, if not actual research. Respect copyright and fair use. Do not plagiarize. Give credit where due by citing and linking to the author of a statement or passage.

Identify yourself and write in first person. Make it clear that you are not necessarily speaking for the firm as a whole. Be sure to disclose any information necessary to keep your statements from being misleading. Use the following disclaimer on all your publications, including blogs: Unless indicated to the contrary, my writings are my own opinions and do not reflect the views of the firm I work for, its owners, or employees.

Do not reveal confidential information that could result in liability to you, your practice group, other firm members, or the firm itself. Do not comment on client matters by name except with the approval of those referred to in the post.

Have fun. Communicating, writing, and speaking can be loads of fun and a terrific way to share the best of your personality, knowledge, and business demeanor with the world.

This was inspired in part by a policy (no longer in effect) developed for DuPage Bar Association by attorney and Chicago area blogger Mazyar M. Hedayat.

General Communication Policy

Whether pertaining to verbal, print, or online communications, these are excellent "ground rules" you might consider applying:

Be polite and sincere.
- Use impeccable manners, even when you disagree.
- Listen first, and always in proportion of ears and mouth.
- Discrimination, harassment, and slanderous comments are not acceptable.
- Always speak respectfully of the competition and current or past employees.
- Even when feedback is negative, begin a reply by thanking the person for sharing their thoughts, feelings, or concerns.
Be positive.
- There are two ways to present things: glass half-full or half-empty. For best results, use the half-full presentation.
- Remember Grandma's advice, "If you have nothing nice to say, don't say anything at all."
Be professional.
- Behave with honor and integrity.
- Make promises you intend to keep, and keep them.
- Avoid self-aggrandizing or self-promotion.

- Speak on behalf of the company *only* if specifically permitted by your manager; otherwise, employees are not authorized to speak on behalf of the company, nor represent that you do so.
- Properly and generously cite original sources (including links) to credit the original conveyer of an idea or information.
- Be sensitive to, and respect, any personal/business boundaries set by others. Recognize that there is no assurance of a clear line between the two—know that any information you share personally may inadvertently impact your business life.
- Be transparent online, disclosing your identity and affiliation with the firm and clients (when permitted) to avoid any perception that you are promoting professional or personal interests in a nonstraight-forward manner.
- Use your name—not an alias—and never be anonymous with your postings.
- Only say things you won't mind seeing again, including in a court or in front of your spouse or mother.

Protect confidentiality of clients and the company.

- Always keep client confidences and identity unless written permission is granted.
- This includes information about sales, finances, company strategy, and any other information that has not been publicly released by the company.
- Seek permission of clients, fellow employees, business partners, or suppliers before naming or quoting them in any written piece, or showing, uploading, or tagging a photo or video of them online or in print.

Internet and Email Policy

IT security needs and approaches change constantly, and I don't profess to be an IT expert, but these suggested policy items cover the big bases for Internet best practices in a professional firm.

- All suspicious links and attachments, even from friends, should be avoided. Never click or open links/attachments from people you don't know. Even if you do know them, don't open the file unless you are expecting it. Not sure, ask.
- Do not download programs/applications from the Web—including third-party Facebook or Twitter applications—using office computers, without first obtaining permission from the IT department who can help ensure that the applications are legitimate.
- Streaming video and audio are bandwidth hogs that slow performance of the firm's network. Use them sparingly, and be aware that you may

be asked to refrain from accessing these types of files at times of heavy system demand.

- Take care to avoid inappropriate Web sites using company resources (improper trade, porn, games, etc.).
- Email communications and all other transmissions (such as texts or IMs) are permanent, never assured to be private, and are "discoverable" by law. Never send sensitive client or firm information via unsecured means.
- Email correspondence should follow the same professional standards as written correspondence. And never manage emotionally charged or highly sensitive situations via email—it does not replace real conversation.

Social Media Specific Policy

As mentioned in Chapter 1, social media tools fall into two categories: firm-sponsored publications/forums that include blogs and Web sites, and outside forums such as Twitter, Facebook, and LinkedIn. The following items pertain to both unless otherwise specified:

Quoting others:
- Keep verbatim quotes as short as possible, indent them, cite and link to the original source.
- Know and abide by Creative Commons Licensing terms (www .creativecommons.org).
- Always use "trackbacks" wherever possible.
- Ask permission to quote someone or something if the information is not already public (see General Communications Policy).
Photos:
- Become familiar with Creative Commons Licensing (www .creativecommons.org) terms. Only use photos (such as those found on flickr.com) with appropriate permissions and citation.
- Make sure images are properly credited by citing the source and photographer, if applicable.
- Obtain permission to display photos of others (see General Communications Policy).
Comments:
- Respond promptly to legitimate comments (see General Communications Policy).
- Be considerate about engaging in private feedback where fitting.
- On other blogs, post meaningful, respectful comments—in other words, no self-promotional verbiage (SPAM) and no remarks that are off-topic or offensive.

- Always try to add to the discussion constructively and to ultimately add value.

Recommendations or endorsements:

- Providing positive recommendations for people outside the firm is encouraged, but recommendations for current employees cannot be permitted due to human resources potential liabilities.
- *Financial advisors, registered investment advisors (RIAs), and other wealth advisory firms only:* Accepting for public posting any recommendations received from clients is not permitted in accordance with SEC rules against use of testimonials in any form.

With these suggested policy elements and sample verbiage, your organization will be off to a strong start as you begin adopting social media communications tools. Chapter 3 begins introducing you to the individual tools covered in this book.

Comparing Today's Most Popular Social Media

At present, there are four new media tools that are most suitable for professionals and their firms: LinkedIn, Twitter, Facebook, and blogs. This chapter briefly describes these four tools and compares them to help you discern how you might use them in your firm-level or individual-level marketing.

The pace of innovation is rapid so these are unlikely to be the most popular and effective tools for your business use in a few years. Emerging tools will build upon or replace these tools. Therefore, as you read, and later as you formulate your strategy, consider the objectives each tool helps you accomplish (through its features) rather than focusing on a tool's current popularity alone. Popularity is certainly a legitimate consideration, however, because of the value of critical mass when you set out to locate and interact with specific people. LinkedIn, for instance, is exponentially more valuable than competitor sites due to the sheer number of people who use it.

Recognizing that new tools will continually emerge reinforces the importance of clarity in your marketing objectives—your purpose—behind adopting any specific tool. After discussing each tool, we'll discuss the types of objectives the various tools can help you achieve.

Comparing the Tools

Unless you have the tremendous time and resources it takes to establish a strong presence everywhere at once, you'll want to decide which new media to explore and, among those, what to bite off first. Table 3.1 is subjective, based on my experience with the way CPAs and lawyers would and do use the tools. People in other professions may experience greater or lesser usefulness or concerns with the tools assessed in the tables.

The objectives, benefits, and concerns listed in Tables 3.1 and 3.2 can also be used when you need to evaluate new tools as they emerge. Contrast the features and benefits of the new tools with any tools you are using. After weighing these factors, you can determine if migration from a current tool to a new one is best for you, or whether adopting a tool in addition to a current one is the best course for you. Alternately, you may determine the newer technology is not a good fit for you at all.

TABLE 3.1 Compare Usefulness (more stars = more useful based on moderate to excellent use of the tool)

Objectives or benefits (C = credibility oriented, N = networking oriented)	LinkedIn	Twitter	Facebook	Blogs
Obtain answers to questions (C)	★★★★	★★★★	★★★★	★★★★
Demonstrate your expertise, establish credibility (C)	★★★	★★	★★	★★★★
Increase your knowledge (C)	★★★	★★★	★	★★★
Distribute content (C)	★★	★★★	★★★	★★★★
Sustain customer loyalty when things go wrong (C)	★★	★★★★	★★★★	★★★★
Communicate without distributing content (firm developed or otherwise) (N)	★★★	★★	★★★★	★
Promote others (building goodwill) (N)	★★★★	★★★★	★★★	★★★★
Conducive to deepening relationships, building rapport (N)	★★	★★	★★★★	★★
Connect others together (facilitate mutually beneficial introductions) (N)	★★★★	★★★★	★★★★	★★
Regularly alerted to opportunities for interaction (reasons to reach out as others update) (N)	★★★★	★★★	★★★★	★
Identify resources (N)	★★★★	★★★	★★★	★★★
Maintain contact and reconnect (N)	★★★★	★★	★★★★	★★
Meet new people (N)	★★★	★★★★	★★	★★★★
Promote events and firm-hosted activities (C/N)	★★★	★★	★★	★★
Recruiting (via a firm vs. individual presence) (C/N)	★★★★	★★★	★★★★	★★

TABLE 3.2 Concerns (more stars = greater concern)

Concerns	LinkedIn	Twitter	Facebook	Blogs
Business/personal crossover among contacts	N/A	★	★★★★	N/A
Time investment to be effective	★★★	★★	★★★	★★★★
Noticeable if absent	★	★★	★★★	★★★★
Process needs/considerations for best execution (internal, firm level)	★	★	★★	★★

Taking the time to assess each tool before committing significant resources is always wise. It may be that you will need to test a tool or seek the opinions of others in order to fully assess the new tool. A very good approach, because of its inclusive nature, is to involve your younger or more tech-savvy employees in the assessment if it turns out they are exploring the technology on their own. For specific ways to involve your people, refer to the methodology presented in Chapter 2 in "A Facilitative Approach to Policy Development," as the same principles apply.

Intersection of Business and Personal

If you have managed thus far to maintain good, solid compartmentalization between your business and your personal life, you're ahead of the rest of us. It's not an easy thing to do these days. In fact, for some of us, we couldn't neatly sort the people in our lives into the two buckets of *business* and *friends* if our lives depended on it.

But this blur of personal and professional isn't really a new thing at all, is it? For years, we've become friends with clients, and friends become clients. Coworkers become like family. Sometimes they literally become family. It's not uncommon that lawyers wed other lawyers and so on. With the hours many professionals put in, where else would they meet anyone?

Collecting all your contacts in one place, particularly a place as intimate as Facebook, is complicated, too. There is the clear challenge of deciding how much of your personal side to bare to whom. While you might whip out your billfold to show off some pictures of your kids at a business gathering, you hardly want the same people seeing photos of you in your beachwear chasing your kid or your dog, right? Fortunately, Facebook—the most likely tool to raise the business-meets-personal-dilemma—has excellent, detailed privacy settings.

LinkedIn

LinkedIn is a user-profile-based database that houses users' professional background information, their contacts, and their affiliated groups and associations. These comprise one's "network," and within a user's network various interactions can occur through groups they belong to, events they sign up for, or just periodic updates—a feature added to emulate Twitter and Facebook.

With over 75 million users—49 percent of whom are considered "decision makers"—LinkedIn's success is directly correlated with its widespread adoption—the more participants, the more effective it is. Through its growth, LinkedIn has become an increasingly powerful tool and is regarded as a safe place to "collect" a lifetime of business connections. LinkedIn is decidedly mainstream for business use and isn't going away anytime soon. Plaxo, a competing online business networking tool, doesn't seem to have that sort of foothold and doesn't offer as many features—it also seems somewhat invasive compared to LinkedIn.

LinkedIn is excellent for keeping up with the über-transient, investigating through whom you can reach someone you haven't yet met, and disseminating tidbits of information in a nonintrusive way.

With automatic notifications of changes to your contacts' profiles, LinkedIn is especially valuable to those of us who have experienced a loss of contact with people over time—people who were important to us and with whom reconnecting would be personally or professionally valuable. With so many people using a powerful, mainstream tool like LinkedIn, maintaining contact needn't be a problem in the future. The impact this alone can have on cultivating a strong base of referrals, prospects, and potential employees is unparalleled in the history of professional firm marketing and recruiting.

Researching within your broad contact base to find connections to prospective clients is a brilliant way to use LinkedIn. To optimize this and mimic some of the advantages of pricey contact management systems, employees can upload their contacts and connect to each other or even just to one main person. Then, to explore connections with ABC Company, a search of that company by someone connected to all the others will turn up your contacts' extended networks—three degrees deep—providing possible introduction chains to persons employed or affiliated, past or present, with that company.

Users often post updates comprising text and links that appear, along with notifications of other activities, in users' Weekly Network Updates. LinkedIn status updates permit the longest entries among the social tools featured here—up to 700 characters. These Network Updates often constitute good reasons for you to reach out and congratulate contacts or otherwise engage in dialogue. Further interaction can occur via common-interest groups by posting or answering "questions." After you answer questions, in their periodic Network Updates, your contacts see that you've answered one or more questions on a designated topic and can click to view your contribution. It's a nonintrusive way to demonstrate expertise throughout your network—letting you subtly strut your stuff in front of that influential past acquaintance or the lawyer parent on your kid's soccer team with whom you've hoped to one day talk business.

A challenge with LinkedIn is the unknown context of various peoples' connections. While LinkedIn suggests that users only connect to people whom they'd be comfortable recommending or endorsing, this criterion simply isn't uniform across all users. Some people link to people they've only just met or to anyone that requests a connection. There's nothing wrong with either approach per se, but the inconsistency from user to user illustrates why it's necessary to talk to people before requesting introductions or providing referrals—context is everything. I also strongly recommend that people ignore the automated "introduction" feature because it's cold and much less helpful, in every way, than personal conversations.

There are also concerns with LinkedIn that surround legal implications of good "recommendations" made of employees who are later terminated for performance issues. A policy disallowing recommendations of current employees is wise to prevent this sort of problem. Save your recommendations for referral sources, clients, and other outside business partners. A goal of providing a recommendation every month or two is a nice idea.

Finally, since LinkedIn requires only moderate interaction, it isn't too time consuming. And being a business tool, business/personal boundaries are less apt to be crossed when using it.

Twitter

Twitter is a forum that consists of a running thread of 140-character (or fewer) postings called "tweets." Through a very simple (minimalist) interface, users subscribe to or "follow" people of their choice. There is no obligation to follow anyone in particular. Because pretty much anything goes, there is a lot of junk on Twitter—spammers and unseemly types—and an unbelievable volume of information (from annoying to mediocre to excellent) that can draw you in for hours if you let it.

Despite its downsides, there is enormous power to be found with this tool—for instance, all significant news breaks on Twitter—that is part of the lure.

If you follow more than a handful of people (necessary for Twitter to be very interesting) you will find that "keeping up" is not an option—you needn't try. Twitter offers a "list" feature to help you group and filter those you follow, and most want to read—and you can view others' lists to find good people to follow or to save time in your reading. Third-party applications like Tweetdeck help users manage and prioritize the information they are most interested in capturing.

Monitoring Twitter is a wise public relations activity so that positive mentions can be met with an appreciative thank you and negative mentions can be remedied with helpful attitudes. Waiting until a problem occurs to set up a presence on Twitter is suboptimal. That's exactly what US Airways did an hour and 24 minutes after its airliner landed in the Hudson River. This was 56 minutes after MSNBC had interviewed the first person to tweet the story, and 30 minutes after competitor Southwest Airlines had tweeted "our friends at USAir and their customers are in our thoughts this afternoon."

A Twitter presence by human representatives of the company (individuals are far preferable to a "logo" account face) can be a worthwhile marketing initiative for the purpose of public engagement and brand management—especially in the face of publicly announced service problems or issues—even if you are not a major airline.

Twitter is especially effective for business development relative to niche specialty areas and when tied with blogging initiatives or other content the firm can share. A large number of Twitter users also author blogs—they work well together.

Twitter is about sharing information. While some users do share inane facts (e.g., "I had a PB&J for lunch") most business users share tips and links to articles or news they feel is worthwhile or controversial in order to spark interest or conversation. It's best to provide a mix of content that includes works of others' and one's own works. Maintaining a high ratio of others-to-me postings can prevent you from coming across as a shameless self-promoter, a huge turnoff in all social media circles. A good rule of thumb is to promote, recommend, and "retweet" (which is to forward another person's tweet) others at least 10 : 1 for each self-mention. A side benefit of using this tool is that posting in 140-character snippets definitely teaches brevity.

Facebook

Facebook is a social networking platform initially established by a Harvard student. When made available to the public, it grew rapidly, in part because it was more private, and more professional looking, than it's closest comparative product, MySpace, which isn't appropriate for a professional firm to use for business development. Facebook is far more conducive to ongoing conversation than LinkedIn. Like LinkedIn, it facilitates group discussions and event promotion. Like Twitter and LinkedIn, Facebook also has a "status update" feature, allowing 420 characters, far more than Twitter's 140-character limit. Facebook's popularity stems from its relative ease of use, particularly as a photo-sharing and conversation hub.

Facebook's average user age is now over 40 for a couple of reasons. One, reconnecting with former classmates is free through Facebook, so it quickly outpaced paid alumni sites like Classmates.com. Another reason is user-friendly photo sharing. Digital cameras make it more efficient to share photos with relatives and friends electronically than the old print way, and Facebook facilitates this securely and for free. Grandparents find they need to get on Facebook to see their grandkids' photos. Now parents also set up accounts to keep in touch with their college-aged or teenaged kids. Since family connections are the genesis of Facebook's growth spurt, a big issue for many users is pressure to invite business contacts into their personal circles. Some users have two accounts—one each for business and personal use but this violates Facebook's terms of use.

The use of Facebook groups, or company pages, is where professional firms come into play at the organizational level. Otherwise, the best option is for a professional to use his or her personal account for developing or deepening business relationships. The platform can indeed be extremely conducive to the accelerated development of business relationships, but this is better achieved by individual account holders than by a firm-level account.

A corporate presence can make sense if the firm has good content to disseminate or hosts a number of events. Most professional firms, so far, are finding that a corporate presence on Facebook is more fruitful for recruiting than business development. The human resources department can be a good place to house the firm's Facebook page's daily management. Gainer Donnelly & Desroches in Houston does exactly this. Their recruiter leverages Facebook to stay in touch with a large percentage of college students with whom she's nurturing relationships. Postings to the firm's page include photos that show the fun side of the firm as well as things that make those associated with the firm proud, such as headlining news and making a difference in the community.

Because of its highly personal nature, it's best not to require employees to participate in or connect on Facebook (such as they might for LinkedIn). The choice of whether to combine business and nonbusiness contacts is a highly personal decision—one that should be respected.

Also respect that business contacts who are on Facebook may be there solely to interact with family and close friends. They may recoil from the prospect of "friending" a business acquaintance or a corporate presence. Do not take this personally, even if you never hear a peep back from someone you make a request of, because Facebook etiquette is such that it is perfectly acceptable to "ignore" a friend request.

If you want to give the blending of personal and business a try, Facebook does offer very powerful, highly customizable privacy settings so you can limit who views too-personal family photos or most any other information on your account. But you should bear in mind, of course, that nothing put on the Internet can ever be guaranteed private or secure.

Blogs

Technically, blogs are just distinctly structured Web sites that contain short, conversational-style articles (called "posts"), each housed on a separate URL, that are date/time stamped, and can be commented on by readers. For professionals, blogs serve as something of a holy grail in their simultaneous ability to substantiate the author's expertise and draw qualified leads to the author.

But most exciting, from a marketing perspective, is the fact that while blogs house your intellectual capital on the Internet for your and others' perpetual, easily searchable reference 24/7/365, they also disseminate or push your content through RSS or Real Simple Syndication to RSS feed readers (tools that are mainstream now), or to email if people subscribe to receive your postings this way. Blogs can replace or supplement an email content distribution program at far less expense and far greater ease. Traditional push-marketing of content, such as with email and print newsletters, has readership limited to physical recipients and anyone they pass it to, but blogs are "alive" and available anytime, anywhere—this facilitates simultaneous "pull-marketing" for intended recipients and new prospects.

Being that blog posts are written more casually than a technical piece (i.e., journal article) they tend to be written in language that real people use in day-to-day conversation, and that people are more likely to search for, so they are considered "content rich" where search engines are concerned. In stark contrast to the language typically found on professional firm Web sites—fluff and puffery—blog posts open new doors to effective search engine strength. Even two or three blog posts on a given subject, and the firm's search engine rankings can improve dramatically for terms found in the posts.

More helpfully, authoring blog posts lets professionals show a bit of their personality at the same time that it emphasizes their expertise. Since people would rather buy from people they know and like—sort of the way you get to know a particular newspaper columnist whom you read regularly—having a regular reader of your blog is a brilliant relationship accelerant.

Blogs definitely require more energy to maintain than one's LinkedIn presence, though time spent on Twitter or Facebook could range from much more to much less. But blogging provides benefits the other social media channels cannot, dramatically elevating one's standing in the profession, leading to speaking and publishing offers, increasing qualified business inquiries, and significantly underscoring credibility. Blog technology also easily facilitates dissemination, promotion, and storage of podcasts and videocasts should your firm be interested in these methods of sharing knowledge.

Building readership and a blog following (also called "subscriber base") requires producing interesting posts on a fairly regular basis. Readership is fueled by your reading of other blogs on related topics and commenting on posts. These comments create links back to your blog, and readership grows organically. Interacting with other authors and their readers to become part of the Web community that shares interest in your particular subject matter is an important aspect of the blog community. Writing a blog and never corresponding with others is equivalent to speaking at a trade conference and not talking to anyone in attendance before, during, or after. It fails to maximize the opportunity you've created.

To establish and maintain a blog, posting two to three times per week is recommended. Much more is not necessarily better. Less and the benefits decrease, but the endeavor can still be worthwhile.

Summary of Part 1

This first section covering the definition of social media, the origin of the technology, and its distinct tone, have helped set the scene for the next chapter on the ways social media are most effectively used in professional firms today and over the past ten years. Before we jumped into what the tools do and how to use the tools, I felt it was beneficial to address risks and policies because, in my experience talking with firms, these questions are the most prevalent when the topic of social media comes up. They tend to make the arms cross and brows furrow. Hopefully the arms and brows are little more relaxed now.

Through covering "how we got here" and where we're going, I hope to have allayed the greatest concerns that professionals have about social media use in their firms so we can move ahead toward using the tools for outstanding results.

WHY

*The "Why" behind
Using Social Media*

CHAPTER 4

Finding Business Purpose in Social Media

P urpose dictates "why" you do what you do in your practice. It makes little or no sense to pursue use of social media tools without clarity of purpose—a clear sense of why. This chapter begins the Why part of the book, in which you'll explore and decide your purpose and objectives in using social media. First, we'll explore some basic underlying concepts in this chapter.

In Chapter 1, several advantages and reasons behind using social media were introduced (see "What Social Media Help Achieve," "How We Got Here," and "Social Media versus Other Marketing Approaches"). This chapter reinforces a few of those points and introduces a handful of additional business purposes. It covers being findable, being fallible, participating in your reputation or external brand perception, increasing your value through differentiation, and building social capital.

As you set about rethinking how you market your practice, recognize that although it feels like there is a marked loss of control of your reputation or brand because of social media, we actually only had an illusion of control over these things before. The speed and reach of potentially damaging messages have certainly increased but only to the same degree as the speed and reach of very valuable, positive messages to reinforce the strengths of your personal and professional reputation (they are now one) and your firm's brand online.

Setting yourself apart to gain competitive and price advantage requires finding ways to illustrate your skill and intellect and engaging others—particularly those who have influence with your buyers—in meaningful interactions. This builds your social capital, the least measurable but perhaps most valuable of the three types of intellectual capital.

Accomplishing these things might require some shifts in mind-set about your practice, too. This chapter sets out several concepts that support success in social media as you interweave them into your practice development strategies.

Being Findable

Professionals have benefitted from the warm referral for ages. You've probably received a call from a person who learned your name through chatting with a neighbor, hitting up a colleague over lunch, or phoning a friend to ask, "Who do you recommend for . . .?" This type of referral pool was much smaller before the Internet.

People still care what others think—perhaps even more than before. Erik Qualman, the author of *Socialnomics,* says[1]:

> *We can see a dramatic shift in that 92 percent of consumers now cite word-of-mouth as the best source for product and brand information, up from 67 percent in 1977.*

Since Web access is so widespread, most people turn to the Internet first when they need to research future purchases, including business and service needs. Therefore, online peer recommendations have become more influential than ever.

Then and now, we apply filters in validating some recommendations over others. Sometimes we seek objective, third-party reviews (like *Consumer Reports* magazine) and sometimes we want to know individuals' biases—much the way you could anticipate that Bill's movie preferences match your own and Sally's are usually the opposite of what you like. Either way, you know how to filter these opinions. Overall, we consistently regard the reviewer's perspective as more credible than the seller's claims. Current studies reflect this continued reality, "Today, 76 percent rely on what others say, while 15 percent rely on advertising."[2]

Now even "strangers" become worthy referrers, and the Internet has adapted to provide us with contextual filters for validating the reviews and comments of those we don't know. When the young Internet became widely available in 1994–95, as Internet service providers (ISPs) set up in major cities, Amazon.com was emerging. Amazon began as an online bookseller that allowed users to rate books, add reviews, and comment on reviews. Just as in real life, filters organically emerged when we deemed some reviewers ("Top 1,000 Reviewer") as more credible than others, and we can also find average reviewers like ourselves whose tastes we perhaps share and can see other books they've enjoyed, or not enjoyed, to guide our choices. Now Amazon includes user tagging, suggestions based on our buying patterns, and purchase suggestions generated by other users ("people who bought this also bought . . ."). Brilliantly sophisticated, all of this makes sellers more findable. Many other companies followed suit, a perfect example of social media at its finest.

Being found online is now critical. If people search and cannot find you at all, you lack credibility. When you are findable, your presence positive, it correlates with your practice, and you have an effective online presence. Outside social networks, blogs, Web forums, and firm-sponsored blogs and Web sites comprise that online presence. Traditional firm Web sites, because they aren't usually content dynamic and don't include unfiltered buyer reviews and comments, are diminishing in their usefulness and value to the firm. If that's all you have, your presence is limited.

The very best places to be found online are generally outside of your Web site. When you or your firm is discovered in mentions connected with other sites and discussions that your buyers and potential buyers are already involved with, it's like a warm referral of a friend. You must be present in various "places" online and the context of the presence matters greatly.

Unhappy Campers

Today, as buyers share their experiences all over the Web, the speed of word-of-mouth is instantaneous. The old rule of thumb about customer satisfaction—that a happy customer tells three people and an unhappy one tells ten—has been obliterated. An unhappy customer can, in seconds, tell ten thousand. There are many places to publicly voice delight or dissatisfaction, and new places appear constantly. In addition to the social media tools covered in the book, there is email, Yelp, Sidewiki, YouTube, and many others.

While I haven't seen anything comparable to the "United Breaks Guitars" video[3] (a clever, entertaining complaint against the airline that has received more than 8.5 million views) for law or accounting firms, don't think professionals are exempt. A couple of quick Internet searches for "yelp:lawyer" and "yelp:CPA" turned up reviews both glowing and horrible. Fortunately, Yelp, like most other review sites, allows company representatives to respond to each review. Joe Marchese advises[4]:

> . . . *as real-time search improves, so does people's ability to get real-time, unfiltered feedback from peers on products and services. It will be much harder for brands to control or manage their reputation, as with review*

*sites. Instead, brands will need to turn to strategies that encourage posi-
tive conversations to balance out the inevitable bad.*

Our prospects have a new lens into our businesses: the lens of their
predecessors' opinions. Like it or not, we're all forced to be more accountable. We have to behave above average all the time, because we are sure
to stumble sometimes and, when we do, we hope the positive online
reviews and comments about us will outweigh the negative ones.

When you have a well-established online presence, others will see that
your interactions with people have heart, reflect integrity, and demonstrate
care at a personal level. A good presence elevates your stature and helps
you sustain the loyalty of customers and "fans" in the event that any threats
to your reputation arise. Being able to respond to complaints and to coun-
terbalance them with positive interactions are ways to ensure that you
maintain an effective electronic presence.

Credibility through Fallibility

Presenting yourself as perfect is not believable. When you are forthright
about what you don't know, can't do, or don't do well, it strengthens
people's confidence in the things you say you *can* do well. To be perceived
as an expert at something, be willing to *not* be an expert at something
else. This is part of how you build trust.

Mistakes are allowed—they happen, they are a part of our lives and
our businesses. Always admit when you or your firm has messed up, don't
exhibit blame avoidance, (more on that in Part IV: TIPS) and bend over
backwards to make things right. This is how you sustain trust.

Consistently exhibiting trust inspiring behaviors is essential in all your
business relationships but especially online because, as others view you
from afar and begin to know you, they are evaluating your behavior. If
they are considering hiring you, they are ascertaining whether or not you
are worthy of their trust. According to expert Charles Feltman, there are
four distinctions of trust:

- **Sincerity:** "I mean what I say, say what I mean, and act
  accordingly."
- **Reliability:** "You can count on me to deliver what I promise."
- **Competence:** "I have what is required to do the job."
- **Care:** "I have your best interests in mind as well as my own."

Feltman elaborates about the competence distinction elsewhere in his
work saying that while it includes, "I know I can do this," it also encom-

passes, "I don't know if I can do that." The point being that honesty about our limitations is just as important—and maybe more—in conveying trustworthiness as claims of our capabilities.

He writes, "Trust assessments are judgments or opinions we have about our or another's sincerity, competence, reliability and care, and which determine how we will coordinate action in a relationship."[5] Trust assessment is ongoing, continuing throughout a business relationship. Upsetting any of the four dimensions of trust threatens confidence in the others. This is why firm-centric or self-centered communications are damaging, and why it's critical to follow through with promises. He emphasizes that repairing trust requires attention to, and reinforcement of, all four.

No amount of great messaging (to be discussed in Chapter 5) can compensate for significant service and product flaws. Address mistakes head-on, transparently, in a nondefensive way, and then learn from them. We must work harder than ever at being "awesome" in our day-to-day work and service interactions to prevent blunders. There's simply no getting around it.

The main things to remember about online interaction are that you should strive to be authentic (true to who you are), transparent (honest about your actions and purpose), and helpful (by educating, supporting, and connecting others).

The Illusion of "Brand" Control

Lots of professional firms have worked very hard and spent a great deal of money to create and build brands for their firms. It's no wonder they cringe at the thought that others can impact that brand so easily. But that is the nature of a brand. The value of a brand, like a reputation, is in the eye of the beholder. The perception is not consistent from person to person—opinions will vary—nor is it exactly capturable.

While a "brand promise" might be articulated by the seller, perceptions and brand value are ultimately in the control of the people external to the organization. Delivery in accordance with promise can support and build the brand, but the perceptions of, and value to, others may or may not have anything to do with that promise. Promise can *hint* at brand, and delivery can *impact* brand, but neither necessarily equate to it.

Further, a brand definition certainly isn't limited to a company's promise. Companies frequently use focus groups and test markets to define their brand, asking questions such as: "What do you think we stand for?" or "What do you think of when you hear [company or product]?" and "How do you feel when you buy from or work with us?" Smart companies regularly test their brand's current definition and status. Feedback is critical, and the ability to gain continuous, real-time feedback is a wonderful advantage of using social media.

There's no doubt that the brand value of Coca-Cola, for instance, is in the taste buds, heads, and nostalgic hearts of the public. It is definitely not on the company's balance sheet under "equity." If the global population got amnesia, the value of Coke's brand would be zero; their promise would mean nothing if people didn't agree with it. Recall the customer backlash at the introduction of New Coke and the impact on brand value during that time. The company was wise to listen to their buyers, react accordingly, and rethink that change. That was long before social media, but it was a public relations nightmare, to be sure.

Social media has truly opened the floodgates to fan influence and consumers' brand control. There probably isn't a company more protective of their brand and their intellectual capital than Coca-Cola. Imagine their executives in a room discussing the discovery of a fan-initiated Facebook company page for their product, featuring their logo and containing content they could not filter or oversee. This representation of their brand was entirely out of their control. They had every legal right to shut down the page, and other major corporations might have done just that. But, as uncomfortable as it probably was, they sat back and watched it grow—it became the page with the largest fan following of any brand page on Facebook.

Their next step was brilliant. They reached out to the two guys who started the page and invited them to Atlanta as VIPs, giving them their blessing and setting about to collaborate with them to further build the page. The fans remain administrators of the page along with Coke execs. As PR specialist Callan Green observes[6]:

> *By empowering their existing fans, rather than trying to marginalize, shove aside, or steamroll them, Coca-Cola has been able to build on the connections that were already established with fans on Facebook before they even arrived in an official capacity.*

Wisely, to further excite and acknowledge fans, they publicized this story urging the page owners to make a video about the history of the page and Coke's support.

If Coke can't control their brand, no one can. Brand control is an illusion and always has been. It's just that consumers now have a bigger, louder voice than company PR departments. In a tweet interview with Toby Bloomberg, Beth Harte said, "In the era of SM, we need to accept that the only brand management in our control is the name, logo, and brand colors."[7] We have to acknowledge that our reputation is in the hands of others, and set about to engage and interact with those who know us in order to maximize brand loyalty.

Personal Brand: An Oxymoron

You won't hear me talk about building your "personal brand," and that is because I feel strongly that brands are for products and large companies. They are inherently *im*personal. Conceptually, I didn't have a problem with substituting "personal brand" for reputation over the past few decades, as popularized by Tom Peters in his 1997 *Fast Company* article, "The Brand Called You."[8] The concepts dramatically changed how employees set themselves apart from the organizations they worked for, which you could call *personalizing*, but in a way that maintained a corporate-like veil of positioning to the public. But this was before social media came into play. If we venture into social media with a purpose of "branding" ourselves, it's easy to think we ought to represent ourselves in a corporate-like, sanitized, inauthentic way. That's exactly the opposite of how we need to present ourselves in the social Web. The fact is, the social Web has truly lifted and burned the corporate veil. Authenticity is a core value in the online world (any world, actually), as I discussed in Chapter 1. The online community values usefulness, authenticity, altruism, and validation by outside parties.

Branding's purpose is to enable premium pricing, thus higher profits. For professionals in firms of any size, excellent reputation or specialization accomplishes the same. Sadly, of all the professional firms I know who have spent vast sums to brand themselves, very few actually leverage their brands in their pricing. A corporate brand isn't essential for professionals to charge premium prices—a reputation, however, is.

Being a "brand" can even be harmful to professionals. Brands are inherently impersonal. People don't want to buy personalized knowledge and advice from an impersonal entity. Professionals are far better off presenting themselves personally, with a human touch, than as an inaccessible corporate brand. Even the largest corporate brands are trying very hard to position themselves more personally. At a recent marketing event featuring top brands, including Radio Flyer, Tropicana, Ford, Chevrolet, GM, Best Buy, Domino's, Comcast, and Kodak, the single greatest take-away for blogger Jennifer Beese was, "It's not about the product, it's about the soul of the brand. It's about people, not logos. In short, humanize your brand."[9]

Professional firms, too, need to recognize this company-level shift and stop trying so very hard to corporatize themselves. Professionals have a significant advantage over corporations in doing this—the professional *is* the product. Don't worry about a brand, just worry about being true to who you are as you continue to establish and maintain your professional reputation.

Setting Yourself Apart: Don't Compete on Price Alone

Competition is fierce, and without other distinguishing factors that buyers can readily see and know, prospective customers often resort to comparing price for making their decisions. Accepting lower-paying work drives down firm revenues, which impacts the attitudes of those performing the work. Without enthusiasm for the engagement, service and even technical quality are not at their highest. This impacts the quality of the customer's experience, rendering them less likely to rehire the firm and certainly less apt to refer the firm to others. It's a vicious circle (Figure 4.1).

The ability for firms to articulate and convey their distinctions via the Internet is more accessible than ever, costing almost nothing, especially

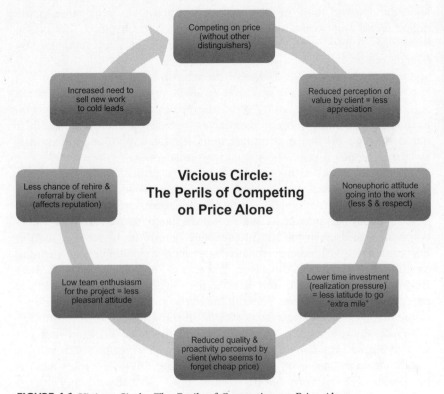

FIGURE 4.1 Vicious Circle: The Perils of Competing on Price Alone

relative to advertising. Firms that are tired of getting beaten up on price and wanting to escape this nasty cycle should embrace the advantages that social media and an improved Web presence afford the professional firm.

Becoming more comfortable with the tools and weaving them into the firm's other marketing efforts lets a firm affordably position itself in a more distinctive way to a broader audience. To do this, focus most intently on the personas and messaging discussed in Chapter 5.

Local Benefits of Global Visibility

When weighing dollars and cents (and time) of different marketing approaches, practitioners sometimes ask me if being known "globally" on the Internet will have much impact on their practices when they are more locally focused. Absolutely, it does. Consider this: in persuading Midwestern prospects to hire you, does it help to have been quoted in the *Wall Street Journal* or to have articles in a national trade magazine for their industry? Of course, it does. Influence is influence, and sometimes we are perceived as being more valuable outside of our market than within it. There's a running joke that a consultant's expertise and value are inversely proportionate to his proximity to "home."

You're likely to find that after garnering some "faraway" attention, you are more in demand locally—CPAs Reed Tinsley and Paul Neiffer both do this (Chapter 7). Use any recognition to your greatest advantage, even when marketing to the company next door. Allow differentiation as an expert and subsequent demand to impact your competitive advantage and your pricing.

Bridging "Social Network" and "Social Capital" to Create Value

Social network and social capital are frequently confused. Though one's social network comprises a portion of one's social capital, social network is not synonymous with social capital.

Social capital is defined by sociologist James Coleman as[10]:

> *The ability of people to work together for common purposes in groups and organizations; the ability to associate with each other, that is critical not only to economic life but to virtually every other aspect of social existence as well.*

I suggest that "the ability" requires effectiveness at building and sustaining relationships. Nurturing a relationship requires caring. Caring requires listening to know what is important to someone.

Activities in social networks enable the demonstration or application of the traits that comprise social capital. Social capital is one of the three types of intellectual capital (IC). And IC is knowledge that can be converted to profit. According to Ron Baker, "It is the interplay among the three types of intellectual capital [human capital, structural capital, and social capital] that generates wealth-creating opportunities for your company."[11] This has strong implications for social media use by people practicing in the knowledge-based professions for whom this book is intended. Social media provide exceptional means of sharing knowledge (held in the minds of human capital) among the practitioner's "community."

In particular, when you write—in the process of sharing ideas and their application with others—you often convert tacit knowledge to explicit knowledge as you give shape to what is otherwise hard to articulate. In a business setting, the chief knowledge officer (CKO) wants to encourage his colleagues to capture and document what's in their minds lest the knowledge leave the company when they do. Ron writes, "The goal is to capture as much of it as we can and place it somewhere (e.g., a file, intranet, Web portal, or blog) where anyone else . . . can get it. . . ."[12] Moving tacit knowledge into an explicit format where others can access it expands the sphere of value of that knowledge.

The beauty of sharing knowledge is that it's a nonrival asset—more than one person can "know" it at the same time. And the ability for others to know it, interpret it, and build upon it makes it infinitely more valuable. This is an exciting aspect of social media. And it's why a CKO is delighted when internal and external blogs are collecting what is otherwise locked in the minds of knowledge workers.

In a discussion with Ron, who is a blog author in addition to having written many books, we pondered how, exactly, it is that social media allow people to monetize their social capital. He said, "I have no doubt that it can and does, even though we can't exactly measure it, because you pick up all sorts of tacit knowledge that will be useful in future." As we interact with others, we glean valuable nuggets of information through the posts people make—information about what is important to them and what makes them happy and what does not. We learn personal details that can bring us closer to people with whom we transact business. Knowing someone loves peonies or is allergic to chocolate, for example, lets us reach out to them in extra meaningful ways. Such knowledge, when you act on it, shows that you listen and care, which helps deepen the relationship, in turn building your social capital.

Trust, authenticity, transparency, and *giving freely to the community* aren't just buzzwords. They are, in fact, core to social capital. Trust, altruism, and willingness of community members to help one another[13] are considered integrally tied to the definition of social capital. Some include, in the definition (and value consideration) of social capital, the depth to which information and sharing takes place among community members, and the very propensity of individuals to work on increasing their social capital. According to the Social Capital Research site, regarding measurement of social capital, "The nature of social capital means that it is necessary to use a proxy or indicator of social capital, as it cannot be directly measured." This concept absolutely has to be taken into account when one tries to calculate the return on investment (ROI) of social media use.

There is no doubt that increasing your value as a contributor within your network also strengthens your social capital. While one way to be valuable is to share your tacit knowledge, another way is to connect others together when you believe they can benefit from knowing each other. In doing these things, your gains are seldom precisely measurable but will be evident to you in a subjective form. You'll see this reflected in Chapter 7 in several of the case studies, particularly of long-time bloggers like Ernie Svenson.

Social capital is nothing without the people with whom you interact and share a purpose; thus, your social capital includes your customers and all your other contacts, including referral sources, vendors, alumni, future employees and customers, and everyone who knows *you* (ideally a much broader audience than just everyone *you* know). When you think of all of these contacts, for every single employee in your organization, it becomes apparent that social capital is, at present, probably the least leveraged type of intellectual capital of an organization. Social media use can significantly improve the value of a professional firm's social capital.

Relevance Requires Thinking Differently

Take a step back to consider how people buy versus how professional firms sell. Professionals and their firms have primarily built their marketing and sales efforts around how they see themselves, not taking into account how customers see their own needs. This is most evident in how firms have presented their wares: their service offerings. It's particularly noticeable on firms' Web sites where the architecture and navigation more closely resemble the firm's organizational chart than a customer's thought process as a user of the site. Examples of this are CPA firms whose sites are split into audit, tax, and consulting sections, and law firms who separately categorize litigation from transactional. Those sections typically house bullet lists of things the firm does.

To shift from a firm-centric to a buyer-centric mind-set, firms have to identify and understand the buyer. We will want to be cognizant of what's important in the buyer's day-to-day role in order to be relevant as a resource and, ultimately, build a relationship. We also need to understand what facts are influential in the buying role during the exploration and evaluation phases; we need to understand circumstances, fears or pressures, accountabilities, the general knowledge level they start with, preconceived notions—everything.

"[C]ompanies need to understand prospects and customers to a greater extent, including how that individual wants to buy and what information they need at particular points in the buying cycle," explains Edward Brice of Lumension in an interview on the Savvy B2B Marketing blog.[14]

We'll explore buyer personas much more in Chapter 5 in "Knowing Your Audience 'Personas.'" First, it's important to consider, and possibly reshape, how firms tend to think of their product offerings. The first instinct for a professional is generally to think in terms of "services I offer," but for greater marketing success, the more effective thinking is "whom I help."

Distinguishing Between Industries and Services

Because you want to be as relevant as possible to the people you interact with online, it's especially important to distinguish between *what you do* and *whom you serve*. Because these are both considered "practice areas" or "niches," they are often lumped together. For example, take this list of a law firm's "services":

- Banking
- Construction
- Employment
- Estate and trust
- Family law
- Litigation
- Real estate
- Workers' compensation

Can you see the crossover? Construction and banking are industries. We can't tell whether real estate is, or if this refers to property transactions. Isn't workers' compensation a subset of litigation? Are construction, employment, and family law intended to be subsets of litigation, too? This is extremely confusing to a customer. The practice areas are unclear, and aren't mutually exclusive. It's important to apply consistent logic.

Construction owners or bankers might need estate planning. A construction company might need an employment lawyer to help write a manual to mitigate risk, a litigator for a workers' comp matter, or a seasoned litigator to help them preventatively with a subcontractor agreement.

For most effective planning and positioning, be clear in distinguishing your products and services (what you do) from those you serve such as industries and other market segments (who you do things for) that include demographic groups and situational buyers—those who buy due to a change, or anticipated change, in circumstance.

A reorganization of the previous list with some corresponding information (italics) filled in to help complete and clarify the picture might look like Table 4.1.

What you do are your services (the perspective from which most professionals position their firms), while "who" needs them and "why" are identified in the industry and situation columns. This chapter is about the "who" and "why"—the considerations that should always be the core of your marketing.

Zeroing In on Industries and Market Segments

For marketing, the more narrowly you can define your audience, the better. Industry focus can be broad (e.g., construction) or very specific (e.g.,

TABLE 4.1 Separate the Offerings from Buyers

Services	Industry	Situation
(Examples: loan documentation, title litigation)	Banking	
(Examples: liens, contracts, dispute resolution, litigation)	Construction	
Employment law	*Any employer*	*(Examples: new hire, termination)*
Estate and trust *(e.g., planning and trust administration)*	*N/A*	*(Examples: persons close to retiring, heirs, one spouse surviving)*
Family law *(e.g., divorce, prenuptial agreements, custody, modifications)*	*N/A*	*(Example: divorcing or divorced couples)*
Litigation *(e.g., business)*	*Any*	*(Example: unresolved dispute)*
Real estate	*Any*	*(Examples: tenant relocation, sale of property)*
Workers' compensation	*Any employer*	*(Example: employee injury)*

heating, ventilation, and air conditioning [HVAC] contractors). For guidance, look at North American Industry Classification Systems (NAICS) or Standard Industrial Classification (SIC) code descriptions (www.siccode.com/naicsearch.php). If you're thinking about starting a blog, consider that a blog geared for HVAC contractors will be very easy to market and syndicate to existing association and trade Web sites (where the audiences already spend time online), whereas a general "construction" blog might be less appealing to those same associations and trade organizations.

Other market segments sometimes require a great deal of thought to drill down. Segments can include age, race, religion, income bracket, and more. There are some excellent accounting practices built around serving people of a certain faith (e.g., Catholic, Islamic, or Jewish); the gay/lesbian community; or Assyrian, Chinese, or Hispanic business owners:

Industries (broad to specific)

- Construction > design/build > remodeling > plumbing
- Health care > medical practices > ophthalmology/optometry

Market Segments (broad or broad to specific)

- Family-owned businesses
- Family-owned businesses > second-generation owners
- Women business owners
- Public companies

Demographic Groups

- Retirees
- Pet owners
- Florida business owners

Situational

- Divorcees
- Parents
- The "sandwich" generation (those caring for both aging parents and school-aged children)

Zeroing in works best because people in these more tightly defined groups share common concerns—they have similar issues—and find the same information to be relevant (to varying degrees, depending on their roles). Further, you are much more likely to be cross-referenced by related groups or organizations catering to those groups when there is a clear audience defined—and you can tap into their readership through comments

TABLE 4.2 Baby Boomers' Web Use

	2000	2010
Percent of Baby Boomers who use the Internet	40%	74%
Baby Boomers as a percent of total Internet population	28%	34%
Percent of Internet traffic consisting of Baby Boomers on a typical day	24%	32%
Percent of Baby Boomers who are online daily	24%	69%
Percent of Baby Boomers who are online multiple times per day	<5%	36%

Source: PEW Internet & American Life Project, March 2010[15].

and trackbacks that you initiate. Finally, there is endless inspiration for new content when you do even a little bit of reading online related to these groups. The clearer you are about your audience, the easier it is to ensure that you remain relevant to those readers.

Baby Boomers are Definitely Online

When I start talking about demographics, professionals are often quite stunned to learn their most commonly targeted demographic, 35+ business owners or high-wealth individuals, are using the Web as much as studies show, particularly the coveted over-50 crowd.

Between 2000 and 2010, Internet user demographics changed significantly, particularly among the Baby Boomer group. Table 4.2 illustrates that the percentage of Boomers who are online at all has nearly doubled, and the percentage of Boomers who are online daily has almost tripled.

The PEW studies show that more than one-third of surfing Boomers are online multiple times per day, which correlates with Nielsen research released in early 2010, showing that the age group with the most hours per week online (includes both home and work) are 35- to 49-year-olds, followed by the 25–34 and the 50–64 crowd. Web video consumption, however, drops to half over age 49, perhaps reflecting a generation more used to enjoying video on big screens as evidenced by the dramatic increase in TV hours for the over-50 audience (Table 4.3). About 59 percent use the Internet and watch television simultaneously.

As recently as five years ago, assuming correctly that their target market was not especially active online, CPAs and lawyers decided not to invest much in their online presence. But business owners, C-suite executives, and the wealthy are definitely online now. There are dozens of reasons to build a strong Internet presence but, given these demographics, *remaining* competitive in a rapidly changing time could be reason enough.

TABLE 4.3 Monthly Internet and Television Use in the United States

Age	Average Hours Using Internet	Average Hours Watching Video Online	Average Hours Watching Traditional TV
65+	2:17	0:06	47:21
50–64	4:53	0:17	42:38
35–49	6:35	0:33	35:40
25–34	5:20	0:35	31:58
18–24	3:45	0:39	26:14
12–17	1:21	0:15	23:27

Source: Nielsen, Three Screen Report, Television, Internet and Mobile Usage in the U.S., Volume 7, 4th Quarter, 2009; http://blog.nielsen.com/nielsenwire/wp-content/uploads/2010/03/3Screens_4Q09_US_rpt.pdf.

Interestingly, CPA Paul Neiffer, when developing his FarmCPAToday blog, considered the use of Internet by prospective clients to be a meaningful filter.[16] In his experience with clients, he observed that the savviest and most successful farmers—those he wants to do more business with—are, in part, successful because they market their farms better than others. He believes that, to accomplish this, they've had to use the Internet over the past decade or two in order to market so well, make informed decisions, and outdo the competition. He says 90 percent of the best farmers are online regularly and warns against preconceived notions about who uses the Web and who doesn't.

Facebook shows some especially surprising demographic trends, considering that it first originated as a resource for college-aged people: students at Harvard University. "The largest cohort of Facebook's user base is the 35–54 age group, and the fastest growing is the 55+ cohort" according to Tom Pick.[17] And age has its advantages. He adds, "On the producer side, the most important attributes are interpersonal skills and industry knowledge. Age is irrelevant in social media usage, and life experience is a plus for social media marketers."

Look Before You Leap

Many companies have eagerly jumped into social networking communities and set up corporate pages without first understanding the tools or discerning their purposes in participating. Setting up a profile and lurking in online communities to become familiar with them is a good idea. Getting too involved or invested without a plan can lead to some undesirable results and the all-too-frequent scenario of firm management questioning: "Why are we 'doing' social media?"

Some undesirable results of leaping before looking are:

- Misuse or underutilization, leading to the incorrect conclusion that the tool is ineffective
- Establishing a profile or page in a suboptimal way, rendering it less effective and requiring significant revision later
- Making unintentional blunders in the space, becoming conspicuous or avoided because of it
- Establishing internal policies that undermine the enthusiasm and trust necessary to succeed in social media

Shoving content, especially firm-centric news, into social media channels without any other interaction is one of the more common clumsy behaviors that firms exhibit. It's unintentional, of course, but merely pushing content "at" people without any other relationship development is simply rude. "Relationships built [within social networks] do impact purchase decisions. Smart brands don't blast messages, they become part of the ecosystem," explains Diva Marketing's Toby Bloomberg.[18]

While content creation and sharing is an ideal foundation for the marketing of professional firms, it's not just any content that counts. Content has to be meaningful. E-marketing consultant Ardath Albee advises, "Influence is a payoff for those who blog selflessly and stay in tune with their audience's interests."[19] What she says holds true for other social forums like Facebook and Twitter as well.

Social media isn't just media, it is "social" first, and "media" second. You would never walk into a networking event and immediately and boldly broadcast your content. Nor should you do that in social networks. Take some time to lurk and explore before you begin broadcasting. You might think of providing your content as "giving," but in social networks, unless content has enormous value (judged at the reader's discretion, not yours), asking people to read your stuff is actually considered "taking." Get a sense of how to get involved in and *give* to the community before you begin *taking* in the form of asking for people's attention.

CHAPTER 5

Strategy Begins with "Who"

While your purpose is the "why" behind what you do in your practice, knowing "who" you want as a customer is critical before you can go down the road of creating an effective strategy. This chapter is about figuring out exactly who you're seeking to reach so you can find them to create the opportunity to interact.

Let's start with some considerations to get you to the right "who." "Who" might include industry or service specialists from whom you can learn and advance yourself in your chosen profession. "Who" might mean future employees or past employees of your firm. And if you're marketing online (versus recruiting or learning), "who" definitely means current and future buyers, and those who influence either.

When it comes to prospecting, it's tempting to say that all types of people are the "who," but that isn't realistic. I don't know any firms that have the time or budget to effectively market to every type of buyer simultaneously. Instead of shooting into the ocean hoping to catch a fish of just any type, figure out what kind of fish you want most so you can find them at their hangouts, observe their behaviors, and determine the most effective ways to reel them in.

Do What You Love (You'll Do It Better!)

Goal setting is the perfect time to contemplate what you actually want to sell. What shall you be known for? Do you want to stick to what you already do, but do a lot more of it? Or do you want to develop or add new offerings?

Give some thought to your firm's current situation. This generally involves a thoughtful assessment of your firm and each practice group as you consider current and potential future:

- Service mix
- Client mix
- Capacity (personnel at the necessary skill and specialty levels)
- Local marketplace opportunities and economic status of the buyer
- Expendable budget for marketing, research, and development
- Internal infrastructure to support marketing and sales efforts
- Likelihood of follow-through by sellers in closing the business

There are a lot of factors that weigh into the decision about which practice areas to grow or promote most vigorously. Ultimately, goals for your practice or your firm should revolve around whatever it is in your practice that you most enjoy doing, assuming you can do it profitably and the market can support it.

In David Maister's book, *True Professionalism*, in his chapter entitled "Are You Having Fun Yet?", he shared a 20-year long poll he'd taken in firms all around the world to gauge their enjoyment of work and their clients.[1] He asks people to divide their work into three categories:

1. "God, I love this! This is why I do what I do!"
2. "It's OK, I can tolerate it—it's what I do for a living."
3. "I hate this part—I wish I could get rid of this junk."

Sadly, the responses are typically 20–25 percent Love, 60–70 percent Tolerate, and 5–20 percent Junk.

He also asked professionals how they felt about their clients:

1. "I like these people and their industry interests me."
2. "I can tolerate these people and their business is OK—neither fascinating nor boring."
3. ". . . these are not my kind of people and I have no interest in their industry."

Again, fairly depressing results: 30–35 percent Like, 50–60 percent Tolerate, and 5–20 percent No Interest.

I agree heartily with David when he says, "Why spend the majority of [your] life working on *tolerable* stuff for *acceptable* clients when, with some effort in (for example) client relations, marketing, and selling, you can spend your days working on *exciting* things for *interesting* people."

In the era of heightened exposure through social media, given what's at stake when a company or person is mediocre or poor at what they do or careless in the service they deliver, none of us can afford to be less than enthusiastic about our work. And when you're highly present on the Web, especially in a blog, lack of passion is fairly evident. The third and most compelling reason to forego marketing the work you don't want is simply that life is too short. Do what you love and do it well—build a specialty around it if you can. Let the rest go.

Knowing Your Audience "Personas"

Pertaining to each area of practice that you've decided you want to expand, your next steps are to identify your prospective contacts and determine what they care about.

Who are the current buyers? What can you do to ensure that you keep them? Who will influence them in making a change? Who are prospective buyers? Who are influential in their buying choices? What do all of these people have in common? Who else might care about those things? In order to fully leverage your investment of time and effort, and get the best results through saturation and diversity of channels, I encourage you to broaden your audience as much as possible, but only as it pertains to the practice area you've selected.

In this book, I sometimes use the terms *audience* and *desired readers,* but I do so reluctantly because I am without better word choices. *Audience* suggests it is okay to broadcast "to" people, and *reader* is rather passive. I just want to be clear that both terms miss the point of social media: that you will view online contacts as people you will engage *with,* not talk *at.*

Communicating Effectively

Great communication begins with knowing exactly to whom you are speaking at all times. When communicating for any purpose, the very first question a good marketing or communications professional asks is: *Who is the audience?*

Designating "everyone" as an audience leads to ineffective communications—a key problem in historic marketing of professional firms. Audience segmentation allows you to create highly focused messages that are relevant to well-defined groups. The more types of people you include in a group, the less specific your messages will be to any one type; they'll be aimed at the common denominator—general in nature. This is how, in professional firms, we've ended up with Web and brochure content that is more about us than our audiences. It's proven that this is not an effective way to position a firm.

I am taking you through the process necessary to inject specificity and relevance into your communications with current and future clients. The process began with prework determining what you want to do more of that resulted in selecting some practice areas on which you'll focus for growth. These might be industry-based practice areas or service-based practice areas. Each persona has unique informational needs and different motivations for contacting you. Even within a single organization, your messaging (any content, verbal or written) ought to be targeted to the persona you are addressing.

Persona Profile Process

One practice area at a time, the development of audience persona profiles involves breaking down the buyers and influencers to individual roles in order to deeply understand each role. What you discern as common traits, needs, or characteristics in a role will be part of the persona profile for *that* audience.

Before working on your audience personas, consider an example of a university's development of their audience persona profiles for the improvement of their Web site and online presence. The example is borrowed from David Meerman Scott, an expert in persona creation, from his book, *The New Rules of Marketing and PR*.[2]

For universities, prospective students are the core audience, followed by their parents. More audience groups are current students, alumni, current faculty, prospective faculty, and high-school counselors who are influential in student placement. This list is not exhaustive.

The university's next step is to understand each persona's unique perspective and needs. Then they'll identify their goals relative to each need they can address. The result is that the university wants to inspire—through nostalgia and pride—students, parents, alumni, and community members to attend and support athletic and art programs, and move alumni and community members to contribute funds and sponsor scholarships. Online, the university wants to ensure that students feel supported and not discouraged or overwhelmed by offering real-time help in their registration process, access to online education, access to faculty members, and the ability to collaborate with one another. These are just some goals, by persona, for the university.

Even within a niche area like universities, various audience groups have their own unique agendas—sometimes their goals are at odds, which can make honest messaging a bit challenging. For instance, a university

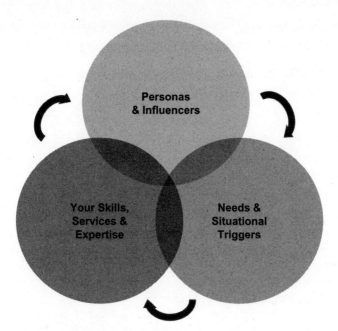

FIGURE 5.1 Persona Development Cycle

Source: © 2010 Golden Practices Inc.

wants to attract students with promises of exciting lifestyle, while simulta-neously reassuring parents about their kid's well-being—that they are not sending them away to a party school, for instance.

For professional firms, prospective clients are a core audience, as are potential employees. Additional groups are current clients, referral sources, alumni, trade association leaders, and the media. Your firm certainly has others.

Now you'll begin the three-step Persona Development Cycle shown in Figure 5.1:

1. Identify Persona Roles, listing all relevant personas by role.
2. List Needs and Situational Triggers from personas' perspectives, defin-ing concerns, symptoms, and problems.
3. Create Messaging Objectives suited to each persona need that you have the expertise to address (and note those you don't).

This sounds like a lot of work, and it does take at least an hour or two for each practice area, but it is well worth the time because the results become a foundation for any marketing efforts related to the practice area.

Keeping these resulting personas in mind at all times changes, for the better, the way you will market your practice.

PERSONAS BY "ROLE"   To begin your persona development, select a practice area (industry or buyers of a particular service) and think of a few companies or buyers you know well (companies of different sizes are helpful).

Ask yourself the following questions:

- With whom do we interact inside the organization as we do the work?
- Who are decision makers within the various buyer roles: user buyers (general counsel or chief financial officer), technical buyers (due diligence gatherers) and the economic buyers (engagement letter signers)?
- What are the roles of people or groups that form buying or oversight committees (e.g., board members, or executive or audit committees)?
- Who are the external stakeholders that care about the success or failure of the organization (e.g., taxpayers, voters, donors, members, employees, SEC or other regulatory agencies)?
- With whom do we interact outside the organization as we do the work?
- Who has the ability to influence the opinions of any of those listed so far?

Get as micro as you can, recognizing that within a particular audience, there can also be subsets. For example, a university wants to position itself differently to recruit high-school seniors than to grad students.

NEEDS AND SITUATIONAL TRIGGERS   Now that you have a list of personas for at least one practice area, work alone or gather team members familiar with the persona or the sector. Spend about an hour. Place yourselves in the shoes of each persona, in his or her business role, and think through concerns, needs, symptoms, and problems they typically or occasionally encounter in their work—whether or not it is related to what you do. Really try to get in their heads. List everything you come up with, and research emerging issues. You might consider purchasing industry profiles from a resource like First Research (www.firstresearch.com), sold individually and well worth the investment.

After you list the needs and issues, group them into categories. Many of these items may tie to "situational triggers" that could lead to the buying process for working with someone like yourself, or for services that someone you know might be able to fulfill through alliances (how often do we wish we could reward worthy acquaintances with warm referrals?).

During this process, it's helpful to humanize your personas, and even to name them. For example, Donna might be your real-life nonprofit executive director, so you may refer to your persona as "Donna" (or Dana) or "Tim" (or Tom) as your sixth-year prospective hire, based on a great past hire named Tim. As you more personally visualize the persona you've named, you can more fully relate to his or her perspective. Also, if you know your real-life Donna or Tim pretty well, consider asking them to help you vet the lists of needs, concerns and triggers. Ask them if your perceptions of their roles and responsibilities are accurate. Often, they'll add to your lists for you.

This brainstorming process results in a list of needs and situational triggers that comprise a detailed profile of each persona. This profile can be consulted for all future interactions. Use it with your team and new hires to familiarize them with client needs and help identify future clients. It will also aid in discussions with prospective referral sources (I wouldn't distribute it to them, though) so they have a better idea of what you know, who you can help, and how you help them.

MESSAGING OBJECTIVES The last step is to establish the purpose—your intent—of your communication with the people you've defined. You should articulate purpose-oriented goals for your communications with each and every one.

The goal of this was expressed well by a blogger in the legal profession, Jordan Furlong[3]:

> *The only point of using a communications and publishing tool . . . is to know who your readers are, know what they care about, and provide it to them. If you do that right, you'll establish yourself as a trusted source of knowledge in an area of importance.*

Your effectiveness will hinge on addressing each unique "persona" in appropriate, relevant ways through the content you share and messages you deliver.

The persona profile is most helpful in message development (Figure 5.2), whether for ads and radio spots, new Web site content, or blog post ideas. This is your core for messaging, and anything on this list is what you might seek to engage them about, regardless of whether it's what you offer or not—you engage them about these things because they are important to *them*—and they appreciate you for knowing that.

When you articulate your business goals and plans for reaching these personas, you can now go much deeper in answering questions about the needs and concerns of each persona at these key points in the purchase process:

- **Researching and investigating:** How can they become aware of you if they aren't already?

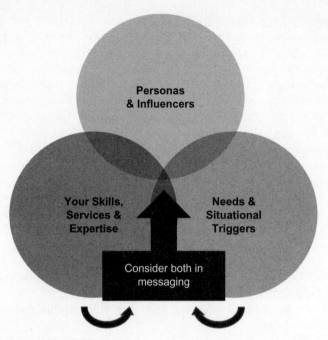

FIGURE 5.2 Messaging by Persona

Source: ©2010 Golden Practices Inc.

- **Evaluation:** What do they need to know about you and about their situation to be sure you're a solid fit?
- **Final selection:** Details about approach and solutions for their unique situation.

Congratulations, you have just significantly increased your social capital. By gathering this information that was previously tacit in your organization, you have made it explicit and it has immensely greater value.

Now the bad news: the information you gathered and compiled related to your personas is not static, so you aren't done. Gathering more knowledge about your personas and understanding their evolving needs is a continual process. Like the publishers of a trade magazine, you have to continually explore what subscribers care about (ask them!) and tackle those subjects in depth.

Erik Qualman advises, "Once you have determined your initial messaging strategy, you have the ability to reevaluate and tweak it for relevancy based on feedback from the marketplace."[4] To help you with some of this ongoing research, solicit feedback through your social media interactions such as embedding questions in your content or running polls on LinkedIn.

Marketing has evolved tremendously as a result of the access we now have to information about people in all industries and all walks of life. We have personal knowledge we gain through customer relationships, but we now have the potential to learn so much more about our buyers through the continuous online dialogue. There's no excuse for not understanding our buyers when we can learn about them this way. This greater knowledge reinforces the value of shifting the focus from how professionals view themselves (how we are used to selling) to how and why people buy.

Finding Your Personas on the Web

To incorporate social media into your marketing—whether leveraging current marketing initiatives or adding new ones—identify where your personas are congregating online. Stepping into social media by creating a presence and hoping they'll find you is Field of Dreams stuff. In the rare instances in which it does occur, it takes a really long time, amazing content, and a bit of luck. It's also passive-level marketing (see Table 1.1 in Chapter 1), and that means it will seldom be rewarding relative to the effort.

Considering your personas' industries, roles, and needs, look for groups that support those sectors, job descriptions, and issues. They don't have to be at all related to your profession (e.g., law or accounting). If you don't find any others "like you" in those groups, don't be deterred at all. You may have struck a goldmine. From experience, I've found that most of the people at the Construction Financial Management Association (CFMA) are not contractors; they are other accountants and bankers. So find out where the contractors *are* spending their limited time. Maybe it's Facebook? Gather the data for running an ad on Facebook to your geographic area for anyone with "owner construction" in their jobs section. See what comes up. If you have or create a company Facebook page geared toward them, run an ad to attract fans to "like" (i.e., subscribe to) your page.

I know a firm that serves the funeral industry. For years, they were thrilled to be the only CPA firm exhibiting at a national convention for funeral home owners. While it may not sound terribly exciting, they were indeed right where they needed to be—and with no competition in sight. You are ultimately looking for the online (or even in-person) equivalent of *that*.

If you cannot find any communities at all related to the group you're looking for, you might want to rethink your group. In *Client at the Core,* August Aquila and Bruce Marcus discuss market segments and write, "If you can't reach them easily, then they're not a market—they are a collection of isolated individuals."[5] Granted, with social media, you have an opportunity to eventually collect individual readers, but when you compare the amount of effort it will take to get some critical mass to the relative ease of joining a group that already congregates in established communities, the wiser choice is self-evident.

In addition to industry-related groups, seek communities that are formed around the shared interests of those in your personas' roles (e.g., controllers/CFOs, general counsel, association executive, chief information officers [CIOs], or board members, to name a few). Search within your preferred search engine for these groups and their associations. Determine who the most influential are in these online communities. You can gauge this by considering a variety of indicators of influence. A single indicator isn't necessarily meaningful, but multiple indicators would be. Some indicators are the number of blog subscribers they have or the number of other blogs that seem to mention them (check Alexa.com for the latter and the blog itself for a "badge" that might indicate the former). In Twitter, consider the number of followers, consistent pattern of tweeting, and the number of mentions or retweets of the person's posts (search Twitter for their @ name to see mentions). Check, also, their score in Twitter Grader (http://twitter.grader.com/), a tool that ranks people in their region by number of followers, retweets, engagement level, and influence.

Search, too, for blogs related to the topics that concern your personas—not just industries, but issue-focused blogs as well. To search blogs only, without the clutter of regular Web sites, try Google's blog search (http://blogsearch.google.com/) or www.icerocket.com/. Note that blog search tools return results differently from other search engines. Blog search results are often shown with the most recent postings first. If you want to find "construction blogs," you are probably better off searching on Google or Bing. But if you want the most recent news on an issue (oil spill or health care reform), a blog search is a good place to look. When you find blogs that are on target, they often link in their "blog rolls" to other related blogs. Scanning blog rolls of good blogs you find can be an excellent way to find several more.

You are also looking for larger social networks that typically have fuzzier boundaries (LinkedIn and Twitter). Look at your competitors' LinkedIn profiles and Web site bios to see what groups they belong to. In fact, for any "real-life" people on whom you've based your personas, go look at their LinkedIn profiles and see what groups they belong to. And if they are on Twitter, skim the list of people and organizations they follow to see if there are some groups there, and visit their Web sites to see what organizations they belong to. The best way of all to learn, though, is to ask. Take them to lunch and pick their brains about all the organizations, resources (publications), and other vendors they consider reputable.

In doing these things, you should have a pretty good list of online communities to explore. Ditch the ones you don't like and lurk to learn about the others. Through discussions in the communities, you'll no doubt learn of more groups—it's an ongoing, organic process from here where you'll pay the most attention to the ones that offer the most value and you'll ignore the ones that don't. But when you estimate the value of a group or its content, remember to value it based not on you, but relative to the personas you are seeking to get to know. If the group gets you closer to your business goals, it's probably worth some level of involvement.

CHAPTER 6

Integrated Marketing Tactics

Integrated marketing is the incorporation of multiple marketing channels—online, offline, or both—to execute a marketing campaign. The simultaneous or consecutive use of multiple marketing tactics and channels typically creates exponential results.

Many companies, even some very sophisticated ones, who use social media quite intentionally, don't really think of their use in terms of campaigns with a beginning, middle, and end, but instead use social media tools in more of a "silo" approach. In other words, they are building social media strategies that stand apart from their other marketing efforts. You can build a strategy that is based around a social media presence, but you will want to promote that presence in many other channels in order to grow it. The more thoroughly you plan the whole thing, the better.

It's become apparent that the majority of companies who enter social media don't have plans at all. It really is still the Wild West in many ways. That's not a bad thing, but for companies who don't want to invest in exploration for adventure's sake—and I think most professional firms fall into this category—going into it with purpose is going to be a lot more comfortable, both from an efficiency and an effectiveness perspective.

Some detriments to employing social media tools without plans are rather interesting. Rajeesh Lawani, in an interview with Toby Bloomberg, said, "The difference between starting social media with or without strategy is the difference between informal and casual where casual means 'I don't care.'"[1] Rajeesh also talked about what having "no strategy" typically results in. I paraphrase:

- Wasting resources that could have added value and reach.
- Social media remains in a silo; not integrated into the organization's marketing strategy, its departments, and its people.
- The blame for social media "not working" is incorrectly placed with "social media," not with the lack of planning.
- Confusion about return on investment (ROI) emerges from thinking that measures come from something other than setting objectives.

I received a great comment on my blog from reader Russell Lawson in response to a post on social media ROI.[2] Russell wrote:

> *When I was in "J" school (back in the Stone Age) we were taught a formula in PR with the acronym "RACE," for Research, Action (planning, message crafting), Communication, Evaluation. Too often, users of social media start with the C step and anticipate the E step will be obvious. Not so. The E will only be clear if you have done the research to define the right channels and targets and then intentionally made the plan for using the tool with specific goals and objectives tied to the features of the tool and the outcomes you require.*

This is exactly right. His comments reinforce the purpose of the persona work in the prior pages, and the planning steps ahead.

Social media tools can sometimes be used effectively as a "stand-alone" marketing tool. Some professionals have built great practices solely through social media use. This works better for practitioners who specialize than for generalists. Tracy Coenen, sole proprietor of Sequence Inc., performing fraud and forensic accounting services, built her practice from her blog—the core of her effective online presence. A full 30 percent of her new business comes from Google searches. Her story is one of several shared in Chapter 7.

A huge advantage to the social Web, as illustrated by Tracy's source of new business, is how search-engine-friendly (findable) social media tool content is. Edward Brice says,[3]

> *While word of mouth is the #1 way that people find information, search engines are #2. If you're not thinking about your content and how prospects will find it in the digital environment, you'll be overlooked. In the world of SEO, getting content into syndication is fundamental to success. You need to think like a publisher about Web 2.0 channels, "If I create this content, where can I syndicate it, and how can I leverage these channels for maximum SEO visibility?"*

If your firm is doing more marketing than just networking or self-publishing, you should be thinking about how you can cross over between social media channels and other, more traditional channels. Several approaches to integrated marketing are presented in this chapter, and some integrated marketing case studies are found in Chapter 7.

What Are You Already Doing?

When you are interested in integrating your marketing to include social media channels, the first question is, "What are you doing now?" The odds are that you're doing some things that can cross over nicely. Take an inventory (in no particular order) of all your non–social Web activities:

- **Print products (brochures, flyers, etc.):** What do you produce? How often? Who sees it?
- **Web sites:** Do you have one or more Web sites? For whom are they geared?
- **Emails:** What email communications do you send? How often? Who sees them?
- **Advertisements:** Do you have any TV, radio, print, Web, or other advertisements? Where, when, and how often do they appear? Who sees them?
- **Print articles:** Do you write articles or guest columns? How often? For which publications? Who is the target audience?
- **Case studies and testimonials:** Do you collect or create these materials? From whom? What do you do with them?
- **Surveys:** Do you take surveys? Of whom? How often? What information do you collect?
- **Membership in organizations:** Are you involved in any trade, peer, general business, community, or charitable organizations? Who else is involved (audience)? How do you interact with others in the organization?
- **Activities or programs:** Do you sponsor any of these? If so, what are they?
- **Events, classes, or seminars:** Do you attend events, classes, or seminars? Which ones? Who else is there?
- **Speaking engagements, seminars, webinars:** Do you accept speaking engagements and for whom? Does your organization host events, or are they hosted by other organizations? Where are they held?
- **Media appearances:** Do you appear in TV, radio, print, or on the Web as a resource or quoted expert?

Any of these activities provide opportunities to promote the other activities, as do your day-to-day activities like talking to people, emailing them, and corresponding in print (including billings).

What Else Can You Do?

When working your way through the list of considerations for what you might be doing, it probably becomes apparent that there are several things on the list that you don't currently do, but perhaps could. You needn't do them all, but if you add any to your marketing mix, be sure to make them relevant to the personas you defined for your practice areas. There are undoubtedly a lot of untapped opportunities to build your reputation as a skilled, credible professional and perhaps even a "specialist."

Another often overlooked angle, especially when creating content, is the opportunity to bring in the voices and wisdom of others—whether influential people or less-well-known experts—including clients, referral sources, academics, industry gurus, media commentators, journalists, and other bloggers. Have them appear as interview subjects or guest speakers, authors, bloggers, or pod- or videocasters. You can receive readership attention for their brainpower and brand power, if they are well known. Plus, their affiliation with you will elevate your stature, and don't overlook the likelihood that they will promote the appearance within their networks.

A lawyer I work with refers to her own marketing "Rule of Three" (not the Rule of Three that proposes to explain market dominance). Barbara Maille says, "Anything I do, I make sure I can use it three ways." For example, if she does a presentation, she wants to invest a little more time turning her content into an article for the Web site (or blog), and then email it out to everyone she knows who would find it of interest.

Just posting content on a traditional Web site is of limited effectiveness—it is a dead-end content route that is not easily found or shared. People don't have a mechanism to learn when new content is posted to regular Web sites, unlike blogs where they are notified of new postings.

Using file-sharing tools on the Web, Barb could put the presentation deck on Slideshare to easily share a link and generate some new visitor traffic attracted to her keywords within the presentation and others she'd add manually when uploading. She could also record the presentation using a video camera if in person, or by using a built-in recording tool, if Web-based, such as the one offered by GoToWebinar) and then post the recording to YouTube. Or she could just audio-record it and offer a podcast. Then she could also post about the session on her blog, embedding the slides, video, or audio files right into her post. And she could also feed the slides and video into her LinkedIn page and her firm's Facebook page. And she could tweet, or ask a friend to tweet, the link to the blog post to drive traffic back to it.

This becomes too messy to diagram. All channels are not required, but intermixing any of these additional channels is a good way to disseminate Barb's knowledge, philosophies, and a sampling of what it's like to communicate with her, to a much more vast audience than her firm's Web site will reach on its own.

Building a Content Ladder

Jay Baer recommends taking a "content ladder" approach for leveraging one piece of content in multiple locations.

He suggests, "Tweak and repurpose content as you move down the ladder." His concept is to consider your channels (also known as social media outposts) as rungs of the ladder. When a piece of content is successful (based on predetermined criteria) on your blog, the first rung, you could add it to the next rung: your email newsletter. He adds, "Of course, this content ladder approach assumes that you do not have the exact same audience for each of your social outlets, and I believe that to be an entirely realistic assumption. You may have some overlap (especially with Facebook and Twitter), but consumption of status updates and consumption of blog posts and email newsletters are meaningfully different activities, and attract different groups of fans."

I've found Jay's observations to be the case when I've repurposed content. I also find it interesting, as a test, to frame linked content with different context-setting headlines in different outposts to see what draws best. Sometimes, if the way I've described a link in Twitter didn't encourage clicks, and the headline in LinkedIn worked better, I'll repost in Twitter with a modified description. Often, I'm rewarded with better engagement.

Source: Jay Baer, blog post, "Build Your Brand a Social Content Ladder in 5 Steps," April 2, 2010; www.convinceandconvert.com/integrated-marketing-and-media/build-your-brand-a-social-content-ladder-in-5-steps/.

Social media allow people to see professionals "in action," especially practitioners in professions stereotyped as stodgy or inaccessible. Let social media humanize you. When you share your words written in a conversational tone (as I am with this book and as I do with my blog), people get a sampling of your personality and might even see your sense of humor. If they read for a while, they get a sense of your values, philosophies, and your true character. It's no mystery that we all prefer to work with people we know, like, and trust. All of these emotional ties are possible to cultivate through interactions in the social Web—if you open yourself to it. Doing so truly accelerates relationship development because we can be developing this level of know-like-trust with thousands of people at the same time. Talk about leverage!

A woman approached me before a talk I gave recently and introduced herself. "Hi, you don't know me," she started, "but I've been reading your blog for years and I feel like I know you! It's so nice to finally meet you in person." She works for a firm I'd love to have as a client. Could this be a warm lead into the firm? Absolutely. This happens often, not just to me, but to scores of bloggers I know. And I feel the very same way about people whose blogs I've read, or whose musings I enjoy on Facebook and Twitter.

When you relax and be "who you are" online, people can envision what it's like to do business with you. If they like what you share and how you share it, your advantages in the marketplace are huge, especially when your competitors share little or nothing by comparison.

Integrated Marketing Strategy Framework

An extremely detailed plan isn't necessary to succeed with your integrated marketing efforts, but it helps. And if you work in a firm where politics abound or the value of your investment in past or future marketing initiatives is challenged, I definitely recommend using the approach I'll lay out, which incorporates setting expectations about what results are appropriate to anticipate—and when—and gaining formal agreement before proceeding. Then, if progress is called into question prematurely by those impatient for results, you have this document to refer back to.

I've fielded many inquiries with responses that went something like this: "I know it feels like we've been doing this for a while without results yet, but you'll recall that we agreed we would be evaluating [reference measure] another six months from now. So far, we are on track for that," or "We agreed we'd consider this effort a success if [refer to subjective measure] occurred, which it has, even if no dollars are directly tied to it."

Busy business leaders sometimes forget what they agreed to, what the plan was, and even why they are doing something they continue to do. In addition to the benefit of having a good plan in the first place, it's nice to have it well documented so everyone can stay on the same page about purpose, actions, and expectations.

Marketing Plan Format

To create a plan that is clear, thorough, and measurable, you need an approach that first establishes your business objectives, and then addresses the details for each marketing initiative. I prefer to work in a grid format for ease of reference. I also find that it's much easier to "fudge" a plan that is in a narrative format yet when the plan is in a grid, it's fairly obvious when a section is missing or incomplete. Table 6.1 is an example of the grid format I refer to.

The framework for a complete plan involves clarifying your a complete purpose, articulating the details in your approach, and documenting your expectations.

Clarity of purpose:

- **Who/Where:** Specifies the company, person, or audience at the core of the initiative (note: this might be a publication or an association)
- **So That:** Clarifies the short- or long-term objective that is the purpose—the desired "effect"—of interacting with the Who/Where
- **By When:** When the objective will be complete or goal reached (note: if this is unclear, your Who/Where and So That probably need more work; try breaking into smaller pieces)

Details of approach:

- **How/Steps:** Defines each step and resource involved in initiative—these are the "tactics"
- **When/Steps:** Represent the chronology of the steps in implementing the tactics

Expectation management:

- **How/Assess:** Documents exactly how you'll know that your objective or goal is met and ties back to your "So That." Sometimes this is statistically measurable, and sometimes it's a subjective measurement. Subjective is okay as long as it is agreed in advance that a subjective measure will be sufficient. Also indicate how periodic "progress" might be assessed if the objective spans many months or years.
- **When/Assess:** Clarify at what points it will be appropriate to gauge progress and perform a final assessment of your outcome.

With this plan format, the process involves going back to the firm or practice area big picture and developing out the plan details in the plan format, for each initiative. Be sure to read the "Monitoring and Measuring" portion of this chapter before you get deep into your planning. It will help guide the expectations that you set.

Calendaring Social Media

When you follow the plan process outlined here, for each step in the plan, you're prompted to consider timing or frequency appropriate for

TABLE 6.1 Marketing Plan Headings

Who (Contact)	Where (Company/Org)	So That (Purpose)	By When (Completion By)	Measure (How & Frequency)	January (Steps&Tactics)	February (Steps&Tactics)	March (Steps&Tactics)
Bill Smith	ABC Company	Earn two inbound referrals from him and send him two, as well	End of the year	Two referrals by December 31	Invite to lunch and send article	Go to lunch, send note of thanks, recommend him on LinkedIn	Forward him a blog post and give at least one outbound referral
Members & leadership	American Construction Association	Seen as expert	Two years: by March 2012	(A) Semiannually by number of personal contacts double every six months; (B) two articles in publication; (C) invited to speak at annual meeting next year.	Attend meeting and seek out current president to introduce myself. Ask who else I should know and how I can be of assistance.	Submit a helpful checklist for the ACA to add to their Web site. Propose to speak on same topic at 2011 conference.	Post to discussion forum and blog. Answer construction questions on LinkedIn. Help at least two people with ideas.

accomplishing your goals (When/Steps). Keep in mind that strictly calendaring social media is contrary to the spirit of spontaneity which has you sharing content you stumble upon or retweeting others on the fly. If you use a calendar, do so as a loose framework to establish "minimums."

For a multiple-person marketing effort, consider setting up shared Google, Outlook, or Sharepoint calendars with your initiatives scheduled out over time. This helps everyone stay on track and also keeps people from overposting to any one medium. Or for your initial planning purposes, you might appreciate an Excel-based social media planning calendar template created by blogger Bob Hazlett that you can download from his One Half Amazing blog (available at http://onehalfamazing.com/blogging/social-media-calendar-template).

If you plan on blogging with WordPress, a powerful content planning and managing calendar plug-in is available that is visible to authors in the blog's administrative backend: http://wordpress.org/extend/plugins/editorial-calendar. It allows you to drag and drop posts around, edit them by clicking on the calendar, and easily visualize posting gaps or overlaps.

Regarding frequency, it's best to post to a blog at least once or twice per week. More often is not really necessary, though it really depends on your format and goals as discussed in the example of the firm that wanted to rely on same-day Google indexing. Some readers find daily blog posts to be too much to keep up with and may not read them all if you post daily. There are definitely pros *and* cons to frequent posting. Once or twice per month really isn't enough frequency to build your blog readership momentum. It simply doesn't convey the level of passion and commitment that more frequent posting does.

It's a good idea to check on your connections' activities and post status updates to LinkedIn once or twice per week. Twice a week would be a minimum for Facebook also, but daily is better. Typical Facebook users check in daily and might update their status one to three times per day, adding a couple of links or other items, as well. More than ten posts in a day is a pretty heavy post volume. Some Facebook users sign in only once or twice a month, but that isn't enough to facilitate relationship development.

Twitter is typically checked and posted to several times a day. Averaging somewhere between two and ten posts per day is sufficient. More than 15–20 posts per day would be on the high-volume side unless you are live-Tweeting an event or attending a Tweet-chat (see Chapter 9 to learn what those phrases mean). Skipping days isn't usually a problem, but I wouldn't skip a full week or more unless you're on vacation. A situation where you're only checking in with Twitter once per week wouldn't facilitate an effective use of the tool for most professionals.

Monitoring and Measuring Social Media

There's a big difference between *monitoring* and *measuring*. Measure to identify where you are in relation to meeting a goal. Monitor to discover what's happening so you can act—either responding externally, or making thoughtful tweaks to a campaign for greater results.

The metrics we hear about that are commonly associated with social media are usually monitoring metrics, not true measurements of the success of one or more marketing initiatives—the latter are unique to you; they tie directly to your marketing objectives. Nate Elliott, a principal analyst with Forester Research, says[4]:

> *Most marketers fixate on easily-available measures like followers or fans—regardless of whether those metrics are important . . . [they] are much more likely to tailor their social media measurement to the tools they're using than to the objectives they're trying to achieve.*

I believe this happens all the time in professional firms because partners demand metrics in order to justify social media use. Yet if proper planning didn't occur initially or if baseline measurements weren't taken, there's nothing specific to measure *against,* so we resort to using the available "volume" and "reach" metrics that mean little in the scheme of things. It's natural to be dissatisfied with these general metrics when there's no context, and they certainly won't indicate one way or the other if your social media efforts are effective.

Just because we *can* measure something doesn't mean we *should.* If you skip the persona work and planning steps, measuring better is certainly not going to get you more business. As my good friend, Ron Baker, says, "Weighing yourself more frequently isn't going to change your weight." The only worthwhile data are those you are prepared to act upon (monitoring) or those that gauge your progress against your target. If you don't have a goal, you don't really have anything meaningful to "measure," you're just tossing stuff out there and seeing what sticks: this is monitoring.

Monitoring is not without value *if* you act on the observations. Monitoring can provide leading indicators as to whether you're on the right track with credibility and engagement, and it's the means by which you discover online mentions—negative or positive. When you act on the former, you get better at using social media, and acting on the latter is a key way that you build social capital.

Whether you or your firm are present in social media or not, and whether you measure anything or not, you should consistently monitor the Web to be aware of those external mentions and make sure everything is copacetic regarding your reputation. The act of measuring is not so important when you monitor as the act of applying what you learn.

Monitoring Online Mentions

Monitoring the Internet for any mentions of you or your firm is a must. When mentions turn up, positive or negative, it's usually best to engage with the commenter. Mentions can turn up anywhere, not just in the social media discussed within this book. There's usually, but not always, the ability to respond on the forum in which you've been mentioned. If you can't respond there and someone is calling you out on service or quality, depending on the circumstances, addressing the comment in another forum might be merited.

When feedback is positive, thank the person for sharing their experience, perhaps adding how rewarding it is to hear that what you do is worthwhile or meaningful to them.

If customer feedback is negative, approach the comments and your replies with a spirit of helpfulness, seeking to remedy the situation. Never resort to dodging or shifting blame—this resolves nothing and makes you look petty and defensive, even if it was someone else's fault. Thank them for sharing their thoughts and take action to "make it right." In the rare chance you encounter a highly irrational commenter, direct engagement might not be the best course of action. But never completely ignore a bad remark. Read more on responding to critics in Chapter 14 in the sections "Complaints, Customer Service, and Crisis" and "Crisis Creates Opportunity."

If no one is talking about you, it might be a relief that comments aren't negative, but it's not great news that you're not present at all. Unless you're a sole proprietor, you should expect to see at least a little buzz in social media. Some firms initially see more mentions among job seekers perhaps tweeting about an upcoming or just-concluded interview than from clients or prospective clients and media. But this can change after even a small investment in social media participation.

Social media and the Web are not just for the bigger firm. A sole practitioner can have an impressive enough online presence to compete with big firms, and many do. These days, the Web levels the playing field between large and small practices. Consider the stories of Tracy Coenen and Reed Tinsley, among others included in Chapter 7. In fact, small firms have the advantage of speed and freedom to jump in without bureaucracy and the need to convince skeptical partners to move forward.

If people aren't talking about you or your firm, monitor what people are saying about your profession in general and those whom you most admire—the thought leaders. You might also watch what's said about your toughest competitors, just to get a sense of positioning and perception. You can match or best any of these ideas with a little focused effort.

FINDING MENTIONS Someone in your organization should be tasked with regularly checking for online mentions. Checking for mentions should be done a couple of times per week or daily depending on volume, and can be done in as little as ten minutes. Monitoring can be accomplished most efficiently with the use of RSS feeds—setting up feeds for various search criteria such as shown below—and viewing them in a feed aggregator such as Google Reader.

Internet Monitoring in Ten Minutes a Day

A good presentation by Hubspot offers how to monitor the Internet in ten minutes a day. They recommend that you spend seven minutes looking at RSS feeds that you will have set up in Google Reader, then spend three minutes manually checking Facebook, as searches of Facebook content cannot yet be fed by RSS.

Hubspot also recommends feeding LinkedIn Answer subscriptions to Google Reader, not for the purpose of monitoring the Web for mentions of you, but to quickly spot questions you could answer to demonstrate your expertise. This allows you to consolidate your social media activities—monitoring and inspiration for posts. The emphasis is the convenience of having these all in one place.

Find the presentation deck at www.hubspot.com/archive/monitor-social-media-presence-daily/.

Google Alerts is a powerful tool notifying you of future Internet mentions of any terms you want to follow, and these can be delivered to your email or to Google Reader, depending on which you specify. I recommend Google Reader simply because it helps to keep clutter out of your email and create a one-stop shop for monitoring.

It's a smart practice to set up Google Alerts and Twitter searches for the following:

- Your name (formal and nicknames)
- Your firm's name (and key people in-house)
- Your URL
- Key clients' names (company names and individuals)
- Key prospects' names (company names and individuals)

- Key competitors (company names and individuals)
- Key products/services
- Key terms related to your primary practice areas

Through these Google Alerts you stay informed about your clients and other contacts. There have been instances where I've seen my clients quoted in major media and sent them a congratulatory message before they knew of the mention—this scores points. And it's so easy—much more efficient than the old-fashioned approach of combing through the business journals to spot mentions of those you know, the approach used when I was in-house in a CPA firm in the mid-1990s. Google Alerts is free—a hefty savings weighed against press clipping services: usually quite expensive.

Adding geographic parameters to search criteria in combination with words that describe what you do and problems you solve can enable you to find people asking their friends about professionals in your area who do what you do. Geo-tagging (i.e., location-based posting) is on the rise and is not difficult to pin down in searches. Be particularly thoughtful about how you'd approach someone that you discover is looking for a service provider—think about what you would consider "too pitchy" and avoid those approaches like the plague.

TRACKING MENTIONS As you find mentions and pickups across the Web, it's a good idea to track them. An increase in mentions is an indicator that your market presence is growing. These are some of the things you may wish to track:

- Where did it appear?
- Who said it?
- What was said? Categorize the nature of the comment and keep a clip file.
- Was the mention about a particular practice, department, or person?
- Was it positive?
- Did the mention include reference to your content or Web site? If so, to what specific content or page?
- Who responded and how fast? You may want to keep the response in a clip file, too.

With regard to counting mentions, the purpose of the count is not to report a "measurement"; it is to set a baseline and seek to improve frequency and quality of mentions. After tracking for a few months, you have a baseline for "average monthly mentions," both positive and negative. The measurement isn't the goal; it's merely the precursor to "now what?"

Evaluate the nature and frequency of the comments. Don't focus on one-offs; look at trends. Do they address product quality or service quality? Do they note a particular practice specialty you are trying to build? Or one you are thinking of scaling back? How can you take action that will result in changing impressions—increasing the positive and reducing the negative? This usually involves the service providers, sales team, and the like. At the core of these matters are operational realities. As I discussed in Chapter 1 in "Advantages of an Effective Electronic Presence" and Chapter 4 in "Credibility Through Fallibility," we cannot hide our flaws and foibles. Social media make service improvement requisite. We simply have to be "more awesome because there's a new level of accountability."

Collected data should be shared with anyone in your firm who is mentioned as an opportunity for them to learn. It may spark interest in improving or increasing the frequency of mentions. There's no denying that it's an ego boost to see your name in "print." Since every firm should aspire to be more "findable," it's a great way to inspire your people to more actively seek mention opportunities.

Monitoring Content Effectiveness

In any marketing, adjusting tactics based on results and experiences generally rewards the company with better results. If you are using social media for any content marketing, you need to know how readers found you and the content that does and does not appeal to them. Knowing this is invaluable for shaping your future content.

WHO IS REFERRING TO YOU? Discover with whom your message resonates by observing who is spreading your message. Referrers can appear all over the Web, but content is most frequently passed along in the social media mentioned throughout this book: blogs, Twitter, Facebook, and LinkedIn.

If you blog, through your blog visitor statistics, identify where readers are coming from (i.e., referring sites). The sources will be search engines and other content authors. See which other authors are most receptive to your current content and check this against your objectives.

1. Explore the referring blog or site and the author's profile to determine if they are your core audience or reach your core audience. Are they particularly influential?
2. Thank the referrer for the mention (regardless of your answer to question 1 by commenting on their post and try to add more value to the conversation in your comment—don't be at all salesy. Then try to reciprocate, if at all possible, by mentioning in your future content something they have written.

3. Is the referrer writing for the same audience you are (e.g., do they fit your persona profiles)? If so, subscribe to the referrer's blog, engage with them regularly, and post more of the sort of content that initially drew them. If referrers seem unrelated to your audience, try to ascertain what about your content might have appealed to them and what changes could make it more relevant for your core personas.

If you use Twitter, Facebook, and LinkedIn, some referrers will be identified when monitoring online mentions, discussed earlier in this chapter. Other ways to see who's sending traffic your way is to look for source activity for downloads, views, "favoriting," and forwards of your tweets, Facebook content, LinkedIn answers, polls, presentation slides, podcasts, and YouTube or other videos.

These sources may not provide the depth of information you would find in blog statistics, but you should be able to discern enough to know whether the referrals are relevant to your personas and goals.

WHICH CONTENT IS DRAWING READERS? Know which content draws the most readers, and who's reading and forwarding them. When your content resides in a blog, you have good access to detailed visitor statistics through your blog software and through third-party tools such as Sitemeter.com and Feedburner.com—just two of many. When readers find your content via search engines, your blog visitor statistics can show you the exact term someone searched when you hover over the inbound link information. Clicking on the referring search engine link (see Figure 6.1) takes you to the search engine result page just as the user saw it. I've found this to be among the most educational information in my blogging journey. For instance, I learned that mentioning the name of a competitor (which I did in a flattering way, of course) got me listed on the first page of Google results for the competitor's name. I also learned that using technical terms in posts is far more effective than words describing who I am or what I do.

In October 2005, five months after I started blogging, I wrote a post entitled, "The IRS Circular 230 Disclosure." Almost five years later, I still receive visitors who click through from search engines *every single day.* Think about that: my "personas" are accountants and lawyers, and these comprise most of the visitors I receive from that term. While my desired readers are rarely searching the term *marketing consultant,* they are searching for answers to their day-to-day questions. Discoveries like these have been teaching moments for me that shaped my future approach to content development.

Study the terms people are searching. People probably don't search the way you thought they did. Once you see some actual search results

home		
general		

Golden Practices
Recent Visitors by Referrals

general		Detail	Referring URL
Summary		1	http://sg.search.yahoo.com/sea...&cop=mss&ei=UTF-8&fr=yfp-t-712
Who's On?		2	http://rpc.blogrolling.com/red...A%2F%2Fwww.farmcpatoday.com%2F
Traffic Prediction		3	http://twitter.com/
recent visitors		4	unknown
By Details		5	unknown
By Referrals		6	http://www.google.nl/search?hl...ia&aq=f&aqi=&aql=&oq=&gs_rfai=
By World Map		7	unknown
By Location		8	http://www.google.co.in/search...rt&aq=f&aqi=&aql=&oq=&gs_rfai=
By Out Clicks		9	http://www.facebook.com/l.php?...rice-be-different.html&h=fb282
By Entry Pages		10	http://www.google.be/search?so...66BE366&q=succes rate proposal
By Exit Pages		11	http://www.google.com.au/url?s...Nw&sig2=6np7BZY0ZNHtfF9vmJ5xCQ
visits		12	unknown
Current Day		13	unknown
Previous 7 Days		14	unknown
Previous 30 Days		15	unknown
Previous 12 Months		16	unknown
visits and page views		17	http://www.google.com/search?h...XJE5TuzASs6pieBQAAAKoEBU_QcbCt
Current Day		18	http://www.google.co.in/search...eting&meta=&btnG=Google Search
Previous 7 Days		19	http://lawyerist.com/links/
Previous 30 Days		20	http://www.google.ca/url?sa=t&...CNG9t_bRz3Yn6aod1XKjWX0XiC3qXA
Previous 12 Months		21	http://goldenmarketing.typepad.com/
page ranking		22	http://whataboutclients.com/
Entry Pages		23	http://www.google.com.au/searc...=teaching basic accounting fun
Exit Pages		24	http://sg.search.yahoo.com/sea...&cop=mss&ei=UTF-8&fr=yfp-t-712
support+service		25	unknown
KnowledgeCenter		26	http://www.google.com.au/url?s...CNFRQzTK9hq
Submit Support Request		27	http://www.ask.com/web?q=short...ncial reports&
Upgrade Account		28	unknown
		29	http://www.google.com/search?q...hl=en&safe=active&start=0&sa=N
		30	http://www.gerryriskin.com/cat-law-firm-advertising.html
		31	unknown
		32	unknown

Tooltip: http://sg.search.yahoo.com/search?vc=&p=circular 230 disclosure&toggle=1&cop=mss&ei=UTF-8&fr=yfp-t-712

FIGURE 6.1 Referrers and Searched Terms

of your readers, ask yourself how this changes your assumptions. What terms seem to interest your target personas? If the bulk of your readers aren't the personas you seek, judge how you might alter your content accordingly.

To view a big-picture comparative of your content's draw, overlay a graph of your Web or blog traffic patterns with the release of certain content and another layer with an inquiry timing chart. Do you see spikes? Explore the visitors on these days to see if they are your target personas, or if they influence your target personas.

A technique for tracking sources that refer to your Web pages is the use of a special landing page. For example, the Web page you list in your Twitter profile might be a special URL set up just to greet Twitter referrals. Used effectively, the page doubles as a reader-friendly, relevant welcome while simultaneously improving conversion or action results by an industry-accepted 25–50 percent. Custom landing pages are often used to greet people who click through from specific Web sites, blog posts, or marketing campaigns. If you run a multichannel campaign for service A and it runs on radio, in print, and online, you can create one landing page for the campaign regardless of where they heard the message, or you can create separate landing pages for each channel to see which drove more results.

WHICH CONTENT ISN'T DRAWING READERS? If you're like most blog authors, you'll be surprised at times that a piece you've shared doesn't get the readership you expected it might. Even seasoned bloggers find themselves surprised at which content strikes chords with readers and which content does not. The problem could be one of irrelevance or lack of clarity. Ask yourself if perhaps your audience and the content are misaligned. Could it be that what you thought was relevant to them might not be? Be sure your content was truly interesting. Is the content unique and innovative or easily found elsewhere?

The subject matter alone can't always be faulted if the draw is poor. Try to be as neutral as possible and read your post as a stranger would. Is your point clear? Was your "headline" unappealing? You can try promoting the same content with a couple of different headlines to see if one draws better than another. Maybe it's too hard to read. Was your post too long and rambling or concise? Did you employ subheadings to make it easier to skim?

Your content quality will evolve as you learn from both what you see and what you *don't* see with regard to content draw. For much more information on how to create great content, see Chapter 12.

Measuring the Right Stuff

The goals and objectives against which you'll measure are articulated as you go through the planning process described earlier in this chapter in the "Marketing Plan Format" section. When you arrive at the "How/Assess" aspect of your plan, it's essential to specify exactly *how you'll know* if your objective is complete (or partially complete). And the "When/Assess" aspect of your plan designates at what point you should measure progress and the final outcome. Once your plan is established and under way, you're going to be eager to assess how effective you are. Without agreement up front on when it's appropriate to assess success or progress, it's impossible to manage expectations well. The eagerness tends to morph into impatience, and I've seen plenty of firms throw the baby out with the bathwater on marketing initiatives long before social media were prevalent.

Tempting though it can be, watch that you don't fall into the trap of measuring efforts instead of outcomes. "Efforts" too often measured in lieu of results include the number and frequency of interactions or posts you initiate, or responses you deliver. Certainly, your plan states that you'll employ various tactics, but simply doing them is not the desired business outcome—the tactics are a means to the end. We can check these off the list as done or not done, but success must be measured against the final objective, not the process steps.

SAMPLE OBJECTIVES   The "end" goals are sales of the right type, of course, but can also be solid additions to the sales pipeline, like warm inquiries or qualified referrals or generating conversation on defined topics. If your goal includes establishing a strong reputation in a certain practice area, some measurable objectives to get you toward the goal might be:

- Increase retweets and mentions (by anyone) related to [practice topic] from [baseline #] to [goal #] by [date].
- Obtain [#] retweets and mentions by target personas including peers and thought leaders in the specialty (i.e., Get on their radar. Knowing exactly who they are in advance is best.) by [date].
- Receive at least [#] unsolicited invitations from trade organizations to speak or write by [date].
- Earn [#] appearances as media "expert" in [publication or station] by [date].
- Receive [#] questions or requests for advice from [define personas] every [frequency].
- Build up to [#] of [define persona] Twitter (or blog) followers (or sub-scribers) by [date].
- Move [# define persona, or specific names] from digital to personal conversations by [date].

All of these particular objectives require your efforts to develop worthy content or provide tips and other resources to earn the mentions and communications you seek. These efforts are the "tactics" you'll use and are broken into steps in the plan process. But measuring the efforts is not meaningful; measuring the objectives is.

TAKING BASELINE MEASUREMENTS   If you intend to account for results, it's necessary to gather baseline measurements before you begin planning. If you are pursuing growth (volume or profitability) before committing to goals, evaluate where you stand today with regard to clientele:

- Number of current clients
- Revenue (average and standard deviation)
- Revenue change percentage year over year
- Client longevity (length of stay with the firm)
- Frequency of client interactions
- Frequency of transactions (purchases)

- Number of clients lost per month, quarter, or year
- Number of new clients per month, quarter, or year

All of these should be captured not just in total, but also "sliced" by sector, practice area, service type, and relationship manager. This data can sometimes be quite surprising. Your findings might put into perspective the areas you would most benefit from addressing first, aiding in your goal prioritization.

Some other baseline measurements to capture in advance are current Web site and blog traffic statistics, current inbound and outbound referrals (by number, quality, source, and status), and current media mentions and pickups (by person, practice, and publication).

If your goals are already established, and even if you've already started implementing a plan, it's still wise to gather baseline measurements at the earliest opportunity and measure against them periodically. This is a foundation for any marketing effort whether using social media or not. If we don't know exactly what success looks like, we cannot determine which approaches work and which do not.

COMPARING CHANNELS When you employ integrated marketing, measure marketing effectiveness at the initiative level, not the tool level. However, you can take some steps to compare how some channels perform for you over other channels. One method of doing this is to use trackable links, preferably in combination with URL shorteners like bit.ly—see Chapter 14 in the section "Link Shorteners" with different links for each channel. Understand that if you change the wording, color, style, or anything at all from one channel to the next, your results will not be scientific but more anecdotal. This is still helpful in seeing which approach is drawing the most interest. Test and refine as you go.

Note that such a comparison does not tell you that Facebook works and Twitter does not. All it tells you is that the way you used Facebook and Twitter in these applications generated these results.

To help demonstrate results from net-of-activities when it is hard to pin down the "source" of results, try a multilayer chart (see Figure 6.2) where you overlay actual sales data with some of the larger milestones in your marketing plans.

Marketing is as much art as science, and it requires modifying the approach as you go. Periodic assessment and monitoring helps determine if and how you should modify your approach.

Beware of the Follower Fallacy

For the most part, corporations still delude themselves into thinking that social media plays by the same rules as "mass media," therefore they

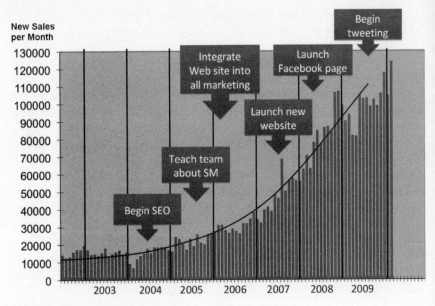

FIGURE 6.2 Sample Sales Report with Milestone Overlay

think audience size matters most. It doesn't. Two things matter much more: the audience quality (relative to your goals) and the richness of your engagement with that audience. These are what lead to loyalty, referral, and ultimately, to sales.

Don't be too impressed by follower, friend, or fan counts—these are often gamed. Size isn't totally meaningless; it can reflect influence so it should be considered. But quality must always trump quantity. As Chris Cree says, "While big Twitter follower numbers are good for your ego, having the right followers is much more valuable to your business no matter what size the list."[5] The same is true for other social media forums, as well.

There's an interesting evolution in the understanding of Web statistics. The early days were all about measuring "hits." Developers now often refer to hits as "How Idiots Track Success." It's not nice, but it illustrates the relative unimportance of hits. Hit counts aren't valid measures, as they can include the same users coming back repeatedly or one user viewing lots of pages. We do want to know when repeat visits are good, and we want to know "stickiness." To do this, identify the number of unique visitors—then get averages of pages viewed and time spent by unique visitor. But even these metrics aren't adequate in the age of social media.

What matters most is how active and loyal your audience is—their engagement. Facebook helped bring this to light when it counted downloads to determine which applications were rated most highly. But, as discussed in *Socialnomics*,[6]

If a million people download something but never use it, then in a sense it is worthless to both the user and to the creator. This is why Facebook tracks by active users, which changes everything.

When you integrate social media into your marketing, it's going to garner results only if the people you have access to are engaged in interactions with you. Like trust, you have to earn this initially, and also like trust, you have to continue to earn it. A Twitter follower count is meaningless if the followers aren't the right people and if they don't engage with you, and you with them. Hundreds of Facebook fans (people who "like" your page) are meaningless if they hide you in their News Feed because your posts are irrelevant or too frequent. Once you've been hidden from someone's News Feed or unfollowed, you're opportunity to engage them is lost.

Pay special attention to who interacts with you and who does not. Rather than count hits, followers, or fans, look for evidence of engagement and possible loyalty (e.g., comments, "likes," pass-alongs and retweets, outreach, downloads, subscription to content, or event registrations). The engagement isn't your end business goal, obviously, but it's a leading indicator through actions in the direction of potential conversion to client or referrer.

Seek quality over quantity. A couple dozen great contacts are better than hundreds if they aren't relevant or won't send you business. That said, you do ultimately want lots of *relevant* followers. When you create engaging, helpful content, your numbers grow organically as followers appreciate and forward your content to like-minded people. This exponentially expands your reach to the right people.

Assessing Tool Use and Following Quality

To help gauge and track quality of Twitter followers, look at each new follower that you follow back and, if applicable, add him or her to a Twitter list you will create, naming it for the sector or role of the person (or both). Examples would be CFOs, CEOs, lawyers, manufacturing, and professional services. Be thoughtful about your list names, keeping them flattering and creative if the list will be public (which I strongly recommend), but use private lists if the list names wouldn't be considered flattering or helpful to others.

The reason you want your lists to be public is that the people you add to lists gain credibility for being on lists at all. They will appreciate the addition and you will have earned goodwill for adding them—unless the list name is something they wouldn't want to be associated with. People seem to like fun and descriptive list names better than boring ones. I have lists called "Accounting Awesomeness" and "Legal Brains"; more people follow these than my other lists—and who wouldn't want to be added to such flattering groups? Third-party applications like Tweetdeck also allow you to group followers.

To help track quality of Facebook friends related to your personal page—this isn't possible for company pages at this time—use friend lists, as described in Chapter 10. These lists are for your eyes only, so the list names aren't crucial. You can count the number of friends in various lists and can specify certain communications to go to, or be hidden from, individual lists or groups of lists.

In LinkedIn, a new feature is available (still in beta at the time of writing) for "tagging" your contacts. Each connection can be tagged to count them, and you can send various communications exclusively to specific lists.

Free Tools to Grade Your Social Media Use

If you use Twitter and Facebook, some free tools can "grade" your use. These tools will not tell you if you're meeting your specific goals, but they'll give you a sense of how well you're behaving with respect to the way most people use the tool, and they usually provide specific tips for improving your tool use.

Facebook Grading Tools

Facebook Grader (http://facebook.grader.com)

Twitter Grading Tools

Twitter Grader (http://twitter.grader.com)

Topsy.com and tweetgrade.com show scores rating your frequency, tweet quality, and overall influence as a Twitter user.

Tweet Effect (www.tweeteffect.com) tells you how many followers you've lost or gained in a given period of time. This can provide an idea of which tweets may have helped influence the gain or loss.

TweetStats (http://tweetstats.com/) shows your Twitter frequency and your post timing trends, whom you retweet most, and to whom you reply most.

Why "What's the ROI of Social Media?" Is the Wrong Question

The return on investment (ROI) discussion can be a frustrating one, in part because the question "What's the ROI of social media?" is flawed. Asking that particular question is akin to asking "What's the ROI of a telephone?" The phone is a tool *and* a form of communication. And so are social media. And just like a phone, social media are used for much more than just marketing.

For marketing, ROI for use of phone calls *can* be loosely tied to a specific lead-generating campaign such as telemarketing activities following direct mail. To determine ROI, you would have to isolate the approximate cost of the phone for the duration of the campaign, and the cost of using it, and offset that with the value of making calls, so a benchmark of results for everything else without the phone follow-up would need to be made. What a pain! Unless you're a huge corporation with enormous marketing processes, it's not worth the effort to isolate ROI for any one tool, even within a campaign.

For years I've used the telephone analogy to illustrate the difficulty and absurdity of seeking to isolate "ROI of social media." It's refreshing to see I'm not alone in seeing these tools as parallel and believing in the useless-ness of an ROI equation. I appreciate the view expressed by Edward Brice, Senior VP of Worldwide Marketing at Lumension in an interview for Savvy B2B Marketing. "We bypassed ROI," he said. "Social media is about con-versation and opening up dialogue. . . . You don't need ROI to have a conversation on the phone with a prospect or customer and you shouldn't need it to connect with them via social media."[7]

As with traditional communications vehicles, these new commu-nications tools can be used well, overused, or potentially underutilized. Though overuse of the tools is one of a firm owners' great fears, from a marketing standpoint, underuse is a far bigger problem. Look again at the frequency suggested in the "Calendaring Social Media" section. Was your initial reaction, "Wow, how will I find time for this?" or was it "That's nothing, I'll do twice that"? More often than not, the ROI question is raised when owners suspect misuse or abuse. Planning and education resolve this.

For any marketing initiative, ROI disappointments generally stem from not doing one or more of the following:

1. Determining the goal first, before deciding which technique or tools to apply—know exactly what needs to be accomplished
2. Having a plan based on realistic outcomes for that type of activity—align the techniques with the desired outcome
3. Executing the plan well, in a disciplined manner, with proper prepara-tion and follow-up

4. Measuring according to the plan using criteria decided before beginning

All social media tools are not equal. And all uses for a single tool are not equal. Understand the goals—the driving purpose behind adopting any forms of new media. Make sure the tool suits the purpose with documented expectations. And, for good results, make sure that people bring their use well past the passive stage.

Sometimes the goal is to actively expand communications and build rapport and trust with buyers and future buyers. How do you assign ROI to that? "Many argue that a fixation on hard numbers could lead companies to ignore the harder-to-quantify dividends of social media, such as trust and commitment. A Twittering employee, for example, might develop trust or goodwill among customers but have trouble putting a number on it," reports Stephen Baker in Bloomberg BusinessWeek. He quotes Susan Etlinger of Horn Group, who says, "There is this default assumption that return on investment is the correct measure for everything. Everything needs to monetize within 12 weeks, so we can understand that we're successful. But frequently the thing they're measuring is misleading."[8]

Most companies simply accept that phones, computers, letterhead, and the like are basic business needs and the costs need to be absorbed into the general operating budget, not allocated out by department or questioned as to their ROI. Social media tools will soon be (if they aren't already) as much a part of professional firms' business routine as the telephone is. Social media are, after all, just other communication vehicles—and we certainly don't invest weeks of labor trying to calculate the ROI of our email, fax machines, and telephones.

CHAPTER 7

Case Studies
and Examples

Having read the background information explaining why you'd want to integrate social media into your marketing, and detailed descriptions about how to do so, it might bring a new level of clarity or idea generation when you see how others have made social media part of their practice development.

It's often helpful to see real-life examples that show how concepts can be applied in our own business. Therefore, this chapter presents case studies broken into three sections:

- **Integrated Marketing Strategies:** Combining marketing tactics to achieve a high-level goal.
- **Self-Publishing Successes:** Efforts focused on blogging (could also relate to publishing elsewhere online).
- **Engagement and Networking Successes:** These are practitioners, solo or in large firms, who have built and leveraged networks in different ways.

These case studies feature accountants or lawyers, some I know well as friends or clients, and some I've merely observed from afar.

The formats of the "Goal, Objectives, Tactics" shown in some of the case studies are very simplified, particularly the Objectives, compared to what is described and recommended in Chapter 6. The case studies contain only vague specifications both for brevity and to protect firms' detailed strategies.

Integrated Marketing Strategies

These are firms that combined various marketing tactics to achieve one or more high-level goals.

Freed Maxick Battaglia

This case study discusses a CPA firm's 10-week campaign to attract new business by encouraging use of the firm's "Tax Credit Locator tool."

Background Information

About the firm:	Freed Maxick Battaglia is a large CPA firm based in Buffalo, New York.
Online at:	Web site: www.freedmaxick.com Twitter: @FreedMaxickCPAs LinkedIn: www.linkedin.com/companies/ freed-maxick-&-battaglia-cpas
Goal:	To expand the firm's marketing footprint beyond western New York, achieving 50 leads over 10 weeks equating to sales of $25–30K

The Firm's Approach

Objectives	Tactics
1. Enhance online presence and establish credibility as experts.	Develop specific Web site content and white papers; practitioners commenting on others' blogs related to key topics; practitioners participate in LinkedIn groups and answer questions about key topics
2. Improve visibility and reach, both online and offline.	Search engine marketing; direct mail; radio advertising; guest expert radio appearances; earned media placements; digital Twitter billboard ads on major thoroughfare; print ads; ads on LinkedIn and Facebook; strategically timed LinkedIn status updates by practitioners
3. Engage target audience in using complimentary Tax Credit Locator research tool.	Practitioners' use of LinkedIn; company Facebook page; firm Twitter account

Over the past seven years, the firm's marketing manager, Eric Majchrzak, completely overhauled the firm's previously outbound-only marketing approaches. Eric's career background includes several years in broadcast radio, developing strategies and promotional campaigns for various companies, so he knew the value of multichannel marketing and understood the potential the Web offered. At Freed Maxick, he blends "old" media (e.g., print ads, direct mail, radio, and earned media placements) with various Web touch points, including high-value content on the firm's Web site; interacting on Twitter and Facebook; leveraging LinkedIn via strong profiles, group activities, and questions/answers; and leveraging external blog communities (they don't currently have a blog of their own).

In a recent campaign featuring the benefits of using his firm's Tax Credit Locator service, the firm used radio very effectively, both for paid advertising and feature opportunities. But where success recently exploded was in promoting one of the CPA's featured radio guest appearances on Twitter, *not* just online but with a rotating digital billboard on a busy highway. The billboard flashes the firm's most recent tweets streamed live, so messages are carefully planned during these media buys, and during Freed Maxick's live radio guest appearance, the billboard tweets alerted drivers to tune in: "Dave Barrett Talks Estate Taxes on WBEN-AM 930. . . ."

Eric's emphasis on Web-based content is based on knowing that, for maximum effectiveness, paid advertisements must have a call to action that's valuable to the audience, "Seminars, checklists, white papers, survey results, consultations, diagnostic tools, and the like are all good value offers," says Eric, "These value offerings differentiate you and engage people, which aligns perfectly with social media integration."

He also goes the extra mile to stretch the firm's radio dollars. Eric explains, "I get the MP3 of our radio spots—most stations will give them to us for no charge—then I distribute them across our social media outposts." Eric also watches closely to learn what engages readers and listeners and what doesn't. He uses unique identifiers (source-specific URLs and phone numbers) to track responses to learn what works best and to discover what he might modify for greater effectiveness.

The results of this single campaign using all media above to promote the firm's Tax Credit Locator service over ten weeks were 522 new leads generated, of whom 37 percent were tax-credit eligible, and over $75K in closed sales. The firm runs 10 to 15 such campaigns per year.

Mark Bailey & Co., Ltd.

This case study discusses an ongoing campaign for audits of small, public companies.

Background Information

About the firm:	Mark Bailey & Co., Ltd. (a client) is a small boutique CPA firm with 2 partners and 20 employees.
Online at:	Blog: *Gray Matters*, http://cfo.markbaileyco.com
Goal:	To obtain proposal opportunities with a set number of prequalified prospects, closing at a set percentage point

The Firm's Approach

Objectives	Tactics
1. Establish credibility as thought leaders who outthink the "big" firms and a higher profile for their top caliber people.	*Gray Matters* blog; publications authored by firm personnel who are university professors and internationally recognized experts; direct mail; email.
2. Create an inbound marketing channel.	*Gray Matters* blog; search engine marketing.
3. Generate interest among companies most likely to switch auditors with targeted content.	Prospect qualification through research; direct mail; phone.
4. Nurture prospects with well-timed, helpful content and personal interaction.	Email; direct mail; practitioners' use of LinkedIn.

The firm had used direct mail and email for years with moderate success, first researching companies likely to be in the market for new auditors, then reaching out based on the prospective client's unique situations. The firm decided to create the blog and allow it to be the "backbone" of their marketing campaign; one of their partners, Marty Weigel, was particularly skeptical. But being a small, boutique audit firm, they needed to prove they could outthink their competition (including the Big 4), and so Marty, one of the primary would-be authors, was willing to give it a go.

They built the blog and prepared it with a good number of starter posts. Shortly after the blog went live in 2009, they received comments on posts (it's a little unusual to receive comments from anyone but friends and family on a new blog) and a lead directly attributed to something Marty wrote. When those first responses came in, Marty proclaimed, "I am a convert!"

The firm's prospects were carefully analyzed to determine if and why they'd most likely be in the market for a new firm. Personalized letters and emails went to the prospects, referring to further information—a carefully selected blog post—about their particular situation and concern. An initial, large-scale mailing went out to grab the attention of these corporate decision makers. An ultra-thin, high-quality, well-designed (to match the blog banner) mouse pad was enclosed with a letter in a completely clear envelope. The response, as measured by page views and phone inquiries, was phenomenal. Mark Bailey described:

> *Right after mailing to top prospects, our blog was garnering 30–35 unique visitors a day—even on a Sunday—with over 240 page views. Averaging seven page-views per visitor is outstanding "stickiness" since the typical blog average is lower than two. And when your competitors and the Big 4 are also regularly visiting your blog, you know you're doing something right.*

Much of the success with the ongoing readership of *Gray Matters* can be attributed to the fact that its authors aren't wimpy about sharing opinions. Why is this an advantage? Because it's not boringly, safely predictable. People—both the firm's desired readers, and their peers in other accounting firms—enjoy the editorial. The blog would probably be way too technical for most client audiences, but chief financial officers (CFOs), chief executive officers (CEOs), and some board members of public companies are familiar with the issues the blog tackles and related jargon. As a topic, it doesn't get much more complex than the fuzzy issues in Securities and Exchange Commission (SEC) compliance. On theoretical concepts, the blog authors provide meaningful analysis and useful advice—in layperson terms.

The firm also has a CPA firm management-oriented blog called Innovative Practice Management. This blog has had a significant impact on hiring, as well as unexpectedly inspiring, many prospect calls. Companies know that happy people equate to a better-quality product and service.

The campaign resulted in increased Web traffic and traffic quality, frequent inquiries resulting in good conversations, many proposal opportunities, higher credibility, and an undisclosed number of new clients.

McKonly & Asbury

This case study discusses Scott Heintzelman's approach to earning the trust of, and ultimately business from, local family-owned businesses.

Background Information

About the firm:	McKonly & Asbury is a large CPA firm in Pennsylvania with 13 partners/principals and more than 100 employees.
Online at:	Blog: *Exuberant Accountant*, www.exuberantaccountant.com
Goal:	To increase credibility and build relationships with area business owners while providing updates and ideas to benefit current clients.

The Firm's Approach

Objectives	Tactics
1. Build and maintain extensive network and high profile in the community.	Face-to-face networking; community activities; calls to action on blog
2. Establish credibility as a knowledgeable advisor on leadership and business who stays current on new developments and is always willing to help others.	Blog on business leadership issues; educational presentations and webinars; Twitter; earn continued readership and interaction on blog.

Scott Heintzelman, a partner, was an avid networker well before social media. He was inspired to start his blog, launched in 2008, after hearing about blogs at a conference at which I happened to be speaking on the topic.

In a business where a sales cycle can take six to seven years, a key goal of Scott's remains building relationships over time. He was already going to nine or ten business development breakfasts and lunches each week, and a personal goal was to better leverage some of his time across more contacts.

He is also a strong believer in the concepts of *Permission Marketing*, promoted by Seth Godin in his book of the same name. Being known well enough to be invited in is possible in ways other than meeting people in person. It struck him that, "A key is realizing that it's not 'who you know' so much as 'who knows you.' The goal with the blog was to be known in my marketplace and the blog has done that. I've definitely cut back on lunches but I'm reaching a lot more people in the same time expenditure—and I'm reaching higher-level people."

When Scott launched his blog in 2008, it was only the 51st CPA practice blog. As he began, Scott had some questions about writing approaches and other normal concerns (e.g., Am I doing this right? Are people really going to subscribe to my blog?). Some early blog comments from friends and strangers served to encourage him on his journey. A year after launching, Scott emailed me about the first (known) 100 percent blog-driven referral he received. He said: "I had never met this gentlemen before, but his quote to me at breakfast was that he felt like he knew me and what I stood for because of the blog."

Scott writes primarily for family-owned and second-generation businesses. He did his persona profile work (see Chapter 5), so every post Scott writes is written "for" someone in particular. He explains, "When I write, I specifically write for three family business owners and their CFOs. The business owners all experience family-related business issues. Some of the correspondence back to me indicates they struggle with succession. I have since included more content about this area."

Out of the blue, Scott received an email from one of his business owner (persona) people. The gentleman thanked him for all the effort he puts into his work and said, "We all learn a lot." How rewarding that must have been for Scott to receive affirmation from the very person he aspires to engage with his writing.

Just over a year in, I asked Scott, "How does your blogging reality compare with what you anticipated?" He replied,

I intended to post once or twice a week, but I actually post three times per week. It takes me about one or two hours per post, compared to what I thought may take half that time. The thing that is easier than I expected is certainly content—I was scared about content and having enough to write about. The reality is that I have way more ideas than days to blog.

I definitely didn't realize the value and convenience I'd find in being able to forward archived posts to people and how much it emphasized my expertise." Scott also says he checks his blog statistics and referral information several times a day to learn what's working and what's not.

He also said he better appreciates "the 'social' side of 'social media.'" It's not a one-way vehicle. Even though you can mass communicate, it has to be personal.

Asked his opinion about the slow adoption of blogging by CPAs, he responded,

Clearly, the legal concerns are greatly overplayed by some partners. Blogging is no different than writing newsletter articles, presenting

information at a seminar, or sharing information during a lunch meeting. Also, the concerns about ROI for the time expenditure are big, but CPAs not blogging is okay with me—frankly, I wake up every day concerned my competition will start blogging and doing what I am doing.

About other social media such as Twitter, Scott says,

I'm on Twitter but my key targets are not really there yet. However, I think they will be and I want to be established and seen as a leader to them. Something that has surprised me about Twitter is how much I can learn and educate myself in such a short time through little bursts of information that I can read where and whenever.

His results from blogging are impressive. He has his foot firmly in the door with several of his target companies, and he has just closed two very significant new engagements directly as a result of the blog. More than 400 prime contacts subscribe to his blog, of which 40 are "key" targets. According to Scott, "Most are servant leaders, over 55, who 'get it.'" He regularly receives positive feedback and can count on garnering five to ten responses whenever he puts forth a call to action. He has a lot of reader-initiated interaction. "I know who's reading, who is engaged," he says. "It's meeting my expectations," Scott said, "Even busy, older CEOs opt in! I 'help' them (with their permission) by signing them up and advising them to click to accept the email verification that they will receive."

Media mentions include being named as one of five helpful financial blogs for business owners in *Entrepreneur* magazine. He was invited to have a blog, and he's received and accepted invitations to participate in other high-profile blogs, including two financial community sites: AccountingWEB and Toolbox for Finance. Several speaking and consulting opportunities have also arisen. He consults on including social networking with consultations with contractors, nonprofits, and law firms, and speaks to accounting peers and a wide variety of business associations about blogging consulting. In March 2010, he presented his first webinar to engage his readers. The topic was "Selling a Business to Your Employees Using an ESOP," and the reports said it was a huge success. He wrote me, "I posted about the event on the blog twice and had 16 sign up. I followed up with all of them and already have a lunch meeting scheduled to talk through an ESOP with one. All without leaving my office and only investing just two hours in this process. Amazing."

On his blog, Scott recently announced his decision to write a book on family business issues. He wrote,

I saw blogging as a way to give back to my network and business community; little did I realize how much I would gain. . . . I have learned

so much about various topics and it has forced me to learn and question ideas that have helped me grow in my profession and also personally. I have also become passionate about adding value. Many advisors throw those words around, but seldom understand what a busy CEO or CFO values. During this journey, I have tried to focus on what keeps them awake at night and have attempted to be a source of valuable information to them. The success of my blog has given me the confidence to pursue a lifelong dream of writing a book. . . . Starting my blog two years ago seemed like such an inconsequential decision at the time, but has turned out to be one of the most impactful things in my life.

In 2009 and 2010, the firm launched five additional blogs: www.mckonomics.com, www.affordablehousinggurus.com, www.thermcadvisors.com, www.contractorscenterpoint.com, and www.leanaccountants.com.

Mercer & Hole

This case study discusses the significant increase of the firm's online presence.

Background Information

About the firm:	Top 25 Chartered Accounting firm in the United Kingdom. The firm (a client) is led by Howard Wilkinson.
Online at:	Web site: www.mercerhole.co.uk
	First blog: *Insolvency Blog*, www.insolvencyblog.com
	Subsequent blogs: *Tax Plus Blog*, www.taxplusblog.com; and *SME Plus Blog*, www.smeplusblog.com
Goal:	To strengthen online marketing, defined as: update Web presence; elevate search engine rankings; humanize the firm's professionals; and demonstrate expertise across select areas of practice.

The Firm's Approach

Objectives	Tactics
1. Reengineer firm's Web site, weaving in several practice blogs for dynamic content on practice-related pages.	Develop Web site; develop blogs; seamlessly integrate blogs (separate platform) with Web site.
2. Establish credibility in key areas of practice.	Identify areas of practice to feature; identify and train blog authors; create and launch blogs accordingly.

Chris Laughton created and launched *Insolvency Blog* promptly upon hearing a presentation I gave in Dublin in October 2006 on blogs and Really Simple Syndication (RSS) technology. He is a partner with Mercer & Hole, self-described as a "U.K. licensed insolvency practitioner with a keen interest in European and international cross-border restructuring issues."

He immediately grasped what a blog could help him accomplish and jumped in with both feet studying personal blog software, buying his URL (insolvencyblog.com), and self-starting. His blog's goal, to which he has stayed true, offers useful, timely information relevant to his referral sources and prospective clients. Right away, he realized he enjoyed this avenue of communication as a new way to serve as a resource. Born in November 2006, his blog caught the attention of a reputable publisher within three months. He declined a book offer, but the opportunity for this visibility and additional credibility cannot be overlooked as an indication of success. Chris showed tremendous initiative, and the blog was immediately successful in generating conversation among his peers.

Mercer & Hole's chairman, Howard Wilkinson, and tax partner, Lisa Spearman, were at the same presentation. All agreed blogs were the firm's next major marketing initiative, but they knew their Web site should be updated at the same time. Howard wrote, "Your session, which in particular opened up the 'world of blogs' to us unsuspecting accountants, made everyone sit back and really think about how we should change our internet sites." The firm was eager to move and within six months' time had a suite of blogs integrated into their newly reengineered Web site. During the build, Chris's existing blog was moved into the LexBlog platform selected to house the firm's three practice-related blogs: the *SME Plus Blog, Tax Plus Blog*, and *Insolvency Blog*. Through LexBlog, the firm's many bloggers receive continuous help with desk support and training.

"It's important for professionals to have the nice, cushy back-end LexBlog offers, as well as their solid and patient support," I explained in an interview with Rob LaGotta for *Real Lawyers Have Blogs*. "When you're going to have a whole team of contributors, the marketing department shouldn't be 'tech support' for the firm's bloggers—and LexBlog does this so well."[1]

Initially, the firm believed partners should be the blog authors, with team members helping behind the scenes in content development. However, the team members did such a great job that even before launch, the firm decided the team members would also be featured authors. This provided more recognition for the team and helped elevate their stature and visibility in the public eye—enabling them to become stronger marketers.

As I advised Mercer & Hole and discussed with Rob LaGotta in the interview, "Blogs also give nonpartners a way to shine. I tell firms that blogging isn't something partners, or just partners, should be doing. It is a way to tap into the next generation and lets them put their great social media skills to work."

Another early concern for the firm had been technical quality control. The firm's initial plan was to run content through a rigorous review process before it went live. Again, once the content was under way, the firm's management realized much of their concern was unfounded and that a strict preposting review process wasn't as warranted as they imagined, plus it became an unnecessary bottleneck hindering timely postings. Now, within a day or so, each new post is quickly perused to ensure that all is good. Seldom are changes needed.

A valuable lesson learned a few months into their new blog ventures, is how posting patterns impact the pace at which search engines will index the blog for new content in the future. For instance, if you post once per week, Google establishes a schedule to match your frequency, "checking" your blog only once a week for new posts. If you post once per day, Google will begin to check daily and if you post hourly, it will check hourly.

This may play into your strategy if you determine it's desirable for your blog to be found readily when there is emerging news related to your topics. In Mercer & Hole's case, one of their blogs had an eight-day average post frequency, and six months into the blog's life, the UK Preliminary Budget was announced. Their eager bloggers pounced with several very timely posts and were disheartened when the posts didn't appear on Google even a day or two later. They saw that to achieve a faster pickup on time-sensitive news, a precedent for daily postings was needed. Realizing the importance to them as a timely budget commentary resource, the posting strategy was altered going forward.

A nice measure of success, in May–June 2009, Mercer & Hole's *SME Plus Blog* was listed in *Entrepreneur* magazine as one of five accounting resources for small businesses[2]:

> *SME stands for small and medium enterprises, which is the focus for this accounting practice. Many of the firm's staff accountants write for the blog, which means a steady stream of blog posts, usually one a day. While this blog is definitely focused on issues pertaining to the UK, such as the many posts that deal with the HMRC (Her Majesty's Revenue & Customs), some posts are general topics that could apply to any business in the world. But if you are based in the UK and you want to read about accounting and tax issues that will impact your business, this blog is a great one to read.*

Success is evident in the frequent media attention and recognition the firm receives—some of extremely high value. Chris shares some examples related to *Insolvency Blog,*

After blogging about the collapse of Northern Rock at the start of the credit crunch, I was invited to speak on its prospective insolvency on BBC National Radio and Television, which of course is advertising you can't buy! Somewhat more routinely, financial journalists from the trade press such as Accountancy Age, *and from time to time from the national broadsheets, call me when something in the blog catches their attention. My comments on Portsmouth Football Club, a high-profile insolvency here, prompted a conversation with* The Times *recently.*

He is confident the blog has been extremely good for raising both his and the firm's profile and credibility. He says,

Within the insolvency industry, acquaintances or even people I meet for the first time do mention that they enjoy reading the blog, and I probably get slightly more of these comments than acknowledgment of my editorship of the UK quarterly trade journal, Recovery. *The blog is also something of a lead generator. I have had two or three inquiries and a reasonable piece of advisory work directly as a result of the blog.*

Naden Lean

This case study discusses a campaign to grow the firm's dental niche practice.

Background Information

About the firm:	Naden Lean is a CPA firm in Timonium, Maryland, with experience in many industries.
Online at:	Blog: *Dental CPAs*, http://dentalcpas.blogspot.com/
Goal:	To build a dental client base in the Northeast and nationally

The Firm's Approach

Objectives	Tactics
1. Strengthen online presence and support expertise and draw prospects through search.	Build and launch micro site (Web site dedicated specifically to dental niche: www.dentalcpas.com); build and maintain dental practice blog; strengthen search engine performance with keyword strategies, articles, case studies, and the blog; buy Google Adwords.

Objectives	Tactics
2. Demonstrate thought leadership, credibility, and commitment through professional association for dental CPAs.	Launch and build Institute of Dental CPAs, a peer organization—necessary competition to an existing dental niche CPA association which limits CPA firm by region.
3. Networking, locally and nationally, with dentists and referral network: those who influence dentists in their service purchase decisions.	Strengthen relationships through in-person interaction and LinkedIn (by marketing department and practitioners); Twitter and Facebook by marketing department; and blog correspondence by author, Tim Lott; actively participate in local and national dental association events and activities; civic involvement; and support of charitable organizations.

Andrew Rose leads the firm's marketing efforts and is both a superb networker and expert in search engine marketing. When he began this effort, the firm had a great reputation among the dental practices that they already served. They also enjoyed the work and the clients. With this good core and room to grow, it made sense to expand this practice area. Two things to leverage in this growth effort would be the very good networking habits of the people involved and the great testimonials and word-of-mouth marketing they could count on from current clients as well as influential referral sources.

Andrew Rose, the firm's marketing and business development director since 2003, performed extensive competitive research. He evaluated competitors' service offerings, delivery track record, and pricing. Among other things, Andrew determined that many of his competitors overcharge in relation to what they provide—his firm charges about the same, but delivers more in terms of service and advice. He quips, "I often say that every dollar one of my competitors spends [on marketing] is one less than I have to. He conditions his clients to pay higher prices, then when they meet us, they see the same price, but a greater array of services." To borrow from Andrew's experience, knowing your competitors' weaknesses provides a great starting point when determining which sore points to counteract with solutions.

He also assessed the people with whom they network most—peers and referral sources—in order to ensure that they work with people of the highest integrity—people who share the firm's values and whose reputations for quality are excellent. "You can never have too much intelligence,"

Andrew explained. "I speak to other trusted people about potential connects, check their online reputation, and occasionally secret-shop them to ensure they are delivering the quality of service or product that we expect from ourselves." In addition to that, the people have to be likable. "Is this someone I like as a person?" Andrew qualifies, "If we are doing a seminar together, they may technically be good, but can they communicate that in a way that puts folks at ease?" While this might sound tough, it assured they'd spend their limited personal networking time with the right people.

The preceding approaches that are advantageous for traditional marketing approaches carry over to a firm's online activities, as well. Naden Lean has a solid sense of what to talk about online that customers care about and others aren't delivering. And they know whom to align with and whom to avoid.

Their more effective online presence began with a new Web site enhanced for search engine optimization and more focused messages about the differences in working with Naden Lean. The next big step was the dental niche blog.

Andrew had put off building a blog because he thought it would be hard to do and hard to maintain, but in 2008, he went for it. More recently, on behalf of the firm, Andrew started using Twitter. He says, "The blog gives me a reason to post on Twitter (www.twitter.com/dentalcpas). Typically within minutes of posting a blog and then tweeting about it, I have half a dozen clicks on the blog. These tools cost the firm nothing!"

On results related to the blog, he reports, "Not only was blogging easier than I could have imagined, the benefits were far greater than I expected. I didn't think anyone would read it, but we've obtained several clients that saw our case studies that were identical to their own situation and so they contacted us." In addition to generating some immediate new business, the blog and search engine marketing efforts are paying off regarding the firm's longer-term goals to stay prominent in search engine results. "The blog now ranks on Google's first page when you Google 'Dental CPAs.'"

Andrew has also experienced good results with PPC (pay-per-click) advertising on Google. More recently, he began exploring Facebook advertising with extremely narrow targeting. Very quickly, he reported that Facebook "is the third highest referring site to the www.dentalcpas.com micro site. The click-through rate (CTR) is still painfully low, but impressions are 54K and rising."

The firm's dental niche is experiencing growth, and Web visitors and inquiries are coming from outside of the firm's previous geographic presence. This is due to a combination of efforts, both with their more focused networking and improved online presence.

Self-Publishing (Blog) Successes

These stories are gathered either from interviews with the bloggers or are merely outside observations. In this mix of examples, you'll find a mix of firm sizes (from solo to large) and stories from blog pioneers as well as newbies. You'll also find a variety of "reasons" for blogging, which, of course, means widely differing expectations. What I ultimately want to illustrate is the depth to which blogging has impacted these practitioners, both personally and professionally.

Tracy Coenen, *Fraud Files*

This case study discusses a campaign to grow a fraud and forensic practice niche.

Background Information

About the firm:	Sequence Inc. is the company of sole practitioner Tracy Coenen. Based in the Chicago/South Wisconsin area, she provides fraud investigation and forensic accounting services nationwide.
Online at:	Blog: *Fraud Files* launched in 2005, www.sequenceinc.com/fraudfiles

Tracy worked for Arthur Andersen (AA) and had a strong interest in forensic accounting; her undergrad was in criminology.[3] AA promised her she could focus in that area but she didn't do much, if any. Once she left AA, she found it very easy to specialize, "I decided to focus like a laser beam. It wasn't hard at all to let go of all the other types of work." She knew that simplicity of message was her friend and that, when specializing, everything she would do would reinforce her expertise. She was also strategic about her pricing, "I was determined, from day one, not to compete on price—I don't want to sell time, I want to sell expertise." She prices by phase usually, and hours sometimes. "The more I've raised my prices, the more I've found it easier to get the right business," she says.

Tracy was an early CPA blogger. Writing and pitching articles was already in her plan, but a "new" option, blogging, was also a natural choice for her, because she knew, instinctively, that grassroots marketing was the most effective. She explains how blogging fits into her schedule: "I read every day anyway. I spend about an hour a day working on it. Part of my motivation was actually to be able to easily remember links later on [by documenting them]." She built her forensic practice network from scratch, and her blog was part of that—word-of-mouth is the source of much of her business.

Only two years into blogging, Tracy shot me an email,

> *Just wanted to let you know that my blogging and marketing has paid off! I just got a contract with Wiley to write a book on fraud! Who'da thunk that [I'd] get a contract with a great big publisher for a book that I've not even written yet!!! . . . I have been doing so much cool stuff . . . . business has never been better. (And has never been more fun too!)*

Tracy's results are exceptional. She now gets 30 percent of her business from the Web. She had successfully pitched some articles to publications before starting her blog, but the blog led to many more opportunities for being published in peer and trade publications as well as writing a second book for John Wiley & Sons. She was invited to write for the personal finance site, *WalletPop*; the stock market site, *BloggingStocks*; and the consumer finance site, *DailyFinance*, in addition to which she is consulted frequently by media for her "expert commentary" and all of this has significantly elevated her credibility in her specialty area.

To those who might be worried about the time investment and return on investment (ROI), Tracy advises, "Shut up and just do it!"

Dan Hull, *What About Clients?*

This case study discusses the blogging experience of litigator Dan Hull.

Background Information

About the firm:	J. Daniel Hull of Hull & McGuire PC is a litigator (federal courts, mostly) and lobbyist whose main office is in Pittsburgh, but his practice takes him all over the United States and Europe. He lives in San Diego and spends much of his time in DC and abroad.
Online at:	Blog: *What About Clients?* launched in mid-2005, www.whataboutclients.com

Dan started blogging because of two "official" reasons described on his blog: "(1) the level of service at even the best global law firms is often inattentive and erratic, and (2) even where the service is sound, it can still be a lot better."[4] The unofficial reason Dan started his blog is that he's always had much to say and now he has a broader place to say it—he's enjoyed writing professionally since his early twenties.

He also says "*What About Clients?* has nothing to do with Hull McGuire PC, my law firm," but I disagree. First, one can hardly ignore the fact that the *Wall Street Journal* names the firm and Bill Clinton in the same sentence: advertising one can hardly buy.[5] Second, when you're a practitioner whose entry in Google is associated with dozens of posts talking about how most firms treat clients poorly, how could you not begin to think if you hired this firm, they might well be different. In fact, if you click through to Dan's blog's "about" page, it reads:

> *While I love litigation, it's expensive, and nearly always overdone. Lawyers need to do more to stop or minimize business disputes that waste client time and money, and keep clients from doing business— and lawyers need to stop treating clients like they are "the equipment" needed for a game.*

His first blog post, "Are Lawyers Just Kidding Themselves About Delivering True Service to Clients?" nicely illustrates the meaningful discussions he provokes:

> *Reviews on lawyers always have ranged from architects of great nations and the world's commercial markets to necessary evils who add little value to any project. We are said to be manipulators with at best convenient notions of truth. And horror stories about our botched or inattentive services are legion.*

> *True service to clients: are we delivering this and, if we aren't, can we talk about why? Do we lawyers have a "we versus them" or adversarial mentality about clients when our main focus should be doing the job we promised to do and protecting clients from third parties or bad events—the real "them"—which would harm our clients?*

> - *Has lawyer camaraderie evolved into such clubbiness that we have lost sight of the client's primacy?*
> - *Do we regularly lie to and slight our clients? (Professionally, is that really any different than cheating on our spouses?)*
> - *Are there built-in barriers which prevent true service to the client? (Are contingency fee arrangements with clients a built-in conflict of interest which can never be justified—even in the name of "access to the court system?" When we represent insurance companies, are we fair to the real clients—the insureds? Will we ever put the interests of the insureds first?)*

- *Are lawyer jokes funny to us because they sound like the truth?*
- *Has the overpopulation of markets with lawyers forced us into a free-for-all?*
- *Do many of us wind up selling clients short because we are disillusioned or burned out?*
- *In short, did we forget the main event—the clients themselves? What do you really think?*

When professionals ask me what I mean by "authenticity" in blog and other online content, this is one fine example. Be real about your, and your profession's, shortcomings.

But Dan also writes about business and environmental litigation, the American legal system, and cultural aspects of international law practice. He is frequently engaged to speak on these topics. He has compiled a long list of non-U.S. legal blogs in his blog's sidebar. The blog has received countless mentions in legal and non-legal publications, is an American Bar Association Top 100 Blawg, and is pretty much all over Google.[6]

While Dan will tell you that companies don't hire him from his blog, other lawyers (including general counsel for publicly-traded corporations) read it. The blog solidly reaffims his client philosophies and showcases his intellect, sense of humor, and frequently provocative opinions. You can be the judge of whether the blog has elevated his and his firm's profile.

Dennis Kennedy, *Dennis Kennedy Blog*

This case study discusses the experience of veteran legal blogger Dennis Kennedy.

Background Information

About the firm:	Dennis Kennedy practices in the field of technology law: information technology (IT), software licensing, and e-commerce. After working in prominent St. Louis law firms for 15 years, he became a sole practitioner in 1998. Since 2008, he serves as in-house counsel with MasterCard.
Online at:	Blog: *Dennis Kennedy Blog*, launched in 2003, www.denniskennedy.com/blog

Prior to creating his blog, he was already an established author on the subject of legal technology. In fact, two years before he started his blog, he wrote that using blogs "might be a great idea for lawyers." When he started his blog in 2003, it was primarily to serve as another channel for his legal tech writing and to expand his subject matter. Dennis told me, "Blogging appealed to me as a vehicle to write on other topics and let those writings find a new audience. My other motivation was that I really wanted to have my own RSS feed more than I wanted a blog, but blogging software was the easiest way to generate an RSS feed." RSS feeds are a means to syndicate content to readers who subscribe to receive it.

Dennis didn't start his blog to develop new business. He'd been writing for other lawyers for years, so he figured he'd reach more and different lawyers than through his other publications "The actual audience surprised me in a couple of ways. First, it was less local and far more international than I expected. Second, I was surprised by the number of people I admired who were reading my blog." His blog was initially created as a "new feature" to his Web site, but for years the blog has been his "main Internet presence." From his increased visibility, there continue to be numerous speaking opportunities, referrals, and a myriad of other projects.

Dennis's interest in technology as a collaborative tool has grown in proportion to the evolving possibilities social media offer. His blogging, as he said, was in part to be able to offer an RSS feed of his writings. In addition to that feed, he and fellow legal technology writer Tom Mighell paired up to produce a podcast series (available through RSS and iTunes) called "The Kennedy-Mighell Report" offered through Legal Talk Network (http://legaltalknetwork.com/podcasts/kennedy-mighell-report/). The two also coauthored *The Lawyer's Guide to Collaboration Tools and Technologies*, a book published by ABA Law Practice Management Section in 2008. Another blog-induced relationship led to the cocreation with attorney Matt Homann of BlawgThink!, an annual event for lawyers who blog. The growth of and quality within the legal blog community has largely been due to support and fellowship among peers.

Blogging has impacted Dennis's life and career in a way that couldn't be imagined in the pre-Internet era. He describes this impact:

I always say that the best part of blogging is the friendships I have formed through blogging. I'm at an age where people do not traditionally make new close friends. I can point to many close friends I now have solely attributable to blogging. The other surprise has been the access that my blog has given me to people who are definitely thought leaders and others whose work I admire. It's also a very nice surprise to meet people who tell me that my blog or a specific post made a big difference in their lives or helped them move to a new path.

After seven years as an author of multiple blogs—his sole blog and several others of which he is a contributing author—Dennis confesses that it's difficult to point to any changes in his legal career that *aren't* in some way attributable to blogging. Dennis says, "If I started out as a lawyer who also blogged, I now feel more like a blogger or writer who also works as a lawyer. That's a fascinating change in mind-set."

Paul Neiffer, *FarmCPAToday*

This case study discusses a campaign to increase business in the CPA firm's agriculture practice niche.

Background Information

About the firm:	Hansen NvO (a client) is a three-partner CPA firm in Washington state; Paul Neiffer leads the firm's agriculture practice niche.
Online at:	Blog: *Farm CPA Today* launched in early 2009, www.farmcpatoday.com

Paul knew exactly what he wanted to do when he set out to launch Farm CPA Today. He didn't have the name in mind, yet, but he knew his theme: his blog would be written specifically for the agriculture sector, and it wouldn't be just about taxes, debits, and credits. It would contain stories and would cover a broad variety of topics that would appeal to farmers. Paul relates to these readers because he grew up on a farm—he misses it and still makes sure to get his combine time in each year on trips back to Kansas City, where he currently owns a farm. In reading just two or three short posts, you will get a sense of Paul's commitment to farming and his genuinely helpful personality.

Paul's goal was to be more findable online by the right people. In particular, he wanted to work with corn and bean producers because a large majority of the world's corn and beans are grown in the United States, and the median farm size is 1,500–2,000 acres, averaging at least $1 million in sales. "I wasn't looking to make money off of the blog," he told me, "but to find the leading-edge people in the industry to connect with— the farmers who are progressive. Being online made sense because Midwestern farmers are hard to connect with from Yakima, Washington!" Many farmers don't hang out online, but Paul wasn't concerned: "I want successful farmers. They aren't going to be as successful if they're not using the Internet to research, run, and manage their businesses. The old-school farmers who don't get on the Web aren't the ones I want."

With his target audience and goals clearly articulated, a short brainstorming session resulted in the firm's name, and the URL was quickly snapped up. The blog design took only a couple of weeks while Paul received some blog author training, and he began creating posts so he'd have several live when he formally launched the blog.

It's powerfully effective to forge relationships with other online authors. Paul did exactly this. Before building his blog, he had researched other agriculture blogs and found Legacy By Design, a company that provides succession planning for farmers. Paul reached out to them through commenting on their blog and then calling to introduce himself, even before his blog was live. When Paul's blog went live in February 2009, Legacy By Design mentioned it on their blog, and Paul started getting subscribers pretty quickly.

"My readership surprised me a little," he said. "Since I write a lot about corn and beans, it's odd to me that a lot of my readers are in the South and from many other countries. But I'm glad they find it helpful."

Some of Paul's rapid success has to do with his writing style. He writes short, easy-to-digest posts that are usually nontechnical. "Some blogs have such long posts, it's hard to get through them," Paul explains, "That's not a good way to attract or keep readers. They've got to be brief." He tends to offset the short length of his posts with greater post frequency: "I planned to do at least two a week and usually end up posting three or four per week. I write a few at a time and use the built-in feature to schedule my posts out so they don't all appear on the same day."

Paul understood he needed to post often enough that he would stay current and credible. He was worried about where he would find "stuff" to write about and whether he would enjoy the writing. "I'm actually surprised how much I enjoy it," Paul said. "I have about 50 sites marked that I check for ideas and I search for additional information as I need it. It takes me no more than five clicks to find something to write about, and I average about half-hour per post—that includes research time."

About content, Paul warns,

It has to be more interesting than just tax-tax-tax. My main piece of advice to others is to be a storyteller. I think back on who my best teachers were in school and they were always the storytellers—they just made you want to hear more.

Paul offers a few more tips for professionals who blog:

- Don't try to be perfect with your sentence structure and all that.
- Be yourself when you write.
- Don't waste people's time with fluff—it also makes posts way too long—keep it short and sweet.

- Grab readers' attention in the first paragraph or two.
- You've got to have a passion for it—if not, skip it.

It also turned out that Legacy By Design is affiliated with Farm Journal Media, the company that publishes *Farm Journal* magazine and *TopProducer* magazine, a leading print publication for the U.S. agriculture industry, as well as AgWeb.com and *AgDay,* a national TV show. Farm Journal Media liked what they saw from Paul—it was the beginning of a beautiful relationship. "I got recognized much faster in the industry than I thought I would," Paul told me.

Only a year after his blog launched, Paul had become a regular columnist for *TopProducer* (print) magazine, had made an appearance on AgDay TV, and posts to a Farm CPA blog on Agweb.com. He reports, "I'm now starting to get many hundreds of unique visitors to my sites on some days. I think it will be great cross-fertilization [wonder if he intended that pun]. I also got a call from our state CPA society, and they are doing an article on my blogging in the July/August 2010 issue." Paul is starting to receive a lot of comments, especially on the Agweb.com blog, and he uses the comments for ideas on future posts, since they seem to reflect what readers are most interested in. He also receives private emails and phone calls, quite a few of which come from other CPAs—some are from very big firms. "It's pretty rewarding," he says.

As far as new business, Paul is sold. Literally. He receives inquiries regularly and has been hired by farmers as far away as Hawaii and Louisiana—all as a direct result of blogging. "So far," Paul says, "my passion for doing this is even higher than when I started."

Dick Price, *Divorce and Family Law in Tarrant County, Texas*

The following are observations about the blog of family law attorney Dick Price.

Background Information

About the firm:	Dick Price is a sole practitioner in Texas.
Online at:	Blog: Divorce and Family Law in Tarrant County, Texas, launched in 2007, http://dick-price.blogspot.com/

I've long held out Dick Price's blog as an example of a very well executed blog by a professional. His blog reflects personality, care, and conveys his expertise. Apparently, others agree as his blog holds the honor of Top Divorce Blog by Attorney.org.

Just by reading three or four posts, a reasonable person would be sure to include Dick in their short list of attorneys to consider. It illustrates that he cares about outcomes, not just the suit. For instance, his content in "Divorce 'No-No': Don't Drag Kids into the Divorce" helps anyone be a better parent, though it is geared to assist parents in going through divorce with greater integrity and focus (no small thing).[7]

His tone and choice of subject matter, even when the content directs readers to other sources like the above post, helps readers understand his approach in his legal practice. Dick's blog suggests what kind of a lawyer he is in a way that a brochure cannot.

His peers appreciate his blog (lawyers are great referral sources to each other) and reference it liberally. And his search rankings are great, so Internet users in marital crisis, especially in Texas, can easily find him, begin benefiting from his advice right off, and can actually see his practice philosophy in action. When we can gain these insights into a practitioner, we are far more inclined to call him than a random name in the phone book.

Jay Shepherd, *Gruntled Employees*

This case study discusses the blogging experience of employment law attorney Jay Shepherd.

Background Information

About the firm:	Jay owns Shepherd Law Group, an employment law firm in Boston with a distinct approach and value proposition.
Online at:	Blog: *Gruntled Employees*, launched in 2006, www.gruntledemployees.com

From the first words on his blog, you see Jay's smart, easy style of writing using short, clean sentences: "If you deal with employees, this blog is for you. As managers, executives, in-house counsel and HR people, you know all about disgruntled employees." This is a perfect example of making a blog's subject matter and audience instantly clear to every reader. It's also hinting at another key thing about Jay: he's more about you than about him. Not a lot of professionals "get" that the underuse of the words *I* and *we* are a bonus for readers. Skimming his three most recent posts, the word "I" appears once. He doesn't need to name the firm because his name, the firm's name, and a little about the firm are at the top right of the blog by design. Jay is very client-centric, and lack of ego is one of the subtle, refreshing differences that is apparent in his blog. Wouldn't most of us prefer to work with an attorney like this?

Shepherd Law Group is unique in its pricing and client service philosophy, too. Jay writes about Shepherd's approaches on a separate blog he started in 2009 called *Client Revolution,* which is named by the ABA Journal as a Top 100 Blawg. The first line descriptor is, "The way American businesses get legal help is broken." Though this blog is more for the law community than for business development, the truth is there is a definite relationship between how you run your business and why people would want to hire you based on that.

Jay started his first blog, *Gruntled Employees,* as a business development initiative, although he wasn't really sure how it would work at first. He explains, "It was something that I felt like I should be doing. I like to write, so it made sense to do it."

Jay's style of writing is very engaging, and his subject matter spans the gamut, but he often discusses current events, tying them to business and employment. From NBA finals and Red Sox clubhouse rules to TV shows like *Undercover Boss* and Conan's premature departure from NBC's *Tonight Show*—where he offers to represent Conan pro bono because the noncompete NBC imposed is unenforceable, and he explains why. He shares tips on motivating employees because the best way to avoid litigation is to keep them "gruntled." His consistent, underlying theme is protecting the employer, but his content makes the employee smarter, too. For instance, posts on noncompetes help both to be more realistic.

"The hardest part is consistency," he told me. "It's been a struggle to run a business and be a dad and still find time to churn out two blogs. My tendency is to write longer posts. What I need to do is write shorter, more frequent posts." I can relate. Blogs, like gardens, can cause feelings of guilt when they aren't tended regularly.

He says he didn't really have a clear idea of how blogging would translate to new business:

> If I expected it to directly lead to new clients, that didn't so much happen. But over time, I learned that the real benefit of blogging was to raise my profile and develop my brand as an expert. Before I started blogging, my firm was reasonably well known in Boston as an employment-law boutique. Three and a half years later, people around the country know me for my employment-law expertise, and people around the world know us for our Open Pricing model. And it really started taking off when I started using Twitter about a year ago.

Jay was truly surprised by the positive reaction in the blogosphere:

> I hadn't appreciated how generous and supportive the blogging community could be. I'm still amazed by the number of wonderful people

I've met because of blogging and Twitter. (Including the author of this book!)

Among the many relationships fostered through social media, Jay also met Susan Cartier Liebel, who runs Solo Practice University, of which he is now faculty.

As to dollars in the door, Jay says,

I've had a couple of clients call saying that they found me after a Google search turned up one of my blogs, but it hasn't produced a stampede of new business by any measure. But I'm still feeling my way around social media. By no means do I feel like I've figured it out, and I do believe that for me there's plenty more to be done with social media as a [business development] tool.

Ernest Svenson, *Ernie the Attorney*

This case study discusses the blogging experience of veteran legal blogger Ernie Svenson.

Background Information

About the firm:	Svenson Law Firm in New Orleans handles business disputes in local federal court.
Online at:	Blog: *Ernie the Attorney*, launched in 2002, www.ernietheattorney.net

Ernie left his larger firm of 18 years to start his solo practice shortly after Hurricane Katrina—a time that brought tremendous change to him and his city. Ernie, his blog, and Katrina are forever part of one another because he blogged his experience riding out the storm. One of the many people unable to get out of the city beforehand, he became very well known to thousands of readers around the world as a "during and after" voice from New Orleans.

Ernie was among the first legal bloggers:

I started it mostly as an experiment. Someone showed me their blog and explained what it was, but I still didn't completely grasp what they were. I had no business objectives for my blog, and don't think most bloggers did back then. I was mostly just trying out a new way of communicating. My main objectives were satisfying my curiosity and wanting to discover other ideas and connect with new people. Those are still my main objectives.

Among the things Ernie is known for are his passion for law, techie tools, local politics (especially after Katrina), and human behavior. Ernie's writing has a vulnerable yet intellectual quality to it—maybe somewhat different from what you'd expect given his blog's name. A lot of people ask about the name: "I noticed that other bloggers had clever names for their blogs so I pondered what to name mine," he said.

There was a local magistrate I had been close to (and who died tragically when her bike was hit by a drunk driver) who called me "Ernie the Attorney." I decided that would work because it quickly described something about me, and it reminded me of her.

Another aspect of the name is that it is anything but stodgy. In an interview with Lexblog, he explained further,[8]

. . . even though I didn't call myself Ernie, I just thought it was a good way of lowering the barrier that lawyers have when encountering people. If you tell them that you're Ernie the Attorney they immediately kind of laugh and say, "You must be a cool guy."

Without a specific business goal in mind, Ernie (he doesn't mind going by that now) expected he would just be writing for his immediate circle of friends. His initial writing was mostly about the law, commenting on topics discussed in the press:

I felt like it was my role to talk about the law in a down-to-earth way (just as my magistrate mentor had done with me), so that people didn't feel like the law was some intimidating, complex thing. I disdain the aloofness that law seems to convey to ordinary people. So, I guess my goal was to talk more to people than to lawyers. I didn't ever know what to expect, but I was happy with the feedback I received and I continue to be pleased.

In other words, Ernie humanizes himself.

Blogging was helpful for me because it gave me an outlet that I would never have had otherwise. I always liked to write, and while I enjoyed writing lawyerly stuff, I longed for the chance to write in a more journalistic or reflective style. Some people have said that my writing is very "self-revelatory" or something like that. I guess that comes from the fact that my dad was a psychoanalyst and so I grew up being oriented to consider how psychology influences our behavior. From time to time my blog allows me to speak with that voice.

Another key learning for Ernie was the way that having a blog instantly eliminated long-standing barriers to sharing knowledge and opinion:

I knew intellectually that it was possible to connect with many people on the Internet. But blogging transformed that dim abstract awareness into something visceral and practical. Initially, I didn't grasp that readership might go beyond my friends. However, people outside my geographic area discovered my blog—in many cases because I was one of the few attorneys who was using one and the blog's name signaled my profession.

Having a blog has been a great way to meet people that I enjoy but would otherwise have never met. For example, one of my good friends now is a judge in another state who I met because one of his lawyer friends read my blog and connected up with me when he came to New Orleans to visit. He brought his judge friend and we chatted, and eventually we got to be good friends, too.

Asked how blogging has impacted his practice and legal career, Ernie considered:

Has it helped me professionally? I don't know how to support my view that it does, but I feel strongly that it does. Sometimes I vent on my blog, and that's probably not good for business or anything else. But I try not to censor myself too much. We all have a tendency to do that, especially lawyers.

Reed Tinsley, RTACPA Blog

Below are observations about the blog of Reed Tinsley, a CPA specializing in the health care sector.

Background Information

About the firm:	Reed Tinsley is a Houston CPA specializing in serving physician practices.
Online at:	Blog: *Reed Tinsley & Associates*, launched in 2005, www.rtacpa.com

Reed was possibly *the* first CPA blog focused on a single industry. His blog has been enormously helpful in developing his practice. After one of my mentions of his blog on mine, Reed emailed his thanks and wrote, "I put a lot of effort into the Web site and that effort has garnered a great return on investment—I get a lot of business from it. I just wish more and more CPAs would understand the importance of having a GREAT Web site (not just a good one)."[9]

His blog continues to be a fine example of an effective niche blog. His approach isn't as time intensive as writing 100 percent original content all the time. Instead, he aggregates health care news and resources, posting a brief snippet every weekday, in the categories of Human Resources, Managed Care, Medicare, Personal Finance, Practice Management, Practice Mergers, Regulatory, Taxes, and Miscellaneous. Intentional or not, he is a reliable "filter" of information for his well-defined reader base. His choice of content, much of it from outside sources, reflects that he's in touch with his readers' needs, wants to help them, and seems qualified to.

Reed doesn't appear to be as dominant in Google as some of his peers who blog, and if I had to hazard a guess as to why, I'd suggest it might be that he doesn't participate much in the blog community or other social media. However, he is very findable online (try an Internet search for "healthcare + CPA" which is how I found Reed several years ago) and he has plenty of business, so it seems to be working well for him. Years ago, he used to come up #1 in Google through his good, organic content, but keyword competition has risen immensely. Still, he remains on the first page of Google search results—not bad for a sole practitioner.

Citrin Cooperman: *Corporate Governance Blog*

Below are observations about the former blog of Citrin Cooperman written on the subject of Sarbanes-Oxley.

Background Information

About the firm:	Michael Rhodes, a partner with the Top 100 New York firm, started a blog during the height of Sarbanes-Oxley (SOX) implementation. Citrin Cooperman was the second largest CPA firm to start a blog. PKF Texas was the first.
Online at:	Blog launched in mid-2006; discontinued mid-2007

Although the blog was suspended (and removed from the Web) about a year after it launched, the blog and its author received some excellent media attention during its brief run. Tracey Segarra, the firm's former marketing director, reported[10]:

> *[Mike's] blog led him to being quoted as a corporate governance expert in many national media, including Reuters and Forbes.com. Unfortunately, time constraints made it difficult for him to give the blog the time and energy he felt it needed to serve its mission as a clearinghouse of information related to corporate governance. He is still regularly quoted in the media, and truly enjoyed the blogging experience.*

At the time I had speculated—based on what I'd seen in other firms—as to why the blog had not been sustainable. The chief reason I guessed was relying on one person to carry the blog, which is consistent with what Tracey reported. (A team approach can help distribute the necessary time commitment if you have the option of including multiple people.) Another solution or work-around is to broaden the topic a bit so more people can contribute.

PKF Texas: *From Greg's Head*

This case study discusses the blog initiative of Greg Price and PKF Texas.

Background Information

About the firm:	PKF Texas is a top regional firm based in Houston. Blog author Greg Price leads PKF's Consulting Solutions practice, working internationally with companies on technology-related business issues.
Online at:	Blog: *From Greg's Head*, launched in 2006, www.fromgregshead.com

As Karen Love, the firm's director of practice growth, reported in an interview[11] with LexBlog, the company that designed and built *From Greg's Head*, the firm had ambitious goals: to stand out among the top 25 accounting firms in the [United States'] fourth largest city, to gain market presence for their Consulting Solutions niche practice, and—most boldly—to revamp the "old, stodgy accounting industry image" by attaching a dynamic face to their ideas.

That face would be the face of Greg Price—they wanted to position Greg as a maven. When the firm built the blog, very few CPA firm blogs existed and no large firm had a blog presence yet—theirs would be the first. It made sense that a CPA focused on business technology would lead that charge. In fact, the majority of small firm blogs present at that time were by tax- and technology-focused CPAs.

Because Greg was already well connected and highly visible among those who were the blog's intended local audience, the firm had high readership from the very start. Word-of-mouth marketing and aggressive prelaunch PR built the blog's subscriber base quickly and garnered the desired attention.

In the interview, Karen explained that the blog had unintended positive effects on their demographics by creating awareness among youth:

> *At a Texas A&M recruiting fair, blog [postcards] and promotions created quite a stir with the recruits, and was met so favorably that although 15 firms were originally invited, only four were invited back. Texas A&M stated that including us as one of the four was a "no brainer."*

The LexBlog interview was conducted one year after the blog's launch, at which time the blog had received coverage in at least 13 major publications, far exceeding their expectations. It had been honored by the 2007 Houston American Marketing Association Crystal Awards in the categories of Best Integrated Public Relations and Maverick Marketing; was bestowed five Excalibur Awards from the Houston chapter of the Public Relations Society of America (PRSA) receiving the Grand Excalibur Award for "Best in Show," and took home three Marketing Achievement awards from the Association for Accounting Marketing, including Best of Show.

The "mavenization" of Greg resulted in the invitation to participate on a number of high-profile advisory boards, including Louisiana State University Stephenson Entrepreneurship Institute Advisory Board; the Houston Technology Center Advisory Board (former chairman); Texas A&M Center for New Ventures & Entrepreneurship Advisory Council; the Audit Committee & Finance Council for the Archdiocese of Galveston-Houston; and Rice Alliance for Technology & Entrepreneurship Advisory Board. He is also the lead scorer for the Rice Business Plan Competition and the accountant for the Aggie 100 and FastTech 50 award programs.

Greg was a featured guest on Talkradio 950AM's BusinessMakers radio show and, by July of 2007, he was offered a regular slot on the radio show with his own best practices segment called "PKF Texas—The Entrepreneur's Playbook®." The scripts from each show are posted on the blog as a regular feature. In 2009, the PKF Texas—The Entrepreneur's Playbook® scripts were compiled and published as a book, adding another element to the reach and success of the blog.

The blog has also served as a vehicle to feature guest bloggers, spotlight friends of the firm, and promote key initiatives in Houston. Through the blog, the firm definitely achieved its goals of standing out, increasing visibility, and overcoming the stodgy accounting image. According to the firm, "in the four years since its launch, the blog has become the center of the PKF Texas strategy map and is continuing to evolve as the demands of the marketplace change."[12]

Weaver: *Energy Blog*

This story is about the *Energy Blog* initiative of Weaver.

Background Information

About the firm:	Weaver (a client) is a Top 100 firm based in Dallas. The Energy Blog was the passion-driven idea of partners Bill Newman and Wade Watson—together they coauthor the blog. The firm is a client.
Online at:	Blog: *Energy Blog*, launched in late 2009, www.weaverllp.com/industries/energy-oil/energy-blog.aspx

Both Bill and Wade work exclusively in the firm's Energy/Oil & Gas practice and, as part of their dedication to their chosen field, they read daily to stay abreast of what's happening in their industry. Basically, they figured, "We're reading, anyway; why not share the most relevant stories with clients and prospects on a blog." They quickly initiated the design of a brand-appropriate blog, and Bill and Wade both had a little blog author training to address blog etiquette, best posting practices, and to learn their blog software. They did their due diligence, investigating other industry blogs and becoming familiar with specific authors, different blog writing styles, and gathering topic ideas. They began writing their backlog of blog posts so the blog wouldn't be bare on launch, and then they were ready to roll.

The firm used traditional media for initial promotion of their new blog, promoting it broadly within the energy sector as well as in their local and national media. Within a week of dropping their initial press release, they had three article requests. Key pickups of the press release, including *Ethanol Producer Magazine* (online), were valuable in creating early buzz and permanent inbound links to the blog from reputable, relevant sources.[13] This is very good for the blog's search engine rankings.

The second month after the blog went live, visitor stats reflected over 400 page views by just under 300 unique visitors, meaning an average visit length of 1:10 per visitor. This was more than double the views during the launch month, and internal traffic stats were not included in those numbers. It's too soon to expect new business results, but so far the blog is doing its job in providing the most relevant energy news to its readers, conveying the practitioners' passion for their practice area, and drawing traffic through search results.

Engagement and Networking Successes

These are practitioners, solo or in large firms, who have built and leveraged networks in different ways—the examples illustrate how primarily using Twitter, LinkedIn, Facebook, or all three, have benefitted them.

Accounting Tweeters

As with blog usership, there are fewer accountants than lawyers using this social media tool; however, there are far more accountants on Twitter than there are using blogs. At my request, some have shared their success stories and value perceptions:

- CPA firm Moody CPAs (@MoodyCPAs) of Charleston, South Carolina, said: "We've picked up a client or two just from using Twitter—they liked what we posted and initiated the contact."
- CPA Rod Humphrey from Indianapolis recently left his firm to start his own (@HumphreyCPA): "I am using Twitter to keep up on the developments in the profession. Good practical advice, especially as I roll out my new firm."
- CPA Brian Wendroff (@wendroffCPA) from Virginia was ranked number 52 in the Top 100 Amazingly Insightful People You Can Learn From on Twitter by OnlineCollegeDegrees.com, a list that includes Zappos and Barack Obama.[14] One of Twitter's most followed CPAs, Brian has almost 14K followers and is on more than 100 lists.
- Monica Lawver (@TheTaxCPA) wrote to Rick Telberg: "Twitter . . . provides an easy way to network with other professionals, and easy access to the latest acctg news."[15]
- CPAs Donna (@CharlotteCPA) and Chad Bordeaux (@CLT_CPA) from Charlotte, North Carolina, reported on JournalofAccountancy.com that they use Twitter to "keep current on the pulse of what is going on locally and in our industry," and say they "obtained two new clients by their awareness of us in Twitter and have received a few mentions in blogs based on our social media presence."[16]
- CPA/CITP Bryan Patrick of Baltimore says he is "able to follow the people whose opinions I respect and no longer need to hunt for

the information I want.[17] It's delivered right to me. . . . Personally, I have expanded my network exponentially with very little effort and, hopefully, provide some value to those I am now connected with."

Legal Tweeters

Lawyers shared their brief stories and thoughts about Twitter for a LegalTech West Coast conference and to appear on the blog of Kevin O'Keefe, president of LexBlog.[18] Kevin permitted the sharing of these stories here:

- Employment attorney Daniel Schwartz (@danielschwartz) of Pullman & Comley in Connecticut: "Got invited to the ABA Diversity summit and speaking engagements bc of my use of Twitter."
- Defamation attorney Adrianos Facchetti (@adrianos) from California: "Got a speaking gig at the Los Angeles County Bar Association . . . another potential speaking gig . . . met an older attorney who is now my mentor and put me in contact with a writer at the *ABA Journal* . . . will probably be writing a piece in the *Los Angeles Daily Journal*. . . ."
- LEED AP and construction attorney Chris Cheatham (@chrischeatham) of Watt, Tieder, Hoffar & Fitzgerald, LLP, a 200-attorney firm in Washington, DC, made connections with huge names in green building, including United States Green Building Council executive committee member Rob Watson.
- Health care and private equity attorney Jayne Juvan (@jaynejuvan) of Benesch Friedlander Coplan & Aronoff, LLP, a large firm in Cleveland: "Even more so than my blog, I've used Twitter to demonstrate that I'm knowledgeable about business news and the economic crisis, as well as developments in corporate law. And today, I landed a new client because of my blog and my Twitter page!"
- New York Internet and intellectual property attorney Deena Burgess (@DeenaEsq): "Twitter has been great for my business. Developed many client relationships through it."
- New York law professor and technology attorney Jonathan Ezor (@ProfJonathan): "I've had quite a bit of success with Twitter, in terms of meeting new folks, getting prospective clients and good PR. . . . Beyond that, using Twitter has helped me counsel about the risks of using Twitter."
- Estate planning attorney Howard Collens (@howardcollens) of Michigan: "Made a nice contact with a local title company through the power of Twitter."
- Texas appellate lawyer D. Todd Smith (@dtoddsmith): "The TX AmLaw affiliate called and asked me to write another article about Twitter."

These are 100% Twitter-generated leads and experiences. Several led to media pickups and article or speaking opportunities that further increased credibility and valuable, new connections.

Mitchell Freedman, MFAC Financial Advisors, Inc.

This case study discusses Mitch's use, as a wealth manager, of LinkedIn, Twitter, and Facebook.

Background Information

About the firm:	Mitch Freedman, CPA, PFS, AIF®, owns MFAC Financial Advisors, Inc. and Mitchell Freedman Accountancy Corporation. He's based in Southern California and specializes in serving artists and entertainers and other affluent individuals.
Online at:	LinkedIn: www.linkedin.com/pub/ mitchell-freedman-cpa-pfs-aif®/6/871/826 Twitter: @mitchpfs Facebook: www.facebook.com/mitchell.freedman

While most wealth managers avoid social media, fearful about crossing lines that their compliance officers and attorneys warn them sternly about, Mitch has a strong, active presence in LinkedIn, Twitter, and Facebook. Mitch's LinkedIn headline reads "Consummate Wealth Manager."

He is a member of many LinkedIn groups with sporadic participation, and even at that level, he's obtained two good leads through entertainment groups he belongs to. He got to know one of the two better after mentioning they share a mutual contact (which he spotted by viewing the person's profile). The other is someone who needed financing—a service Mitch doesn't provide—but leveraging his contacts, he was able to connect the person with the right resource. Both contacts are very likely to become clients.

Mitch has two recommendations on LinkedIn, neither of which refer to his role as a financial advisor because that would be in violation of Rule 206(4) of the Investment Advisors Act of 1940 (see Chapter 8 under "Recommendations"). The two he displays are from a colleague who describes Mitch as his "first and most influential mentor" and someone alongside whom he served on a nonprofit board. He respects the compliance requirements, and he is careful to approve only recommendations that are benign, suggesting that financial advisors needn't be so skittish about social media as long as they observe the rules and apply good judgment. This seems to be a sufficiently cautious way of dealing with the limitations on references for financial advisors that can be perceived as testimonials—a no-no per the above rule—while still having the benefit of third parties vouching for his character.

With Twitter, he shares news and articles, a little humor, and interacts with others. When he talks about articles he's appeared in, he does so in a helpful way such as:

> <u>Mitchell Freedman:</u> *Documents you need when disaster strikes, via bankrate.com: http://bit.ly/cxEb3S—with a couple of cites from yours truly.*

On Facebook, he sees what his contacts are up to and chimes in with friendly comments from time to time in order to stay in touch and let people know he pays attention to them. He also selectively posts his tweets to Facebook. People appreciate what he shares, as evidenced by this comment on Facebook to the above tweet that he cross-posted:

> *Cash in hand is super important . . . in the 1994 earthquake we were out of power for days, and cash was all that we could use . . . and the gouging was rampant so have lots of cash!!!*

Mitch receives calls from the media to provide expert quotes—though he cannot say which social media outpost may have driven those calls. "In the past, I've provided advice on disaster planning and elder care, and then I get calls. It's definitely related to being perceived as an expert." But Mitch doesn't claim to be an expert in social media:

> *I'm still learning what to do in social media. It seems to me that Facebook is a much more social place than Twitter or LinkedIn. I'm very careful not to spam people too much, especially when I put Twitter posts on Facebook. It's rare for me to put more than three things there in a given day.*

I asked Mitch how he got started using Twitter:

> *What really got me started was a comment made by a colleague at CalCPA. He said, "Back when you started your practice, success depended on who you know. Now and in the future, it depends much more on who knows you." This made sense to me, especially when it came to Twitter. The "knowing" had to happen online . . . when you look around at younger people, they have no wristwatches, and they got rid of their landlines—it's all about the computer.*

And when I started tweeting, I didn't know what to tweet about. At first I did post what kind of wine I was enjoying. But it didn't take long for me to see what role I wanted to play in the space. I want to provide useful information that people who follow me can use in their day-to-day lives. I also promote the Jumpstart Coalition—something I really believe in—it's about financial literacy for K–12 kids. With a little practice, it's amazing how much you can communicate in just 140 characters.

A firm believer in the importance of social media for a professional practice, Mitch says: "I love it. It's crazy *not* to be there. I've found it to be one of the best forms of practice development out there."

Daniel Stoica, Daniel Stoica Accounting

This case study discusses Daniel's use of Twitter and LinkedIn.

Background Information

About the firm:	Daniel is a sole practitioner in the Chicago area.
Online at:	LinkedIn: www.linkedin.com/in/danielstoicaaccountant
	Twitter: @DanielStoicaTax
	Blog: Daniel Stoica Blog launched in 2009,
	www.danielstoica.com/blog/

Daniel is an accounting and tax professional who is very selective about his clientele—he develops business by developing relationships. He has more than 500 LinkedIn connections and a huge Twitter following. To get an idea of his Twitter follower growth (not that numbers mean everything), in two months he went from about 13,000 followers to over 20,000 followers. And a more meaningful number is that he grew from being listed by 1,200 people to being on 1,700 lists.

He has developed some new business, but his purpose is 100 percent "to contribute to others' success in a direct and meaningful way. The contribution must be measurable, containable, and I have to be discerning about it." He budgets ten hours per week to achieving this goal—much is online but some is offline, too. He views his social networking activities exactly the same as his offline networking: "I am here to initiate, develop, and nurture long-lasting business relationships."

Daniel started on LinkedIn because it was the most business-oriented social media tool. "I liked that I could easily discover small but immediate ways to help people, partly by answering questions or participating in group threads, but even more so by being a connector," he says. "Sometimes we sort of miss this—we almost forget that connecting people is the most important part of networking. Do this in person, and then repeat this in your online marketing.

He acknowledges that in person, circles are smaller and more intimate, but as your reach multiplies, the assistance you can provide to others increases exponentially, too. When your network is extremely large, there is a different expectation about how well you know and qualify introductions. Daniel explains,

> *While the context of how you know someone—or how well you know someone—online is a little looser, the people you are connecting understand this and realize they still have to do their own due diligence.*

Daniel also has a blog where he posts tips on accounting and on social media use. "Social media is not for everybody," he says. "Everyone has to develop his or her own reason to venture into social media. But if your reason doesn't have anything to do with building relationships, then don't do it." I couldn't agree more.

Joel Ungar, Silberstein Ungar PLLC

This case study discusses Joel's use of LinkedIn and blogs to market his CPA practice.

Background Information

About the firm:	Joel is one of the two partners at the small Detroit firm Silberstein Ungar, an audit and tax firm of seven people. Joel is a LinkedIn power user and was among LinkedIn's early adopters.
Online at:	LinkedIn: www.linkedin.com/in/joelmungar
	Blog: *Ungar Cover*, launched in 2007, http://joelmungar.blogspot.com/ and www.accountingweb .com/blogs/accountingweb/ungar-cover

Joel has had his private blog since 2007, and the name was recently changed to *Ungar Cover*. He also maintains a blog on AccountingWEB, and he has a sizable "friend list" on Facebook, where he participates regularly and, from personal knowledge, quite amusingly. Though Joel uses multiple media, his approach is solidly defined as networking across LinkedIn and Facebook. While the blog is a good means of communicating with peers and clients, and serves as a way to boost the firm's Web presence and credibility, it isn't used with other marketing channels in an "integrated" way.

Intrigued upon reading *Never Eat Alone*, Joel was inspired to try social networking online. Joel was one of the first 2.5 million people on LinkedIn—this might not sound special until you consider there are now over 60 million. His LinkedIn profile sets him apart. It reads: "Exceptional CPA helping SEC companies, franchisors, franchisees and restaurants with their auditing & accounting needs." His "summary" is unique, also. It's written as a friendly, businesslike letter that describes his service approach and articulates—very specifically—what he does.

Joel tries to update his status about twice a week. He uses the paid level of LinkedIn because he likes being able to send messages to people he wouldn't otherwise be able to reach, as well as having access to the extended search results. He greatly values the Outlook Add-In, especially as a way to easily get people's information into his Contacts folder.

He maximizes LinkedIn by asking and answering questions and is listed as an "expert" in several areas: accounting, auditing, social entrepreneurship, blogging, and using LinkedIn. He achieved this through his answers to questions being voted as "best answer" by other LinkedIn members. Through these answers, or even the summary that says he provided them, people see that Joel is regarded as helpful. This is third-party validation at its finest. He doesn't hesitate to ask questions either, and appreciates how helpful others are in sharing what they know. This encouraged him to answer more questions—kind of in a "pay it forward" spirit.

In fact, other than the relationship-building aspect, his only other intention in using social media is to be a person who shares: "I believe you should give to get. There's a divide between people who share or give and those who don't. I don't give away *all* the cookies, but giving *some* cookies builds credibility." About social media, he says: "It pays off, even though it's not all measurable."

Not only is it apparent to others that Joel is willing to help solve problems, but in his word choices and delivery, people can see how Joel thinks and if they are lucky—especially if they get to be his Facebook friend—they get to experience his zany sense of humor. I know this firsthand through "reading" Joel. Though we have known each other online for at least three years, until we talked by phone about his social media use for this book, we'd never actually spoken and have not yet met in person. Yet I know Joel better than many people I have met face to face and even worked closely with for several years. I know in my gut that he's a trustworthy, credible guy. That's as good as it gets, isn't it?

Joel dabbles in using Twitter but doesn't really enjoy it as much as the others. He says,

Facebook utterly fascinates me. It's my playground. I think it's interesting that when two people who are on Facebook see each other, they already know what they're up to. It brings people closer. When people refer to what I'm doing, traveling and that sort of thing, it shows they are aware of what I'm up to—they are paying attention. As far as clients being on my Facebook account, only 5–10% of my Facebook friends are clients. It is a little weird at first, but all sorts of people, including clients, tell me, "I didn't know you're that funny." They haven't fired me yet, so I guess that's a good thing.

In addition to the personal entertainment aspect of Facebook, and the rewarding feeling of helping people by sharing what he knows, the results for Joel have been the development of a much larger, richer network, enhanced credibility, and a lot of media exposure.

Case Study Recap

Several early bloggers who've become very successful didn't have social media strategies and plans. They blogged simply to contribute their voice and perspectives, and to engage in conversation—all of which are the original, underlying spirit of the Web. A take-away from this is probably that the more you act like you want to make money with the social Web, the more that will preclude it from being. However, we do know that there can be (eventual) measurable value in providing useful content to the people who care about said content.

And in the meantime, there is no debating that journalists, book publishers, and trade publishers are reading professional service firm blogs. If they are good and they like what they see, they are delivering to the professionals opportunities for exposure that were previously difficult and expensive to get. Professionals who are actively sharing their intellectual capital are getting visibility they never anticipated. Some are getting clients and some haven't yet, but they continue because they see value in what they are doing.

Several of the stories such as those of legal bloggers Ernie Svenson and Jay Shepherd convey the same sentiment: yes, it's enormously valuable . . . just can't exactly put my finger on how or why. Two accountants heavily involved with social media, Daniel Stoica and Joel Ungar, also suggest the same thing. There's no question as to the benefits or these smart people would stop.

The knowledge of the value is nearly impossible to articulate—perhaps it's simply intuitive. According to his 1922 autobiography, Henry Ford made many important business decisions intuitively.[19] He was known to say, "Well, I can't prove it, but I can smell it."

It is my firm belief that the most valuable things you'll get out of social media won't ever be measurable. While some of these examples show measurable "gain," even those statistics fail to convey the bulk of the value: visibility, relationships, and the "feel-good" of "doing good."

Summary of Part II

Part II: "WHY" deeply explored why integrating social media into other marketing efforts is valuable, especially for the larger firm. However, even if you don't start with an integrated approach, you may, much like PKF Texas, find that your social media presence becomes the core of your marketing, building other initiatives around it.

Having read more than twenty case studies, and detailed how-to's for your strategic approach, you're ready in Part II: "HOW" to move on to setting up and using the tools we've been discussing.

PART III

HOW

How to Set Up and Use the Tools

CHAPTER 8

LinkedIn

Of the various social networking tools, LinkedIn is a perfect entry point to social media because it is purely business and yet offers features that mimic some elements of Twitter, Facebook, and even blogging. This allows you to discover which components or practices of popular social networking tools you might enjoy most or be most comfortable with.

LinkedIn is very easy to use and follow. It leverages grassroots marketing by capturing, building, and maximizing relationships. This works beautifully because people generally are prone to doing business with people they know, like, and trust. LinkedIn, like other social media, can help you move to a "know each other better" phase so that "like" and "trust" can be established or reinforced.

Getting Started

Initial setup for your individual profile takes just a few minutes but, in all, it will probably take about three to six hours to populate your user profile in the manner I recommend. Plan another hour to upload contacts and then filter them before you go through a process to selectively invite people. You'll probably end up spending a couple of hours in the days thereafter to correspond with and thank contacts when they accept your invitation. This is a great thing—most people skip this opportunity, and those who act on it almost always renew some good leads in this process.

You needn't do all this in one sitting. You can even spread your setup out, over several weeks, as shown in Figure 8.1. This keeps your time expenditure reasonable and ensures that your profile is set up before you invite people to connect.

159

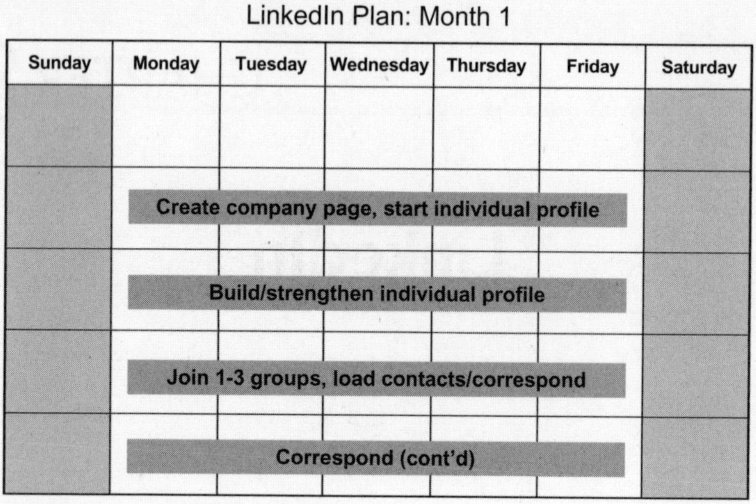

LinkedIn Plan: Month 1

Sunday	Monday	Tuesday	Wednesday	Thursday	Friday	Saturday
	Create company page, start individual profile					
	Build/strengthen individual profile					
	Join 1-3 groups, load contacts/correspond					
	Correspond (cont'd)					

FIGURE 8.1 LinkedIn Plan: Month One

Setup time for a company profile will be negligible, less than an hour for a basic profile and perhaps another hour or two if you enhance it with company data, which is not a requirement.

After your profile is complete, plan to invest 10–20 minutes per day to interact with others. It's okay to skip days, but check your "home" page and happenings a minimum of twice per week for best results.

The Tool

LinkedIn doesn't change as frequently as Facebook and Twitter do, but they may, so the location of the features discussed below might change, but the descriptions should remain consistent. The asterisk is used to indicate where tools may be available only with a premium access package. As of May 2010, the price for premium access ranged from $25–$500/month. The elements found in LinkedIn's top navigation are as follows:

- **Home:** Your hub. It's where you input your status update and see summaries of a number of things, including:
  - Recent inbox messages
  - Questions posed, which you might answer
  - Upcoming events
  - Job openings

- Automated contact suggestions and newly joined people from your past companies, schools, and associations
- The last few people who've viewed your profile (more history* and specifics on who viewed it come with premium level)
- Your contacts' recent status updates, recommendations they've given, and changes to their profiles
- Updates from groups you belong to
- Access/manage some third-party applications
- **Profile:** Edit and view your profile, view recent activity.
- **Contacts:** See and edit invitations, navigate through connections, access contacts' profiles, see network statistics, manage imported contacts, add new connections, access profile organizer.*
- **Groups:** Access and manage the groups you belong to, see some contacts' recent group activity, view discussions you've marked to follow, find new groups to join, create a group.
- **Jobs:** Find or post* jobs.
- **Inbox:** View all types of messages, requests, and invitations sent to you or by you, view and manage InMails.*
- **More:**
  - **Companies:** Add companies or search by name, industry or location.
  - **Answers:** Pose a question to your network, answer questions, browse by category, see "this week's experts."
  - **Events:** See events your contacts are attending and groups are involved in.
  - **Learning center:** Learn a lot more about how to leverage LinkedIn.
  - **Application directory:** Select from available applications that interact with your LinkedIn account.
  - **Installed applications:** Manage any third-party applications you've installed such as:
    - **Amazon:** Edit your reading list, see connections' lists, view updates.
    - **Blog Link** (if installed): Check your blog feeds and those of your contacts (great idea but suboptimal functionality, runs very slowly).
- **Search:** Run quick or advanced searches (save up to three at the free level). Paid level returns hundreds more search results and provide access to expanded member profiles.

Creating Your Individual Profile

A complete and compelling profile on LinkedIn supports your online credibility, and if it is the most robust information on the Internet about you—which it can be if you follow these recommendations. LinkedIn is almost guaranteed first-page rankings in Google search results, especially when any other defining criteria is included with your name that also happens to be in your profile (e.g., your city, your field of practice, your firm name, a school you attended, etc.). Your LinkedIn profile can and should serve as a hub for all your professional information.

Your profile is completely within your control. If you work in a firm with inflexible practices when it comes to your firm's Web site and your official "bio" (or if you don't have a biography on your firm's Web site), this is the best place to describe the detailed credentials you have that support your practice development efforts. Even if you *do* have a firm bio that is largely within your control, LinkedIn is highly searchable and so well ranked in Google, that it behooves you to have a robust profile. Don't be surprised or worried if your LinkedIn profile comes up higher in search engine results than your firm's Web site pages. This is a good thing and another reason you benefit from a strong LinkedIn profile—it may be someone's first impression of you. As long as people can find the right person quickly when they seek you out, your mission is accomplished.

GENERAL PROFILE TIPS The goals with your individual profile are to help people find you, convey your differentiators and specialty areas, and reflect your personality. This is *not* your resume and shouldn't be approached like one—instead, it is an introduction. Here are several tips to keep in mind as you write the "story" that becomes the body of your profile, and maximize some of LinkedIn's features.

- Keep your profile in the present tense (e.g., "He works with Fortune 100 . . ." instead of "He has worked with . . .") so people realize you are *currently* in demand. People don't want to hire a "has done"—they want to hire an "is now."
- Refer to yourself in the first person, not as she/he or Mr./Ms.
- Also avoid "I, I, I" and "we, we, we" (e.g., start a sentence with "Solving . . ." rather than "I solve . . .").
- Instead of using the impersonal word *client/s,* use *you* or *people* because it is much more engaging and personal.
- If you speak multiple languages, in the Edit Profile view, choose the option to Create Another Profile in an alternate language where, with a dropdown box, you can select the language of your choice—if it applies, this is potentially a huge differentiator for you.
- Mix up the wording throughout your profile instead of repeating the same verbiage. In different places, you'll summarize your work, indicate specialties, and also elaborate on past roles. For instance, you might say "nonprofit" in one place and "not-for-profit" in another. This is where variety trumps consistency: it helps you pop up in more searches.

- Settings for who can view your profile should be wide open (i.e., "Full View"), and allowing your contacts to be visible is usually best, too, but there are a few circumstances where it makes sense to keep them private; those are discussed later, in the Interacting section.
- If you use a browser with no spell-check built in, type your descriptions into Word first, and copy/paste into LinkedIn when finished.
- For sections with more than two or three lines of text, use bullets or special characters to distinguish lists.
- If you use slash marks, use spaces on either side (e.g., show "either/ or" as "either/or"); otherwise, search engines won't recognize them as distinct words.
- List all your past and present companies, schools, and organizations— not only will it help former colleagues find you, but LinkedIn notifies you when new people join whom you may know from your past. This makes it very easy for you to invite those past contacts to reconnect—a great way to renew acquaintance with "long lost" contacts.

PROFILE FIELDS   Your profile should reflect your skills, qualifications, experience, your involvement in organizations, activities, and even social media. Take the time to build a good profile and revisit your profile a few times each year to make sure it is current.

Name

- Use the name you use professionally—if everyone knows you as Jim instead of James, use Jim, but otherwise avoid nicknames.
- Leave out maiden name and credentials—it messes with search results.

Photo

- For best results, it must be a great one—smile or look approachable. The importance of a great photo cannot be overemphasized. (See "Smiles Sell" at http://goldenmarketing.typepad.com/weblog/2007/10/ smiles-sell.html.)
- Must be current, per LinkedIn rules: "A photograph that is not a current image of you is considered inappropriate."
- A head shot, one tightly cropped on the face is strongly recommended; this works especially well for the square shape displayed.
- Precrop (before uploading) your photo to a square of at least 80 × 80 pixels in size (using a smaller size will cause fuzziness or distortion after uploading).

- If necessary, have someone with some photo editing skills to help you size and crop your photo to the exact pixels specified to avoid graininess or distortion.
- A nonstudio picture will be fine, especially since you want to look natural and relaxed, and most or all of the background will be cut out.

Professional Headline

- This should be different from your job title and company name—it's your personal tagline. The default will be your name and the job title you entered, so you should manually change it to be more complete and more descriptive (see tip below).
- It's visible everywhere your name is on LinkedIn, including lists (such as other people's contacts) and under your name when you participate in groups.
- Use 120 characters to explain what you do—replace the automatically populated info (taken from your "current" title/company). LinkedIn's own help screens tell you "your own headline will be much more effective than the one we select."
- Follow professional/ethical guidelines and restrictions in your states of licensure (use of "expert" or "specialist" may be restricted), and never self-proclaim "guru" status.
- Leave out all nonobvious acronyms (spell out credentials aside from JD, CPA, or C-suite references, which are widely recognized).
- Project confidence and effectiveness and be descriptive. Good examples are:
  - "Tax and accounting professional with over 20 years of experience serving doctors, lawyers, and other professionals"
  - "Visionary lawyer in the real estate industry"
  - "President, [FIRM], mergers and acquisitions. Growth and succession strategies for privately held companies."
  - "CPA specializing in integrating business and tax expertise in problem solving"
  - "CPA; Licensed Insolvency Practitioner; Partner, [FIRM]; Business Restructuring Expert"
  - "Investment Counselor & 'CFO for Your Family'—Major League Investments, Inc. (Family Office)"[1]
  - "Consummate Wealth Manager"
  - "Lawyer—[FIRM] (International Business Law Firm)"
- Example of an unhelpful description:
  - "Partner [FIRM]" Without the words *lawyer, attorney, CPA, accountant, architect,* or *engineer,* how can anyone quickly discern what you do?

Summary

- This is your virtual elevator speech—it's where you articulate the sort of results you deliver and the qualifications that make you well suited to deliver them.
- Reinforce the industries or types of business you serve—the less vague, the better.
- Contains two separate fields: "Professional Experience and Goals" (2000 characters = about 330 words) and "Specialties."
- The former is where you tell your "story."
- The latter, Specialties, is generally used in a "keyword" format with commas separating one- to three-word descriptive phrases. Being repetitive is okay, but this also gives you a chance to use alternate yet similar wording. For instance, you might say "long-term care facilities" in one and "retirement homes" in another.

Positions—Multiple Items as Needed

- List current and past positions.
- Fill out each section completely, although past job descriptions needn't be lengthy (1,000 characters are allotted). A big-picture overview is adequate unless you really want to load up on those key words and phrases.
- Consider reflecting any board terms and other organizational leadership roles as additional "Positions" you've held.

Additional Information—Multiple Items as Needed

- Include all associations and organized groups you belong to if you believe they add credibility, show social responsibility, or otherwise demonstrate strength of character and commitment.
- Use both an organization's acronym and its full name spelled out, and then reflect the years of involvement.
- List all honors and awards, the organizations that bestowed them, and when.
- Consider bullets or > marks and hard returns to separate multiple items.

Education—Multiple Items as Needed

- Include years and activities—it helps people find you.

Web Sites—Up to Three

- LinkedIn provides three "places" for you to list your firm's Web site and other links of choice. By default, they are labeled My Company,

My Website, and Other. These are the words that will show up on your profile as "hotlinks" (aka "anchor text") unless you change them. Most people don't realize they can be changed, but indeed they can and should be.

- Be strategic in naming your links. Get better search engine optimization for your Web site or blog by putting the name of your firm and other descriptive keywords in the box to create good anchor text (e.g., Smith & Jones Web site).
- Make one of the links a direct link to your bio on your firm's Web site if you have one.
- When you click to edit the link, drop down the menu where you see the words *My Company* or similar.
- Show and select "other."
- Then an additional field will appear beside it for the words you would like to use to describe the link.
- For example, see Figure 8.2: "Description" would be "Robert Smith's Bio," and the link is "http://www.smithjones.com/robert.smith.html".

THIRD-PARTY APPLICATIONS Various applications are available to spice up your LinkedIn profile. Using any of these is optional. It really depends on how you intend to use LinkedIn and what other sorts of social media or intellectual capital you plan to share or integrate. Available third-party applications are:

- **Blog integration:** Feed blogs into LinkedIn for more exposure.
- **Twitter integration:** Feed select (not all) Twitter posts into LinkedIn and vice versa for broader exposure.
- **Book lists:** If you're a reader, consider sharing your favorites.
- **Travel arrangements:** Sharing when and where you'll be traveling can lead to get-togethers with contacts at your various destinations.
- **Presentations and documents:** Different tools let you share PowerPoint slides, PDF, Word, and other files.
- Other tools such as polls and file sharing.

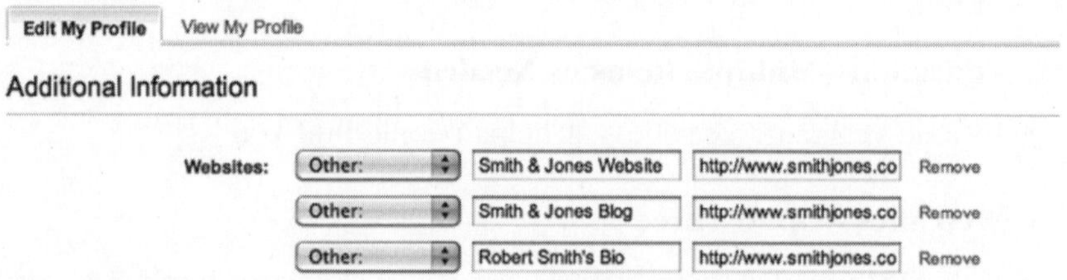

FIGURE 8.2 LinkedIn Profile Web Site Listing Example

Vanity URL or Personal URL

LinkedIn assigns a unique link to every public profile (found on your "view profile" page, the last item in the summary box at the top of the page called "public profile"). The link contains various numbers and odd characters in it (it will look something like this: http://www.linkedin.com/pub/bill-jones/1a/890/ba1), so you should change this because it is impossible to remember and a hassle to type.

The custom URL has to contain 5–30 alpha or numeric characters. Use something as close to your name as possible. If you have a very common name, this will be more challenging, as many are already taken. Avoid using numbers. If BillJones is taken, try BillJonesCPA. The custom link looks something like this: http://www.linkedin.com/in/billjonescpa.

Once edited, the custom URL will be easier to remember and to include on your email signature, your biography, and all your other social media sites such as when you comment in a blog or to list in your Twitter profile as your Web address (if you don't have a blog).

Finishing

Fairly new to LinkedIn is the ability to "drag" various sections of your profile into the order you prefer people to see them. Grab the four-direction arrow to the left of a section name, and move it up or down in order to rearrange sections.

When you are done with your profile, preview it in the "View Profile" tab and ask a trusted friend or two to view it also. Did you spell-check it? Run back through the General Profile Tips above to test for any of the writing styles recommended.

TIP: Updating Your LinkedIn Profile

Plan to review your profile for updates and changes at least once every three to six months.

Building and Managing Connections

People take different approaches in handling LinkedIn connections—some strictly invite only people they know well, and others connect to anyone. When it comes to quantity versus quality, there's no single "right" approach. No matter which choices you make with regard to inviting connections and accepting connection requests, courtesy is key.

Whom to Invite

LinkedIn guidelines suggest we should connect only to those whom we'd recommend. Truth is, that's not how most people use LinkedIn. You certainly can, but do recognize that not everyone is that well acquainted with their connections. Many people start off with strict standards and, as they meet new people and connect to them, standards get looser. These days, it's not uncommon to meet someone online and connect to them because you share a common interest or mutual respect, albeit superficial.

A connection you see elsewhere doesn't equate to an endorsement—connections lack context. If you want to know more about someone's knowledge of, and opinion of, a connection, unless they have written a "Recommendation," you would need to ask.

Some professionals, especially financial advisors and lawyers, aren't comfortable inviting clients to connect because of client confidentiality. This is totally up to you—use your judgment on a client-by-client basis. If you do want to invite clients, there can also be a concern about awkwardness in the event the client would feel obligated to accept the request. This isn't a big concern in reality, but I have some suggested verbiage below that addresses removing any obligation someone might feel to accept your invitation. Some professionals chose to invite no clients, but will accept invitations extended to them. Others invite all clients. Either is okay.

One distinct advantage to connecting to your clients is that you can see if they are connected to your competitors (or, alternately, you can see this by connecting directly to your competitors). This can be useful information to have. Another clear advantage is the extra opportunity to stay front of mind with them in a nonintrusive way.

SHARING OR HIDING CONNECTIONS You will need to choose whether to hide your connections from each other. Under most circumstances, you will want to show connections. Most people do. In the general business world, it's pretty well understood that people who would hide their contacts are either journalists protecting their sources or recruiters protecting their inventory. There are some instances, though, where professionals *might* make a similar choice:

- If you are heavily involved in merger and acquisition work
- If you are involved in initial public offerings or similar sensitive, high-stakes transactions and your contact list is a resource comparable to a journalist's
- If you are a wealth manager with a *very* prestigious clientele

I emphasize "might" in this choice because it would take a pretty substantial contact list for the cons of sharing to outweigh the pros.

Uploading Contacts

People often worry whether bulk uploading to LinkedIn is safe. It is. LinkedIn, unlike some other programs out there, will not spam your contacts—even after uploading, you are required to manually select anyone whom you wish to invite.

Upload your contacts from Outlook, Apple Mail, some Web mail, and .csv, .txt, or .vcf file formats. If you prefer to filter your contacts (eliminating those whom you'd never invite) before you upload, you can—simply export your Outlook to a .txt or .csv file and edit that before uploading to LinkedIn. This isn't necessary, however, because you can filter after uploading, as described below.

Once you upload, you'll see all your contacts and they'll appear with a checkbox beside each, as shown in Figure 8.3. Do *not* "select all"; I'll explain:

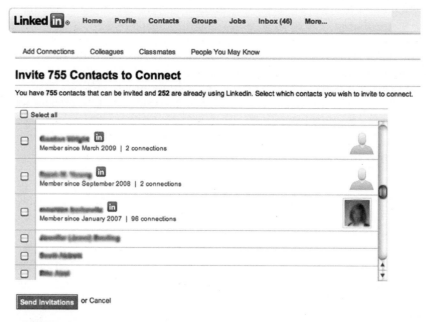

FIGURE 8.3 LinkedIn Contact Upload Screenshot

- In addition to the checkbox, you'll see a LinkedIn logo beside some names. I strongly advise you to invite only persons who have the logo by their name because it means they already use LinkedIn. The logo appears because their email address matches what they have on file with LinkedIn.
- If you invite people who don't already use LinkedIn, you will almost certainly receive a slew of emails asking you: "What's LinkedIn?" "Is it worthwhile?" "I keep getting these invitations, should I join?" Unless you want to spend a lot of time answering these types of emails, forego sending invitations to nonmembers.
- A cool thing about LinkedIn, though, is that when any of those people do join, later, LinkedIn will let you know and you can easily click their name and invite them.

Read the rest of this section before sending invitations to anyone because there are some good dos and don'ts within.

Note: When you upload contacts, connect, and later view others' profiles, there is a private (for your eyes only) notes area on the right sidebar that includes contact info and a notes field. If you have notes in programs including Outlook or CardScan, they can appear here. Don't panic. LinkedIn assures us that these are *not* publicly accessible.

If you are an Outlook user who also uses LinkedIn, you have some tremendous features available to you. LinkedIn has an Outlook Add-In—a toolbar—that lets you manage your LinkedIn contacts directly from Outlook. You see LinkedIn mini-profiles right in Outlook when people email you. You can add people as LinkedIn contacts with one click to quickly and easily build your network. And my favorite feature is the ability to update your Outlook contact information with LinkedIn profile changes. You can greatly improve the quality of your data through automatic contact info changes.

Sending Invitations

Whenever you invite people, there are some approaches you can take that will be much appreciated. First, whenever you are prompted to personalize the invitation, please do.

Use this personalization opportunity to remind people where you've met unless you're absolutely certain they'll remember you and the context in which they know you: "Mary, it was great meeting you at the dinner last week, thought it would be nice to connect." When you start receiving some rather unhelpful invitations, you'll come to see why people appreciate the memory triggers.

When you invite in bulk, LinkedIn no longer allows you the opportunity to personalize the invitations you send. So consider the advice below before you do initial inviting upon uploading contacts—there are probably some individuals you would be better off inviting personally with individual messages versus sending a bulk generic invitation. Think in terms of three groups of people:

- **Group 1:** Nonclients you haven't talked to in a while. Say something like, "Hi, It's been a long time! I saw you on LinkedIn and thought it would be nice to connect so we can stay in touch better . . . hope you're well. . . ."
- **Group 2:** Nonclients you *have* connected with recently. Try something like "Hi, it was nice visiting with you recently and I thought it would be great to stay in touch through LinkedIn so we have the chance to do that more often."
- **Group 3:** For clients you feel comfortable inviting, ask something like this, "Hi, I see you are on LinkedIn, too, so you know it's good for strengthening business connections. Ultimately, I hope to introduce you to others who could be of value to you and your business. However, my contacts can see one another's names and because you are a client and your privacy is foremost, I understand if you prefer not to connect in a way that is visible to our mutual contacts. Therefore, I won't take offense if you chose to "archive" this request to rid it from your inbox. Thanks for considering."

Do not pitch yourself or your services, either in the invitation or in the thank you. Even saying, "If you ever need a business valuation, keep me in mind . . ." isn't appropriate in an invitation or thank-you message.

When it comes to inviting clients, believe in the power of choice and information. If you give your clients all the information they need, and offer a choice, you'll be pleasantly surprised with how many of them are happy to be connected to you on LinkedIn, just the same way many would come to a party that your firm would throw. You are sharing contacts for *their* best interest. Connecting people is one of the most valuable gifts you can give.

AFTER PEOPLE ACCEPT Be gracious when people accept your invitation. You'll receive a notification email saying they've accepted. Take just a moment to click in the email to view their profile, and from there, in the top right of their profile, choose Send Message, and dash off a quick "thanks for connecting" message. You can add something you might be looking forward to such as "it'll be nice keeping in closer touch" or "looking forward to seeing you at next year's event and staying in touch better in the meantime now that we're connected."

Very few people send a thank you, so you will stand out in a positive way. Also, you'll be surprised at how much dialogue continues based on this courteous outreach. Especially after a bulk upload, do expect to invest some time corresponding with people who accept your invitations. It's not uncommon to find yourself discussing some new opportunities with a few contacts, and scheduling some lunches. Don't wait too long to reply to people who converse with you at this time. It's beneficial to keep up the momentum.

Continue to build out your connection base over time. As you collect business cards, attend events, and meet people online, invite them to connect. After you meet someone at an event, it's a nice gesture to send an invite as a "Thank you for a great conversation—it was nice to meet you," within a few days or a week. A best practice I learned from a recruiting pro friend is to always connect with any candidate who has potential (e.g., 3.5 or better on a "1–5 scale") shortly after an interview, office visit, or recruiting event. This practice will help to build your experienced hire database and allow you to keep tabs on recruits you might wish to contact in the future.

To help users organize and sort their contacts, LinkedIn is adding the ability to attach your own personal "tags" to your connections. This feature is in beta at the time of writing, so it's not available to all users—but it has a lot of potential for maximizing LinkedIn as a robust contact management system. If it's available to you, it appears in your contact view as shown in Figure 8.4.

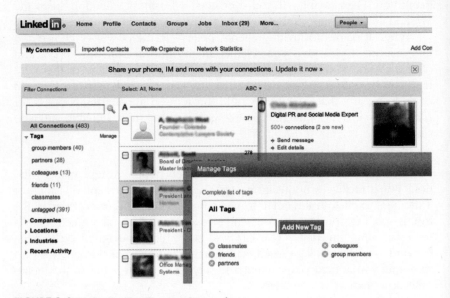

FIGURE 8.4 LinkedIn Tag Feature Screenshot

Building Your Network

Why do you want to have a lot of connections? One reason is that a large number of connections improves the odds that your profile will appear in searches by your connections *and their connections* for someone to do business with—when you are connected to someone in the second or third degree, you are a more qualified potential provider than you would otherwise be.

Print your LinkedIn URL on your business cards. Have it added to your bio, your Twitter background, and your email signature. Your LinkedIn profile will probably be more robust than your firm's Web site bio, and it is definitely going to be more interactive and beneficial for you. Share it liberally to encourage people to connect to you.

TIP: Sharing Your LinkedIn URL

Share your LinkedIn URL liberally to encourage people to connect to you. Print it on your business cards, have it added to your bio, your Twitter background, and your email signature.

GROUPS   While some people advise you to join LinkedIn groups in order to meet new contacts, be very careful about how you do this. Read and respect the rules of any LinkedIn groups you join. Many groups have rules against joining for the purpose of "connecting" to other group members. Some are very strict about overt self-promotion. Your best approach is to join groups with an altruistic spirit of helpfulness.

CONNECTING TO COMPETITORS   Some people are particularly concerned with competitor exposure. It's a valid concern. If you connect to a competitor, they can see your contacts. And you can see *theirs*. On the positive side is the fact that you are able to see if they suddenly connect to a key client of yours, even if you are not connected to that client. Most of us would want to know, and you can by connecting to friendly competitors.

Once you connect, when you visit their profiles, a listing on the right-hand side of the profile displays all your mutual connections. This is good competitive intelligence. It helps you see if they are schmoozing any of your clients (or if anyone you are schmoozing is potentially a client of theirs and maybe you didn't know it). Also, by watching their behaviors (groups they join, questions they answer, etc.) you can get ideas for other ways to market yourself through LinkedIn or other good resources.

You know the saying: "Keep your friends close and your enemies closer." Ultimately, it's about what you are comfortable with.

Interacting with Other Members

Two simple ways that relationships are strengthened in LinkedIn are through members updating their status and their profiles. As your contacts make changes to their profiles—anything from a new picture to a new job—you will receive a notification. You can receive these updates as they happen (possibly too intrusive) or weekly. To change the frequency:

- Go to Settings in your top right navigation.
- Find "Receiving Messages."
- Look for "Weekly Digest Email."

(There are many other settings you can also customize. Poke around the settings and explore—change things if you want to see if something else would work better for you. If not, you can easily change it back later.)

When you receive these updates, allow them to inspire personal notes and outreach. If your goal is to leverage the digital world, it means that you should always seek ways to move interactions "from digital to personal."

In addition to, or instead of, waiting for periodic updates, you can check LinkedIn daily by going to your home page and doing a quick scan of contact updates. Reach out to people to congratulate them, comment on things they share, or just say hello. If this form of interaction is the limit of your use of LinkedIn, you will no doubt experience some positive responses, making these efforts worthwhile.

Status Updates

Like Twitter and Facebook, LinkedIn has a status update feature. However, unlike these other applications, most users refrain from updating their status several times per day, or even daily. Most users update their LinkedIn status once or twice per week. This comparatively slower pace appeals to a lot of users.

The types of things people share in their status updates vary. Watch others for a while to get a feel for what they post. You'll see that some people are much more self-promoting than others. If you think something is "too much," it probably is, so don't emulate it.

A rule of thumb for self-promoting message ratios in LinkedIn status updates is 5:1 or five "about others" to one "about me" post. What this means it that you should post five general interest posts (helpful tidbits, promoting other people and their work, etc.) to every one post about you, your work, or your firm. Because of the less frequent posting on this site, it's a lower ratio than Twitter where you should have a ratio close to 10:1.

Because LinkedIn status updates are limited in space (700 characters), something you'll learn very quickly is the value of using link shorteners. This is covered extensively in Chapter 12, but several great services are out there including Bit.ly (www.bit.ly) which, when you sign up for a free account, lets you keep tabs on how many people click on your various shortened links—a good indicator to watch in order to know which things appeal more or less to your audience.

If you use Twitter in addition to LinkedIn, you can connect the accounts. Integrating your LinkedIn account with one or more Twitter accounts is accomplished via a third-party application (discussed below). If your status is integrated with Twitter, you will have to check or uncheck a box beside your status to cross-post, or not, with Twitter. Alternately, to update your LinkedIn status from Twitter, just include "#in" (without the quotes) within your Twitter post, and it will appear in your LinkedIn account status.

Because of the posting frequency differences, I strongly recommend *against* having every tweet you make flow through to your LinkedIn (or Facebook, for that matter) account. If you're a moderate to heavy Twitter user, the volume is too much.

Asking Questions

Anytime you like, you can ask questions of your network. LinkedIn requires the questions to be in the form of a question (this would seem obvious, but you'd be surprised) and polls are not allowed. There is a field for the question (2,000 characters) and another 2,000-character field for additional details.

You are permitted to ask your connections questions related to recruiting, job seeking, and even promoting your service. You will be asked directly if any of these are your intent. If so, only your current contacts will see the question. If not, your question may be posted more broadly—outside of your network. It is against LinkedIn's rules to ask questions with the intention of trying to connect with people who answer them.

You will also be asked to categorize your question and to indicate if it is geographically specific. Be as specific as you can. When you enter the Question area, there are tips and links to guidance in asking effective questions.

Answering Questions

LinkedIn offers an opportunity to demonstrate your expertise through answering questions and participating in groups. Sharing your knowledge increases credibility.

You can seek out questions in your areas of expertise. Good answers are sometimes tagged "Best Answer." When this happens, it shows on your profile. You will have 4,000 characters to invest in your answer—that's about 650 words—usually more than sufficient.

Whenever you answer a question, that fact, along with the category and a link, are included in the periodic updates your connections receive. So when the value and reach of your answer is extended beyond the people who asked, it is made known to everyone who knows you. Though many people won't click on the link to read the question and your answer, they will notice if you routinely or even occasionally answer questions. By the power of suggestion, this creates a sense of expertise.

Michigan CPA Joel Ungar[2] (read more about Joel in Chapter 7) is very active on LinkedIn. His profile headline, by the way, is very good. It reads: "Exceptional CPA helping SEC companies, franchisors, franchisees and restaurants with their auditing & accounting needs." He uses the Question and Answer feature often and is impressed with how helpful others are when he is in need. This inspired him to "give back." Joel has earned several "best answers" in Accounting, Auditing, Social Entrepreneurship, Blogging, and Using LinkedIn. At the time of writing, he has answered more than 30 questions (Figure 8.5).

At a minimum, people see that Joel is helpful—willing to lend his brain and experience to help solve people's needs. But more than that, people can see how Joel thinks, get insights into his values, and experience his unique sense of humor. Answering questions, even if they are outside of "accounting," doesn't hurt Joel at all. In fact, it helps that he answers ques-

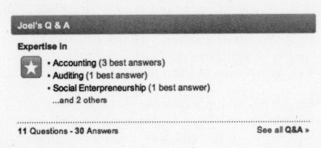

FIGURE 8.5 Joel's Q&A

tion in other topic areas. It illustrates that he has broad interests and knowledge. It also gets his name and excellent headline in front of a lot of new people.

Steve Strauss recommends building some buzz after you answer questions in LinkedIn by "sharing" your answers. He describes[3]:

After you answer a question, look to the far right and you will see a link that says "share this." You can email it out to your contacts or share it using Delicious.com. The permalink function allows you to link your blog or site to your answer.

It's also a good idea to keep a copy of any questions you answer on LinkedIn somewhere else on your local computer or company network, this way you'll have a compilation of your "intellectual capital" in the event you decide to start a blog or use the information elsewhere.

Answering people's questions on LinkedIn provides users with a taste of what blogging is like. Blog posts are usually somewhere between 150 and 500 words, each addressing a micro sort of issue. If you find you enjoy answering questions on LinkedIn, or even by email to clients and prospects, you might be a good candidate for authoring a blog at some point. If you should choose to, you could repurpose your answers to questions on LinkedIn and elsewhere as posts for your blog.

Some people who answer questions are annoyingly sales-y. No one appreciates those folks. Some tips for answering questions without being too self-promoting:

- Consistently approach answering questions from an altruistic perspective.
- Answer only if you can provide new information, perspective, or ideas.
- Stick with the answer to the question and avoid tangents or anything that strays too far from the actual question.
- To sound less self-promoting, avoid the words *I, we,* and your firm's name.
- By providing good info, appropriate in context to the questions asked, you cannot be faulted as a shameless self-promoter.

Joining Groups

To answer questions, you can search for random questions and you can also join groups formed around common interests or industries. Many formal associations have LinkedIn groups, which may or may not have restricted membership. Joining groups is a great way to expand your reach and interact with people who share common interests.

Responding to Invitations

When someone invites you to connect and you accept, accept promptly and take a moment to thank him or her for extending the invitation. Despite the fact it takes about two seconds, you would be astounded at how few people make the effort for what should be a common courtesy—like waving back when someone waves to you. Sadly, I received only one thank you for an invitation in the last nine months. My personalized invitation said, "If you'd like to connect, I'd be honored." Here's what my acquaintance wrote back:

> *My pleasure, Michelle. Glad to be part of your network! I hope you are doing well.*
>
> *Regards,—*

Simple. And he really stood out. You will stand out, too. And a nice dialogue can occur as a result. There is no point participating in social media if you are not going to interact and have dialogue with people, right?

When you receive an invitation from someone you don't recognize, first check their profile to see if it rings any bells. If not, you might want to reply to the invitation, asking, "Thanks for reaching out. Can you please refresh me . . . how do we know one another?"

If, in fact, you don't know them, and you don't want to connect, you have two choices, one of which has unfortunate consequences for the sender. If they haven't been obnoxious, just archive their invitation. This merely removes it from your inbox (or you could leave it in there if you want). The other option, the bad one, is the "IDK" or "I Don't Know" penalty. If you click "I don't know this person" and they get a few of those, they get into trouble—a LinkedIn has penalties for spammers. Therefore, unless the person is pretty obnoxious or spammy, just archive undesired invitations.

If you *do* know the person, and you don't care to connect with him or her, it can be a bit awkward. You can simply ignore or archive the invitation. Or you can reply that you prefer not to connect, but if you do that, you should be able to give a reason. Of course, either ignoring or openly declining someone's invitation can have negative consequences. But, sometimes, it's unavoidable. There may be people you would not refer to your worst enemy—and if they have no clue how you feel, and ask to connect with you, you must decide between the lesser of two evils. While it's okay to connect to someone you may not know well enough to refer yet, it is never a good idea to connect with someone whom you'd never refer in a million years.

Recommendations

Recommendations are a neat feature on LinkedIn because the recommendation comes directly from the other person. Because they are not altered, modified, or created by you, they carry more weight than testimonials you might publish on your firm's Web site or in your print materials. You may receive the random unsolicited recommendation, and this is a treat, indeed. Do be sure to offer profuse thanks to someone who has gone out of his or her way to endorse you.

Despite the exciting prospect of having a large number of contacts flood you with glowing recommendations, *never* click the button that sends an automatic request, en masse, to ask people to recommend you. This is an extremely impersonal thing to do. And, no doubt, there are people from whom it would be inappropriate to solicit a referral—such as someone you just met.

It is also perfectly acceptable to personally ask someone (preferably by email or telephone rather than through LinkedIn) to recommend you. The optimal time to do this is immediately after a very positive interaction. Perhaps you've delivered exceptional service or results. Or you've received a nice email or note of appreciation. You could say, "I'm so glad you're pleased! Thank you for telling me this. If you feel moved to do so, I'd be honored if you could share this in a recommendation on LinkedIn so that other people who are considering hiring me might see it and be more confident about their decision to give me a shot."

You can imagine how good it feels to receive a nice recommendation. A fantastic strategy is to pay it forward and give recommendations to worthy individuals. This is especially fruitful with referral sources. Once a month or two, scan your contact list and see if there's someone you feel inclined to reward with a few words about your positive experience with him or her. Try to be specific. Instead of "Chris is great and does a good job," provide some context and at least one or two details such as, "Chris and I worked together serving a mutual client. I was impressed by how she proactively responded since time was of the essence for our client who needed to secure a loan quickly for some urgent cash flow needs."

Finally, when you give recommendations, not only do you create good will with the person you've recommended, but your name and link to your profile will appear on their profile so others will see you and, possibly, click through. It can make good strategic sense to focus on giving recommendations to people you respect who also happen to have large, influential networks, or at least some key contacts with whom you'd like to become acquainted.

Note: Wealth managers are not allowed to receive testimonials (per Rule 206(4) of the Investment Advisors Act of 1940). Financial advisors and registered investment advisors (RIAs) must write back to the people kind enough to recommend them, explaining that compliance requirements prohibit them from displaying anything resembling an endorsement or testimonial.

Introductions

Introductions are another LinkedIn built-in function, similar to recommendations—a neat idea, in theory, but the actual use of it is cold and unfriendly. Further, the fact that the context of relationships is so inconsistent from user to user means that it's potentially inaccurate to assume someone is well-enough acquainted with his or her contacts to leverage them for an introduction for you.

Therefore, if you see a connection you'd like to ask to make an introduction, pick up the phone and call your contact. Explain what you're trying to do and ask if they know the person well enough to facilitate that sort of an introduction. If you receive an automated introduction request, again, pick up the phone to learn more before using the built-in mechanism for the intro. Your personal handling of it will go far.

Searching and Researching

One of the greatest benefits to firms in using LinkedIn is the information that can be learned about prospective clients, referral sources, prospective employees, and almost anyone through searches. LinkedIn is a third-degree connector. You may be surprised by how small the world really is.

I stumbled upon the name of a past coworker, in another state, from 20 years ago. When I opened his profile, I was stunned by the fact that I know five people from my "current life" that also know Scott. And I'd bet that only two of these five people know each other. A small world indeed.

Research will show you who you know, or could know, throughout your firm and your entire network. Practice growth consultant Gale Crosley discussed its use in the sales process "to smoke out relationships, see who is at the table, get introduced to the right people including board members and other influencers."[4] At any time, you can see the extent of your reach by going to Contacts and choosing "Network Statistics." With over 500 first-level connections, I can access over 4.9 million people at the third-degree level—approximately 7.5 percent of the total LinkedIn user population. That is at the free level. A user can search to find and connect to any of the more than 70 million people at the paid level.

What to Research

Search your prospects, referral sources, and other contacts (new and old) before meetings. It's always good to be prepared. At a minimum, check their profile to see mutual contacts. If you don't know the name of someone who will be in a meeting, but you know their job title, search their job title and company, but deselect the Current Titles Only option so you can see more background information about them, like where they attended school, past job titles, and personal interests, as well as shared contacts. When you meet new people, it's nice to have some acquaintances or interests in common.

You can learn a lot by studying your competition. Where do they "hang out" online. Who do they know? Check the competitor's company page to see where employees usually go when leaving the competitor's company. Also, when your connections include your competitors (some pros and cons discussed earlier) and you search prospective clients' companies, you'll see if you and your competitors have people at those companies in common.

When researching prospects or competitors, it can help to get a sense of their employee turnover—good due diligence if the prospective client would be a big fish in your portfolio. To see if a lot of turnover occurs, or if key people are leaving or have recently left, search for the company name and deselect the Current Companies Only option.

To identify some new prospects, use geographic parameters ("in or near zip codes" works well) and do an advanced search by industry. Once you identify some prospects, look for people who have worked for those companies so you can distinguish cooler leads from warm leads, depending on how many contacts you have in common and who those contacts are.

For recruiting, search for additional references for your prospective hire. This feature is now only for paid users, but is very helpful for human resources. Go into the Advanced People Search and select Reference Search. With an applicant's resume in hand, you can quickly enter their companies and years worked to find people you know who worked there then or know someone who did. Without paid membership, you can do this manually by looking up the candidate's past employers to see whom you may know in the organization and whether they were there at the time your candidate was there.

If you are considering a job change, check your prospective company and its turnover trends.

This is just some of the valuable information that can be found in LinkedIn. It's a wonder how few people do premeeting research when such a powerful tool is available to us.

The advanced search provides much cleaner results than a basic search. Searching by title or industry isn't always effective. Instead, try "keyword" searches, which find text anywhere in the profile. A Boolean search—using operators: AND OR NOT () ""—works well.

TIP: Searching Competitors and Prospects

If you don't want your name or company name to show up in their list of "Who's Viewed My Profile?", check your settings (Settings > Privacy > Profile Views) to control how much information is shown to the users whose profiles you have viewed. At present, there are three setting levels that range from nothing to your name and company name.

Setting Up a Company Page

Setting up a company page is very easy to do. Once your firm has a company page, everyone who works for the company can connect to it. Each person who does so will be listed on the company page. Also, beside the company's name on each person's profile, a small "document" icon will appear where someone can click for more information about the firm.

The company page should be set up by a permanent owner/member of the firm. Someone who leaves the firm and no longer has an email address that has the firm's URL can no longer edit the page and LinkedIn will have to be contacted to adjust anything—it's best just to avoid the hassle.

Also, if you ever need to change your firm's Web site domain (aka URL), remember to edit the firm profile *before* your authorized person's email address changes in order to avoid another big hassle.

Setting up the company page requires only a few fields, including location, industry, type of business, status, company size (number of employees), year founded, and Web site. There is also a description field, a specialties field (keywords like the individual profile), and the ability to upload a company logo. You could also add blogs and annual revenues if you are so inclined.

Calendar of Activities

It takes time to build up your LinkedIn profile to the point where it is highly effective for you. This won't happen overnight, but don't feel overwhelmed. An action plan helps you spread out your LinkedIn project and

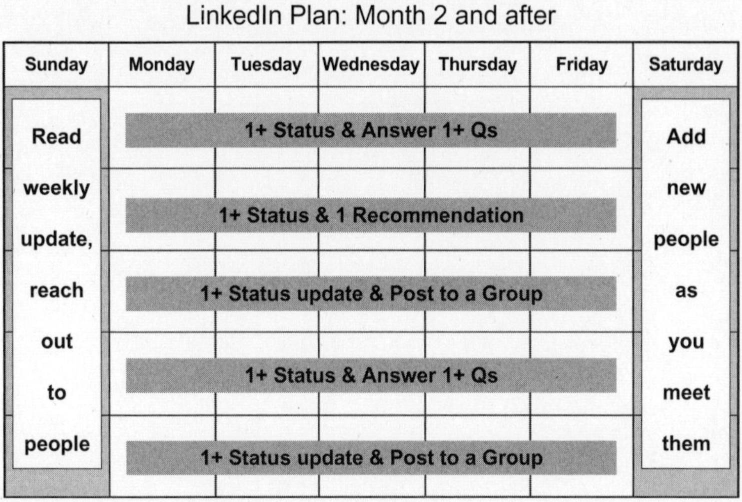

LinkedIn Plan: Month 2 and after

Sunday	Monday	Tuesday	Wednesday	Thursday	Friday	Saturday
Read	1+ Status & Answer 1+ Qs					Add
weekly	1+ Status & 1 Recommendation					new
update,						people
reach	1+ Status update & Post to a Group					as
out	1+ Status & Answer 1+ Qs					you
to						meet
people	1+ Status update & Post to a Group					them

FIGURE 8.6 LinkedIn Month Two and Beyond

reminds you to interact regularly and update your profile periodically. The setup month is represented in Figure 8.1 (earlier in this chapter) and the months following your setup month could follow a pattern like that shown in Figure 8.6. Take it one month at a time.

Month one is to build the foundation: create your profile and invite/correspond with your contacts. Month two and beyond begins consistent interaction.

Weekly:
- Update your status at least once
- Invite new contacts
- Review "Network Updates" and correspond with people accordingly

Once per month:
- Recommend someone
- Answer a question or participate in a group

Quarterly:
- Review and update your profile

LinkedIn is an extremely powerful tool on many levels. With more than 70 million users including Fortune 500 executives, the extent of reach for the average user is outstanding. With purposes ranging from recruiting to positioning yourself as an expert, or from researching prospects to nurturing relationships, it is an excellent entry point to social media for any level of professional.

CHAPTER 9

Twitter

Twitter is extremely simple to navigate, set up, and use: there are only a few elements to learn and master. The setup time will be less than an hour, and a decent presence can be easily maintained with a minimal time investment of just 5 to 15 minutes per day, though some people spend far more time using Twitter. Personally, I don't usually exceed 15 minutes, which are usually broken up over a couple of quick visits.

On Twitter, it's perfectly acceptable to skip a day or two or more, but it's not a good idea to skip weeks without an indication you'll be gone or people may assume you've fled.

A major challenge with using Twitter will be trying to manage the incoming flow of information (tip: don't try), locating the best content (lists are terrific for this), and providing relevant information—this does require some reading. It could go without saying (but I'll say it) that another challenge might be not getting sucked into it too far from a time-consumption standpoint. Limiting your time to five to ten minutes a shot will help.

Another issue with Twitter, particularly in the business space, is frequent phishing and hacking of accounts. Seasoned users are pretty understanding of it, and tend to roll with the tide when this happens, accepting it as a temporary inconvenience. But when corporate brands whose branded accounts are hacked to send out phishing messages, brand managers are more than annoyed—they are horrified, and rightly so.

Firms' accounts are sometimes hacked, and private direct messages (DMs) are sent under the firm's name to everyone who follows. The messages invite the recipient to visit a harmless-looking link, or to view a sexually explicit video, as a means to phish their login credentials and spread the attack. You can avoid this to some degree by not clicking on phishing links yourself, but you can't guarantee prevention of hacks. It's similar to email exposure. However, when you are weighing the choice of establishing a branded presence on Twitter versus blogs, for instance, consider the risk of this type of thing in Twitter, whereas in blogs, authors can control who posts and can manage comment spam—more brand control is possible.

The Tool

The Twitter interface is extremely simple. Its simplicity has encouraged numerous third party programmers to build fancy applications, with lots of bells and whistles, that interface with Twitter. Some users prefer the simplicity of the Web interface at Twitter.com, and others swear by the third-party applications. I'm describing just the Twitter.com Web interface.

Top Navigation

- **Settings:** Where you create your account and manage your minimal profile
- **Home:** Where you view the stream of tweets by those whom you follow
- **Profile:** Where you view your page as others see it (called your "timeline")
- **Find People:** A search mechanism for other Twitter users

Right Sidebar Contents (just for you)

- **Following:** Those whom you "follow," a count and link to the list
- **Followers:** Those who follow you, a count and link to the list
- **@[yourname]:** Links to a list of all mentions of your Twitter handle
- **Direct messages (DMs):** Links to a list of any messages sent privately to you, and those you've sent privately to others
- **Saved searches:** If you've performed a search and saved it, it shows up for your future reference until you remove it—clicking the search term opens a new search for that term.
- **Retweets:** A listing of tweets rebroadcast using Twitter's built-in "Retweet" feature. Shows retweets by those you follow, your retweets of others, and others' retweets of your posts.
- **Trending topics:** At any time, see a quick reference of the 10 most popular topics of the given moment. Keep an eye on this list for breaking news.

Right Sidebar Contents (others can also see)

- **Favorites:** Links to a list of any tweets you've indicated a "favorite" by selecting the "star."

- **Lists:** Twitter recently launched a "list" feature that is very powerful. Any lists you create will show here, and any lists others make, if you choose to "follow" them, will show under your lists.
- **Footer:** If you need to reach the Twitter team, the footer of each page contains navigation for contact information, help, and Twitter's official blog. The Help pages have rich, descriptive explanations of all things Twitter.

Setting Up Your Account

If you will be tweeting personally, it is advantageous to tweet under your own name (e.g., @billjones or @billjonescpa or @billjonesesq) versus tweeting under your firm name. If you have a marketing department or person who will be handling corporate tweets, he or she can tweet under his or her own name (preferable) or establish an account with the firm's name (less preferable) such as @smithjones. Other than a marketing or customer service representative, all individuals within the firm who tweet should do so under their name rather than under an impersonal corporate presence because this makes you more accessible—the only way you can develop relationships.

It's best if you don't use one account for multiple people to tweet. It's awkward. If you have multiple individuals, and especially on a corporate account, each should display a "List" called, for example, "Smith Jones Employees," adding all individuals who tweet to that list. This way, people see you as individuals who collectively comprise the firm and as team members who cross-reference each other.

Following are some considerations pertaining to your account setup. I have not included every field, just those for which choices may impact future usability and effectiveness.

When it comes to picking your user name, Twitter has approximately 20 million users (not all of whom are active), so you'll find that a lot of names are already taken. When you choose your name, consider the following:

- The shorter the better (spelling it all out only if necessary) It's okay to run words together (e.g., @dansmith) to keep it short. Remember, every letter counts when there's only 140 to a post, and you want people to post your name a lot, so make it easy for them to fit in—there's a 15-character name limit.
- To be found and remembered, try to use something easy for others to recall, avoid uncommon abbreviations (e.g., "oklaacctgprof")—again, your name or a variation of it is best.

- Don't use all caps. All lowercase is perfectly fine or capitalize first letters of first and last name, and CPA/JD if you wish.
- Including CPA/JD can be a good enough differentiator for a fairly common name.
- Don't use numbers in your handle—this isn't a typical user name, it will be your identity.
- Don't use an "underscore" between words—they are a pain. If necessary (for more alternatives), you can use a hyphen.

If you already have an online presence elsewhere, and are known as something specific, use that name in your Twitter name if at all possible, as it will give you broader recognition as well as a little extra "link power." Some naming examples are:

www.twitter.com/michellegolden
www.twitter.com/jayshep
www.twitter.com/dentalcpas
www.twitter.com/MitchPFS

TIP: Changing Your User Name

If you started on Twitter with a name you regret, there is a way to switch. If the name is not already taken, you can simply change your user name in your account settings.

If you've already created "another" account with the name you want, a tutorial describing how to painlessly make the switch can be found at www.digitizd.com/2009/01/28/how-to-switch-to-the-right-twitter-username/. By using this method, you don't even need to notify anyone to "change" anything in order to keep getting your tweets.

Main Account Setup

- **Name:** Use your real name, and put CPA, JD, Esq., or other credentials in this space—this displays on the top right of your profile.
- **Username field:** This will be your "@" name, which is your main identifier and will be part of your unique URL (www.twitter.com/YourUsername).
- **Email address field:** Twitter offers you the option of receiving notifications of direct messages received, new followers, and so on. These can be turned off. But if you do wish to receive them, you may want to consider giving Twitter an email account other than your primary

work account. This can help you avoid frequent email interruptions at work. If you don't already have one, you might want to set up a Gmail account for your social media activities.

- **Find sources:** You can skip this for now, we'll discuss finding accounting-relevant people to connect with.
- **Find your contacts:** This feature pulls from Gmail, Yahoo, and AOL. For your corporate contacts, this usually won't be applicable, so feel free to skip this step unless your contacts are synced with one of these services and you want to see if people you know are already on Twitter. I strongly recommend you do *not* invite others who are not already on Twitter, if so prompted.

That concludes the bare-bones sign-up process. But before you do anything else, take care of a few things in your in settings.

Account Tab

- **Tweet Privacy:** *Do not* select "Protect my tweets." This hides your communications from everyone and completely defeats the purpose of Twitter. It reflects that the user doesn't "get" Twitter, and most Twitter users will never follow back someone whose tweets are protected.

Notices Tab

- This is where you can turn on (or off) any email notifications—feel free to leave these off unless you really want them pushed to you. You can view these on demand any time.

Profle Tab

- **Picture:** Add a photo of yourself as soon as possible. It should be a photo that shows you as friendly and approachable. It needn't be a professional head shot. Fact is, it will be so small that you will prob-ably want a close-up (cropped tight on your face) so a home shot versus a professional shot won't be easy to discern. Don't use a pet or kid photo here, or your firm logo (except for a firm account). This should be you.
- **Location:** Add city/state.
- **Web:** Put your firm's Web site address here (include http://first) or if you author a blog, you may wish to use that address. If you'd like to link directly to your bio on your firm's Web site, that is good, too, or you can use your LinkedIn URL or Google Profile if these are better alternatives for you.

- **Bio:** You have 160 characters (20 more than a tweet) to describe yourself. Don't leave this blank.
  - Mention your profession (lawyer, CPA, CFP, etc.) and other credentials, and perhaps name your firm.
  - Tell something interesting about yourself—something personal to help people relate to you. "Father of three beautiful girls," "Die-hard hockey fan," "Avid photographer," "Committed to church and family," "Love helping people," or "Volunteer at my kids' school."
  - About your work, avoid calling yourself an "expert," "guru," or similar—these terms are overused. It's okay to say if you specialize (or "focus" if "specialize" is disallowed by your profession) in something.
  - Possibly include a mission as does @jayshep, "My two missions: 1) Make the workplace easier for employers. 2) Make lawyers suck less. Wish me luck."
  - It's not a good idea to admit skepticism about Twitter in this space: "just seeing if this Twitter thing is all it's cracked up to be. . . ."
  - Do talk about yourself in the first person and active tense. Be positive and friendly.

It's best to avoid changing your Twitter picture too often because this is a visual reference so people will recognize tweets as being yours. It is comparable to brand recognition. Just as changing your logo frequently would cause confusion, so, too, would switching your photo often.

Design Tab

- Twitter has a variety of backgrounds from which you can choose to customize your Twitter page to start off with. Simple is best. You could also upload a favorite picture from your computer as the background image.
- Ultimately, you may wish to sport a professionally designed, firm-branded background image.

You may have in-house or outsourced resources who can do this for you (it requires Photoshop skills) or you can use a free or inexpensive service to create a company or personally themed background image. One is www.twitterbackgrounds.com. This is what @steveburtoncpa (www.twitter.com/steveburtoncpa) did.

Note that background images are not clickable at this time so don't list a large number of links, or very long links, on the background image itself. Keep it simple: one or two Web sites and a phone number.

Finding People to Follow

You will want to add individuals to your follow list as soon as possible in order to make Twitter interesting for yourself. You will quickly find that people post at different frequencies. When you first start out, you may find it annoying that a frequent poster will "fill" your wall with tweets. Once you follow 50–100 people, you will find that the seeming barrage of posts from heavier users becomes more diluted.

Be sure to connect to your state society and any relevant media, both national and local. Follow peers, media, experts in your industries, association representatives, people you respect, and people you enjoy learning from. As you read these people's tweets, you'll find them referencing other "Tweeps," and if you like what you see, follow them, too. This is how your follower count will organically grow. Through this method, my follower count increases by about 100 per month.

Never use a "How to get a zillion followers" service. These are not how legitimate professionals increase their follower base. Like many Twitter services, they require users to provide their Twitter name and password, and some of these services have been associated with Twitter account hacking. You will find people in your followers list who are on Twitter to spam others. These people can have upwards of 10,000 or 20,000 followers, but don't let this impress you. They are probably using a service to inflate their numbers. Follower count is, more often than not, unrelated to one's credibility.

To find specific people you know, you can search their names from the Find People page in the top navigation. There are good-sized communities of most professions on Twitter, and the list feature enables people to compile and group their favorites. To quickly find other lawyers, accountants, or financial advisors, check out some existing lists.

Lists of Legal and Financial Professionals

The following are user-compiled lists that might be good starting points for finding interesting people to follow on Twitter.

Law

> http://twitter.com/kevinokeefe/lexblog-network
> http://twitter.com/AmyParalegal7/legal
> http://twitter.com/JDSupra/lawyers-law-firms-legal
> http://twitter.com/stephaniethum/attorneys-legal-professi

Continued

Financial, Investment, or Wealth Advisors

http://twitter.com/AdvisorTweets/us-financial-advisors
http://twitter.com/JonChevreau/financial-planners

Accountants

https://twitter.com/michellegolden/cpas-cas-who-tweet
https://twitter.com/michellegolden/accounting-firms-corp
http://twitter.com/darlasycamore/accountants-to-follow

By clicking on a list name, see the most recent tweets and you can then click on "listed [#]" to review a listing of the people contained on each list in order to quickly follow them individually. Alternately, you can just follow a whole list, which means that a link to the list will then appear on your Twitter page sidebar for your convenient access in the future.

You can also benefit from seeking out and following back seemingly random people from your local area—they may have more influence than you think. Check some sites like TwitterGrader.com to find out "who has influence" in your geographic area.

When you follow people, many of them will follow you back. This is how your follower base is organically built.

Terminology and Nuances

There are a few weird Twitterisms that are part of the Twitter shorthand. I do see them oozing onto Facebook and LinkedIn, so don't be surprised if you encounter them outside of Twitter, too. Perhaps you already have.

RTs (aka Retweets)

RT, often the first two characters in a post, designates that what follows the RT is being "retweeted" or rebroadcast by another person. The RT is a very powerful tool if you use Twitter for business development. You want people to "RT you" because it spreads your ideas and your content if you've linked to your blogs or other content housed outside of Twitter.

RT Example

I tweeted, "Finishing up the Social Media Toolkit for the AICPA today!!"

A few minutes later, Francine McKenna (aka @retheauditors) tweeted, "Can't wait to see it! RT @michellegolden: Finishing up the Social Media Toolkit for the AICPA today!!"

I reached up to 1,836 followers with my message, and she then rebroadcast to her 4,306 followers. We have some overlap in followers, and not all our followers will catch this tweet, but her RT dramatically improves my reach.

Note how Francine preceded "RT" with her own comment. Some people will put their commentary before the RT, and some people put it after what they are RTing, usually in brackets, parentheses or following an arrow they create to refer to the preceding text (i.e., "← I agree with this"). Remember, characters count. I prefer the approach Francine used because it doesn't require use of precious space for brackets or the arrow.

A third approach is to tweet the original post, but put "via @NAME" at the very end. This is okay, too.

To make it very convenient for people to RT you, leave enough "space" in your tweet so that "RT @[YOURNAME]" will fit with your post intact. This way, other users won't have to condense your post to make space. It increases the ease, thus likelihood, of RTs.

Important note: Always give attribution to the original author of anything you post. It is illegal and very poor manners to tweet someone's work without credit to them. If you are retweeting something already retweeted, and space is at a premium to credit them all, just credit the original poster. It's a plus if you can also credit the person who directly shared it with you.

There's now another way to RT. The "RT" designation was created organically by users and was quickly adopted as the standard. But in late 2009, Twitter built a retweet feature into their tool. Using it has pros and cons, which is why you'll see that most users adopt both, but in different circumstances.

The disadvantages of the built-in retweet are that you cannot append the original tweet with your own commentary, approval, and so on—appending the tweet lets you add value and clarify context. Also, the tweet will not readily appear to others to have "come from you," per se, it will show in the timeline of someone who follows you, but with the original person's photo and a small indication that it was retweeted by you.

The advantages of the built-in retweet feature are that it's fast and easy. Because the tweet is shared "as is," if space is tight, you don't need to manually shorten it to keep it at 140 characters. It will be captured for you, listed in your sidebar Retweets link under "Retweets by You" tab. When others retweet you this way, Twitter stores those retweets under the "Your Tweets, Retweeted" tab along with the number of people who have retweeted you via this method.

A practice that should be used in moderation is begging for RTs. People often RT when asked (usually done by putting "Please RT" at the end of your post). However, don't ask people to RT you unless it is important, such as when you are helping someone find an answer to a question. Don't ask people to RT everything you post.

@replies

In Twitter, when you type the "@" character and follow it by someone's Twitter name (no spaces between) it does two things: (1) a link is automatically created to that person's Twitter page (aka "Timeline" or, informally, "wall") and (2) your tweet will appear in their @NAME list on their right sidebar. In other words, they will see that you "named" them. This is called an @reply.

Because everyone who follows you can see everything you write only if they look or happen to be on Twitter right when you are posting it, you need a way to flag them when you want to respond to, communicate with, or thank anyone in particular. You do this by referencing their @name in the tweet; otherwise, they probably won't ever see it to know you are addressing them.

#hashtag

Hashtags are used often in Twitter to isolate conversations and designate themed discussions. Among the Trending Topics (right sidebar) you will often find hashtagged words or acronyms. This is the way users share information about any given topic.

Hashtags are an essential Twitter tool and support the extremely rapid imparting of breaking news or information. An example of this was an event that changed my perspective on Twitter. I grew up in Orange, California, and the fires in 2008 were very close to my mom, but I couldn't seem to find detailed news anywhere on television or online other than a Google map showing very rough fire progress—that is, until I stumbled on Twitter. Local residents were using the hashtag #ocfires to share information about the fast-moving fires, including what streets were burning and photos for perspective, and *The Orange County Register* (ocregister.com) had streamed a feed (unfiltered) of all tweets containing the tag #ocfires to provide something the newspaper otherwise could not—the *only* real-time source of information. Fire districts, state agencies, and news reporters, local and national, simply could not organize and provide information and photos faster or more completely than real people, on the ground, all over Orange County. The same thing occurred much more recently with highly publicized events, including the #hudson airline landing, #iranelection, and #haiti earthquake. If you suspect there is something important going on in the world, check Twitter first.

Business application for hashtags is growing. If you attend a webinar or in-person conference, your hosts may provide, or attendees may organically create, a hashtag for the event. Hashtags can be searched various ways so anyone can follow along. Find them via Twitter's search at search.twitter.com or in Twitter's sidebar, or on various third-party Web sites that capture hashtagged conversations.

Third-Party Hashtag Sites

Hashtags.org tracks the frequency with which a hashtag is used and lists most recent posts containing a searched hashtag. Tweetchat.com also displays conversation threads.

Hashtags can also be registered with What The Hashtag? (http://wthashtag.com) which is "an encyclopedia of hashtags," and hashtagged conversations can be nicely archived for later reference. See http://wthashtag.com/Haiti as an example.

Anyone can make a hashtag. Simply search it to make sure it's not in current use and then just announce it to like-minded friends. You don't have to, but you might wish to register it with a site like What the Hashtag? (see sidebar) so others can more easily find and follow the conversation either during or after the tweet-chat or event.

Engaging with Twitter

Basically, on Twitter, anything goes. The purpose of a professional's presence on Twitter for business development includes:

- Learning from what others post—you'll begin to recognize who shares the "good stuff" that's worthwhile to read—use these folks as an information filter.

- Interacting with others at least to a moderate degree—you might be surprised at relationships that are forged.
- Sharing your thoughts and content—strive to be that information filter for others.
- Promoting others (building goodwill) by sharing their thoughts and content.

Even in the space of 140-character posts, you can actually achieve all that.

Posting

There aren't really any rules about what you can and cannot post. Each post you make should be a complete thought that stands alone. Whenever you post something off the top of your head, ask yourself, "Would this make sense to me if it had no other context?"

When you post links, use the space before the link to describe why you think it's worth sharing. Don't just write "Great article: [LINK]," which tells people absolutely nothing and no sense of why they would want to click on it. Give some context about the piece. Indicate whose article it is. If the author is on Twitter (use the Find People to search his or her name) refer to their @NAME.

The focus and subject of your tweets should not always be you, your firm, and your content. Some firms' tweets don't branch beyond:

"Congrats to Dave for passing the [CPA/bar] exam."
"Dave's article on estate planning has been posted to our Web site [link]."
"Come to our seminar on estate planning next week [link]."
"Do you need an estate plan? Call us."

Rather than talking about yourself, shift the focus of your content to sharing information that is actually helpful to people and go out of your way to name others outside of your organization. Try to maintain approximately a 10:1 ratio of promoting others or sharing external information to promoting yourself. Not only is it dull when every post links back to your own Web site or is all about you or your firm, it's actually a turnoff to readers because it is perceived as relentless self-promotion—very counter to social media culture.

Recall the shift from "broadcast" advertising to becoming a participant in a community. John McCain (or his people) in his campaign for president, made this mistake: they used Twitter as a one-way broadcast vehicle. Barack Obama (or his people), however, interacted with people and shared content and messages other than their own promotional message. The latter is the correct way to use Twitter. In addition to being more interesting when you feature others, you catch their attention and you create goodwill. You also show you or your firm are givers and do-gooders, not "all about you."

Some community-oriented post examples would be:

"Solid estate planning ideas for 40-somethings in this article by Bill Smith on Forbes [link]."

"@[referralsource] is hosting a seminar on 'Estate Planning Mistakes to Avoid' in Springfield [link]—see you there!"

"The psychology of family business succession is the topic on NPR right now—good stuff—listen online at [link]"

"Met w/ a new client who had no estate plan & spouse passed away last month. Big probs. Always heartbreaking when avoidable."

"Excellent read: RT @[twitteruser] "Don't let this happen to you—4 steps to tax savings for your heirs [link]"

In general, avoid inane "I'm at Starbucks" or "Stuck in traffic" posts. Though people joke that this is what Twitter is all about, that's not the case for business tweets. No one who would be reading the posts of a professional actually cares what you have for lunch unless it's in the context of something more personal, like, "Ate a huge salad for lunch because I'm starting a serious fitness regime." The latter imparts something about your character and priorities that is more meaningful than your lunch menu.

Posting your own material is a broadcast type of activity. Because Twitter is a relationship tool (hence the word *social* in social media), it really is expected that you will also engage and refer to other people with your postings. One way to do this is to post @replies. Another is to RT other people.

If you look at your post timeline and see no interaction in the form of correspondence with others on your page, you should make more effort to interact. Otherwise, people will notice that you don't interact and engage and they may perceive you as more of a taker than a giver.

There is an extreme, however. If you see that your whole timeline (aka profile) is filled with personal @replies (conversation not of general inter-est), this is probably a poor use of Twitter. If you begin a conversation with someone where you are replying back and forth more than once or twice, this is a *great* thing, but take it to DMs, email, or telephone.

Using the "reply" button/link (found to the right of a tweet when you hover over it with your mouse) is the easiest way to reply to someone. When you do this, their name is autopopulated in the tweet field and the post will have a subtle reference under it telling others that your tweet is "in reply to . . ." with a link to the original tweet. This makes it a lot easier to follow a conversation of your own or among other friends you follow. If you click the "reply" button beside a second or third person, their @ name will also fill in the tweet field so you can quickly respond to a few people at once if you'd like.

Note that if a tweet starts with an @ sign, only you, the person you named, your followers, and people who follow *both* of you will see it in their feeds. In other words, the other person's followers don't see your tweet in their stream unless they follow you also. This was a step Twitter took to help reduce clutter.

FODDER FOR TWEETS   The best source for tweets, from a marketing and credibility-building perspective, is content you find on the Web that the personas you've identified will care about. Naturally, some of this should be your own content that is housed elsewhere online (i.e., Web site or blogs) as long as you remember the recommended 10:1 ratio of you:me posts. If you promote others ten times more often than you post links to your own content, you will be in great shape. If you and your firm are not currently generating content, don't worry. There is plenty of additional tweet fodder.

Tweet the content of clients, referral sources, peers, related trade organizations, and even competitors. Read other tweets, online news and articles, print news and articles, or simply mention things that that you see, hear, and think as you go about your business interacting with clients, referral sources, and other organizations—always respecting confidentiality, of course. Once you start reading some tweets, it will probably not be difficult to find things to share. Even five minutes of reading per day can provide ample content, making you a worthwhile person to follow.

As humans, we are complex, so we might tweet about a large variety of things that interest us; it's still a good idea to have some focus in your tweets. If you specialize, share the bulk of your content related to your specialty. If you are using Twitter through a corporate presence, seriously consider having separate accounts for your firm's different specialty areas so that you can maintain this sort of focus to stay relevant to smaller groups of readers—smaller and focused is always better than larger and general.

THANKING PEOPLE   Social media are all about courtesy and sharing. When others do something cool for you, you should thank them. There are many great reasons to reach out and interact with people, either with a public tweet or a DM:

- Following you
- Adding you to a list

- RTing you
- Mentioning you or your work
- Tagging you in a #FF or #FollowFriday (a Friday tradition of listing good people to follow)
- Telling you of a problem they have with you or your firm (rare)
- Hosting Tweetups, Twitter Chats, and other events
- Telling an author that you enjoyed an article, blog post, or book
- When someone teaches you something
- When someone goes out of their way to help you

Direct Messages

When you follow people, you may receive a nice, personal thank you DM from them. This is a very good practice, and it is rare to get a truly personal response.

Likewise, when someone follows you, it's nice to thank him or her. If you do this, make it personal by using their name and maybe reference something else you noticed about them, their profile or a recent tweet. You don't have to DM every new follower. If you just thank some, thank the ones that look like they are related to your profession and might be especially good to know.

Note, you can send DMs only to people who follow you (this prevents Twitter users from getting DM spam from just anyone). So if someone mentions you in a tweet, and they don't already follow you, the only way to thank them is to do so publicly with an @reply.

Whenever people RT you, follow you, or otherwise mention you (with an @reply or other @mention), it is proper (and good manners) to thank them. You can do this with an @reply (which all will see), or it is always acceptable to send such thanks in a DM. If you have many people to thank, it's better to DM them than to fill your followers' streams with a long list of thank-you messages that won't add value to them.

It's advisable to avoid clicking links sent to you in DMs. There are some nasty Trojans and phishing scams that circulate via Twitter, sometimes even coming from trusted friends whose accounts are hijacked.

AUTO DMS   When you follow people, you will also receive some "auto DMs." There are third-party software applications that help people "manage" their Twitter activity. Many of these offer automatic follow-back and thank-you DM features that can instantly send a canned message to everyone who follows them. At best, this is an annoying practice. Auto DMs are often cheesy and include a link to view something—legitimate or not. Frequently, these canned messages are completely out of context. This does not serve to build goodwill, so refrain from using such a service if you want to establish yourself as a caring professional.

An example of an out-of-context auto DM is when I followed back someone who followed me. She wrote: "Thanks for following! How'd you find me? And what would you like to learn/read/see more from me?" She found me—that's how I found her. Also, I don't know enough about her to know what I want to learn from her. This is *not* effective social media engagement.

How to (and How Not To) Thank People for Following You on Twitter

Cheesy

Thanks and I'm looking forward to your tweets. Check out this site for a FREE [x] [link].

Thank you for following me. If you'd like to immediately know more about me, visit [link].

Nonmemorable

Thanks for the follow! If you need any help with [x] please DM me. I look forward to your tweets.

Thanks much for the follow. Drop me a line anytime. Cheers, [you].

Better

Thanks for the follow, [name]! Happy to add you to my circle of friends. I'm a [mom of five, writer and actress], and I tweet to maintain sanity.

Glad to have you among my friends, [name]. Happy to follow you back—looks like you share good stuff. Have a terrific day, [you].

Excellent

Thanks for the follow! Other users you might like: @[name], @[name], @[name].

Thanks for the follow, [name]! The thing on [something they wrote] was a really good article. I think you have a lot of great content, so I've listed you.

While auto DMers do get some click-throughs (or they wouldn't keep doing it), the sincere, personal thank-you message can help you to be remembered in a positive way. The obvious auto DM won't.

Joining Gatherings (aka Tweetups)

There are opportunities to join "gatherings" of other Twitter users both online—called Twitter Chats—or in person, which are known as Tweetups. Since a core purpose behind using Twitter is to meet and develop rapport with a broader group of people, participating in both of these types of events is beneficial.

You're likely to stumble upon these gatherings as you participate in Twitter. The more people you associate with in your areas of interest, the more likely you are to come across events that would be meaningful for you. There are also great tools for seeking out and finding nearby Tweetups and Twitter Chats: two are TweetMeUp.net and Tweetvite.com.

When you attend a Twitter Chat, you'll be exposed to new people who share a common interest in the topic at hand. If you are an active participant in the conversation, you're likely to pick up some new followers. And be sure to follow participants who have interesting perspectives and who add value to the conversation. They'll follow you back and expand your network. This is exactly the purpose of Twitter: broaden your contacts, extend your reach, soak up the learning, and share as you go.

As a courtesy, if you are participating in a Twitter Chat, your tweet volume will probably be heavier than normal. While this probably won't bother your followers who follow lots of other people, it can flood followers with small networks. Therefore, it's courteous to send a tweet informing your followers that you are joining a chat, or live-tweeting a conference, alerting them to possible heavy tweet volume (e.g., "Am attending the #WIE10 conference. Warning: I might be tweeting more than normal").

If you plan to attend an in-person event, ask if there is already a designated hashtag for it, then search to see if anyone is talking about a related Tweetup. If not, initiate one. With more than 20 million people using Twitter, hardly an organized event is held without at least a small Tweetup.

Once you know the event hashtag, tweet that you are attending the event in order to help spread the word, and try to tweet some of your key take-aways (or things with which you disagree) related to the meeting. When you meet other tweeps, tweet about them, too. It's a way to thank them for going out of their way to meet with you (e.g., "Great time hanging out with the brilliant @diannahuff at the #IGAF conference. She's even more delightful in person!").

Managing Followers

People will follow you; some will be legitimate and others will not. Among the "not" will be bots and spammers—with both business and adult content. You needn't follow back everyone who follows you, but unless they look shady or they post junk, it doesn't hurt to follow them. At least once per week, open your followers link to review the list and follow back anyone who's followed you if they seem legit.

Sometimes people (or bots) will follow you just to get you to follow them back. When you look at their timeline, it doesn't seem to contain spam but once you follow them, they can spam you with DMs. This is an unseemly practice. If this happens, feel free to unfollow them. And if they are pushing products or if you feel they are truly abusing Twitter (such as by submitting multiple DMs to you), you may go so far as to "block" them. Twitter keeps an eye out for people who get lots of blocks. Don't do this unless they are truly offensive.

TIPS FOR SPOTTING SPAMMERS   To quickly evaluate whether a follower is legitimate, consider their user's photo, user name, and most recent post. If you still cannot tell, right click their user name to see their profile page. This is where you can see how active they are, how long they've been on Twitter, what their description and background image convey, and what sort of content they post. If you'd like some help identifying potentially spammy followers, see Table 9.1.

UNFOLLOWING PEOPLE   If you follow someone you later regret following, you can unfollow him or her at any time. Reasons might be that they post too much, post off topic, or just get on your nerves. They will notice their follower count drop but won't usually be notified about who it was that unfollowed them unless they use a third-party application to monitor this.

PEOPLE UNFOLLOWING YOU   People will also unfollow you from time to time. Don't take it personally. Your follower count will rise and fall. Sometimes spammers get booted from Twitter, so when Twitter does a bulk cleanup, your numbers can drop by a dozen or more at a time. If your count suddenly drops by hundreds, there could be a problem and you would want to contact Twitter about that. Consider whether you posted something offensive. Odds are you did not and that changes in your numbers just reflect some housecleaning.

Managing Inbound Information Flow

Once you follow more than 50–100 people, you are likely to have a heavy enough stream of inbound tweets in your timeline (your main Twitter "home"

TABLE 9.1 Is My Follower Legit?

What to Evaluate	Possibly Good to Follow	Possibly Spammer
Photo (preview)	There should be a photo. Does it look authentic? Like someone you'd want to associate with? A logo?	Inappropriate? Looks like a stock photo? No photo? A logo?
Username (preview)	A legitimate-sounding name? Credentials or organization included?	Does it feature a product name? The words *marketingseo, guru,* or *free?*
Most recent post (preview)	Does it seem related to your field of interest? Does it contain an @reply that seems thoughtful?	Refers to "making money" or "getting followers""free" or "affiliate" offers? Offensive? Poor grammar or low maturity?
Most recent posts (profile page)	Demonstrates conversational, interactive person? Interesting content? Do they mention @names you recognize? Fewer tweets are okay if they look good or credible otherwise (good people have to start somewhere).	Repetitive posts (same links)? Any product pushing (weight loss, teeth whitening, etc.)? Way off topic? Offensive? Too few posts (fewer than 50 unless otherwise credible)? No interaction with others (just broadcasts)?
Bio (profile page)	Appropriate or interesting?	None? Includes the red-flag words mentioned above?
Web (profile page)	Appropriate or interesting?	None?
Followers/ Following ratio and # tweets (profile page)	Balanced ratio?	Following tons but few followers? Tons of followers but few tweets? Tons of followers but poor content?
Listed	Are they listed by anyone? Whom? Okay if none and they look new.	Do they have a lot of followers but few people, if any, "list" them?
Background image (profile page)	Appropriate or interesting?	Cheesy? Get rich quick or too slick? Inappropriate?

page) that you'll no longer be able to keep up with all of it. Don't bother trying. And don't feel pressured to "catch up" with tweets you've missed.

A good way to make sure you don't miss tweets of favored people is to create one or more lists of those specific people. You can make lists that are private, perhaps one called "friends" and another called "referral sources" (definitely don't make a public list with the latter title), and you can provide a helpful service for others by creating public lists that both you and they will value as filters for certain types of content. For instance, people who tweet often on particular subjects might fit into lists for "Estate Planning," "Construction," or "Employment." People can be added to multiple lists—they need not be mutually exclusive.

What you are likely to find is that a quick five- to ten–minute check of Twitter each day can provide you with a few worthwhile articles you would have otherwise missed. No time to read the article right away? No worries. Simply "favorite" it and the tweet will easily be found in your favorites list. To favorite a tweet, hover over it with your mouse and click on the little "star" to the right of the tweet. Unclick to remove it from your favorites. Others can see your favorites, and you can see theirs.

Third-party software applications help users manage their Twitter streams. These were a necessity before, but have become less essential since Twitter introduced their "lists" feature in 2009. A lot of people continue to use third-party Web-based applications, and Tweetdeck is considered a leader in this space. Twirl is another. To keep an eye on what other people seem to be finding most useful, look at the bottom of a tweet, where you will see an indicator as to how it was posted. "Web" means it was posted directly on the Twitter Web site, and the rest are other apps people use on their desktops or smartphones. You can also view the previously mentioned http://oneforty.com link for the most current and highest rated apps that improve the Twitter experience.

I no longer use a third-party desktop application for Twitter, preferring to work directly in the Twitter interface, and my (iPhone) mobile preference is Tweetie, recently bought by Twitter and renamed Twitter for iPhone, but choosing what's right for you is highly personal, so if you become a frequent user of Twitter, exploring these applications may help you discover an interface that you'd greatly enjoy using—one that enriches your Twitter experience.

Summary of Twitter Tips

Twitter is simple but flexible. Here is a brief recap of best practices and etiquette for Twitter users. Also find some practices to help prevent being hacked or phished.

Best Practices

- Good ways to use Twitter: linking to articles, RT others, respond to questions, offer tips, link to reference tools or checklists, share pithy observations, and recommend books, movies, or restaurants.
- Don't send automated response messages (aka auto DMs). It's obvious when a message is automated, so you appear impersonal—the opposite of what social media are about, and these messages are considered annoying, spamlike, or just plain tacky.
- Tweeting as an individual is best. But if you're dead set on a corporate Twitter account, at least consider having a separate Twitter account for each of your most active practice areas so you can tweet by "topic" areas to better appeal to your target audiences.
- Tweet about others far more often than you tweet about yourself. A 10:1 ratio is a good rule of thumb. When you do post about yourself, or link to your own content, be transparent that you're doing so—don't mislead people to click to read your stuff without their realizing it.
- Don't use automatic posting services like Twitterfeed to post your blog content to Twitter, partly for the reason above, but also because it's better to do it personally so you can frame the post with some context that will encourage readership.
- Having multiple Twitter accounts is a "spammy" behavior, especially if you post the same information on two or more of the accounts. If you have multiple accounts, they should be for separate audiences or purposes; therefore, they should feature unique content with very few, if any, cross-posts.
- If you also have a blog, periodically assemble your best tweets into a blog post (courtesy of Jordan Furlong).

Twittequette

- Look for and always thank people who retweet you, Follow Friday (FF) mention you, or add you to a list because they are promoting you. A private thank you by DM is nicer than a group "thank you" posted publicly, and it has a greater chance of starting a dialogue.
- Add good prospects and referral sources to lists that are flatteringly named such as "smart people" or "good to follow" and they will definitely notice you. (Tip within a tip: don't ever name the lists "prospects" or "referral sources"!)
- If you are going to tweet a heavy volume, such as live-tweeting a conference or participating in a tweet-chat, it's considerate to forewarn with an explanatory tweet.
- Watch your tweet frequency. If you tweet more than 10 times a day or more than five times an hour (unless you're at a conference, then

forewarn), you may be flooding your readers. Another side effect of this is that you might appear to have too much time on your hands, raising the question as to why you're not busier in your professional practice.

- When people DM you or @ you, they are engaging you in conversation and you need to respond.

Be Savvy to Prevent Hacking or Phishing

- Don't click on links in DMs unless it is *extremely* obvious it is a personal and legitimate message from someone you know. Personal context of the message is a good clue. And it's always okay to check with the sender first, to make sure they intentionally sent you the link.
- Don't be someone who sends links in DMs, especially not in auto-replies to new followers because savvy users know that people shouldn't click on links from *any* automated messages. In fact, don't send auto DMs because they are usually annoying.
- Never enter your Twitter login credentials when asked for them through DM.
- Be extremely wary and selective about giving your Twitter login credentials to any third-party application. Verify their authenticity and reputation first. Even if they look popular, they could be malicious.

Twitter is the Wild West of social media, but there's actually a pretty large number of professionals using Twitter and finding value in it. Read about some of them in the case studies in Chapter 7.

The Best Current Twitter Tools

New tools and resources for Twitter users are emerging every single day. To seek out the newest and highest rated (by users), visit www.oneforty.com.

CHAPTER 10

Facebook

Facebook is fairly easy to use, though it's more complex than Twitter and LinkedIn, especially if you intend to use the rich privacy settings to manage the nearly inevitable "intermixing" of your business and personal worlds.

Your setup time will be less than one hour for a personal user account, which includes creating your account, populating basic information, and inviting some friends to connect. Expect to spend a couple of hours or less to set up and populate a company page—this would not include fancy programming or including third-party applications in your company page.

For ongoing use, in order to be effective, estimate a time investment of 10–30 minutes per day. It's okay to skip days, or even a week, but not several weeks if you wish to maximize Facebook in your business development. Once you have more than a couple dozen friends, it's pretty easy to get sucked into spending much more time than this. You'll have to decide your how much time you're willing to invest, and find your comfort-level regarding mix of personal and business. From my own personal experiences, I recommend keeping a very open mind—you might find pleasant surprises in your results if you let them mingle.

When I started using Facebook, it was to keep in touch with close, personal friends and family. For a long time, I resisted adding business contacts unless we were already very close personally. But the lines blurred more and more (like figuring out where to cut off wedding invitations) and I caved. Now my close friends and family comprise less than one quarter of my Facebook contacts. Building more personal relationships by participating in the lives of previously distant contacts has been, by far, the most fun and financially fruitful of any of my online activities, in just one year's time. Speaking as an early blogger and active participant in other social media, this is a strong statement.

Clearly, my mind-set shifted and my time expenditure increased, but with 75 percent of my interactions business related, it's a very enjoyable place to spend some of my "marketing" time while also keeping tabs on friends and family. Not everyone that combines business and personal on Facebook does so to the degree that I do. I take advantage of the privacy settings related to my children as well as selectively share some photos, links, and music, but as far as wall conversation, I allow the blending of friends, family, and business colleagues. There is no one "right way" to do this—you have to be comfortable with what you share. But I will say that I believe this "letting down of the hair" (aka authenticity and openness) is at least partly responsible for the business development success I've found with Facebook.

For your decision purposes as you get started, aside from time management, the biggest considerations are going to be distinguishing who sees what, related to your personal account, and assuring that you or someone else keeps your company page (if you have one) fresh, acting as an effective community manager.

Deciding on an Approach

Will you use your individual account for development of business relationships? Will you or your firm maintain a company page on Facebook? Will you do both? A personal Facebook account, if intermingled with business, could serve to achieve one or both:

- Deepening relationships with business-related contacts
- Sharing content that demonstrates expertise and credibility subtly promotes the firm's image

A company page might serve either or both of these purposes:

- Engage and cultivate relationships with prospective employees, clients, and referral sources by inspiring them to "Like" (formerly "Become a Fan" of) your page and to participate.
- Update and engage employees, family, and friends of the firm, who can follow what's going on, view photos from firm events, and participate in dialogue, polls, and activities you create for them.

If you create a company page, refrain from creating a mini-version of your firm's Web site. Seek to put at least some content on your Facebook page that is unique from your content elsewhere, though it certainly can and should point to it. Which type of content you choose to offer is, of course, dependent upon your purpose—who is your audience.

As a result of their experience interacting with it, people who are exposed to your company page should have a better sense of the firm's capabilities, awareness of the firm's corporate responsibility, and impression that the firm's team members interact well and enjoy working together.

A 2009 survey conducted by the Kbuzz provides great examples of company pages with features that engage or impress.[1] View "Facebook Top 40 Pages" at www.thekbuzz.com/casestudies/top40.aspx.

If you'd like to see some good recruiting examples, law firm Curtis, Mallet-Prevost, Colt & Mosle LLP has a careers page (facebook.com/Curtis. Careers) on Facebook that uses an application known as "Static FBML" (FBML stands for Facebook Markup Language) for tabs containing summer program details, law school interview dates, and awards and rankings. An even more impressive site is that of Ernst & Young Careers (www.facebook.com/ernstandyoungcareers). There is more about custom content later in this chapter.

I'm unable to find a reference listing of accounting firms with Facebook pages, but a fairly broad list of law firm Facebook pages is on JD Supra, here: http://scoop.jdsupra.com/2009/07/articles/law-firm-marketing/lawyers-and-law-firms-on-facebook/.[2] Interestingly, few of the firms added in the comments section have customized their URL. Instructions for how to do that appear later in this chapter.

Individual Account

Here's the dilemma. People often begin with the intention of using Facebook strictly for friends or strictly for business, but it's probable that you'll end up mixing the two at some point—especially since it is a violation of Facebook's terms of service to create two accounts.

It is quite possible to invite business contacts into your personal Facebook and limit, to varying degrees, most of your Facebook content. The one part that gets tricky (subject to change anytime, given how often Facebook alters its site functionality) is visibility of your "wall," which is where you and friends post content that includes various personal messages, a running list of status updates, notifications related to activities, and photos. Photos and activity-related messages are easy to control without continuous effort. But wall posts, in totality, are not. At present, your wall—and the ability to post on it—is either completely suppressed from a person's view which can be considered antisocial, or it is entirely visible with the option of your limiting, post-by-post, what shows for whom—cumbersome, at best.

However, if you can get past the business/personal separation challenges (this bothers some people more than others), you will find that, as I described in my own situation, business relationships can deepen far more rapidly through Facebook than otherwise. This happens when both parties participate with some regularity on Facebook, and not all Facebook users do.

Company Page

A company page can be established for any organization. Per Facebook, only the official representative of a business may create a page. The page creator can designate others to help manage the page. It is best that the page is initiated by an owner or "lifer" with the firm, not by an employee who could depart, leaving the page awkwardly tied to his or her account—avoid having to deal with disassociating the company account from a user who is no longer with the firm. The official company representative can establish the account from his/her individual Facebook account, if one exists, or can establish what is called a business account to create a company Facebook Page.

Note: I don't recommend the business account approach because it provides very limited access to Facebook.

The business account holder cannot view anyone's individual Facebook profile page. His or her access is limited to administering the company page and managing any Facebook ad campaigns. Moreover, a business account user cannot add any additional applications, and these are necessary for piping in blog or Twitter feeds to the company page. Also beneficial might be installing a useful app called Static FBML, which is necessary to create customized elements on your company page, like many of the examples you may have explored in the Top 40 link in Deciding on an Approach, above.

If the "lifer" already has a Facebook account, he or she should initiate the company page, then designate one or more employees as administrators of the account. The employee needs to "Like" (formerly "Fan") the page before the creator can assign admin privileges. Each page admin will then be able to update and edit the pages from their own accounts. The administrators have unlimited permissions with the exception of removing the account creator. The creator, however, can remove administrators and designate new ones, as desired.

If the "lifer" doesn't already have a Facebook account, my recommendation, even if they don't want to actively use Facebook, is to create a regular user account for him or her. In this scenario, it's advisable to establish the account using an alternate (not commonly known) email address, so people won't easily find the user when they upload their contact list as prompted by Facebook and which could lead to friend requests the person would rather not have to field. Setting up a new Gmail account, for instance, is ideal for this.

> ## TIP: Managing Your Mail
>
> It can be helpful to route all your social media accounts through a single, separate email account in order to avoid constant email interruptions at work and to better manage your time.

Another question that may arise is whether the firm should create a company "page" or a Facebook "group." Generally, a "group" is less formal, and groups are typically formed around a common interest or a particular topic. A "page" is Facebook's recommended approach for an officially branded business presence on the site.

As an aside, it is not appropriate to require employees to participate in your firm's presence on Facebook. People use Facebook in all sorts of different ways, and it's considered the most personal of social media tools. Individual privacy and preferences should be respected. Some firms have been known to direct employees to create a second account if they oppose using their existing account for business purposes, but this is distinctly against Facebook's terms of service, so don't encourage it.

The Tool

Facebook changes continuously, more often than the others tools featured in this book, so the location of the features (within the navigation scheme) is absolutely going to change—probably even before this prints—but the feature descriptions should more or less remain the same.

Main Navigation

- **Home:** Contains your news feeds (information posted by all your friends, groups you've joined, or companies you've liked). Also on this page as well as your profile is your "publisher" box at the top, where you can change your status or post a variety of media or links. This page also houses access to content viewing and editing filters:
  - **Messages:** Where you receive and send private messages
  - **Events:** Upcoming events, past ones, and friends' event activities, plus birthdays of all your friends by month (very helpful reference)
  - **Photos:** Displays photos and videos recently added by your Friends
  - **Friends:** View news (aka recent postings of friends) filtered by any lists you've created

- **Applications/Games:** Lists Facebook standard and third-party applications you use
- **Ads and pages:** View ad campaigns you're running and any Facebook pages you are authorized to administer.
- **Groups:** A quick reference of group activities and updates for groups to which you belong
- **Videos:** Displays videos added by friends and is a hub from which to upload or record your own.
- **Notes:** Lists notes posted by friends
- **Profile:** View your own Facebook pages (see Your Profile Navigation, below).
- **Account:** Contains links to Facebook's robust help information as well as editing your friends, user settings, privacy controls, and third-party application access.
- **Chat:** Facebook's built-in instant messaging tool is found at the bottom of the Facebook screen.

Profile Navigation

Each person's profile has a series of tabs that may or may not display for others, in full or in part, depending on individual privacy settings. Aside from the basic tabs described below, additional "custom" tabs can be added (optionally) when offered by third-party applications installed by an individual.

Basic Tabs

- **Wall:** Houses your posts and activities, the posts of your friends (if permitted) and contains the "publisher" box, which is where you enter status updates, share links, photos and more
- **Info:** Displays basic, personal, contact, education, work, groups, and other information that you add
- **Photos:** Your albums and pictures tagged to you
- **Links:** Your posted links, in reverse chronological order, useful to share links to content and events you are interested in promoting
- **Notes:** Appear in reverse chronological order, a great place to share articles or short pieces you write, even duplicating blog posts (I'm not a big fan of this, but it's done often)
- **Videos:** Your posted videos, in reverse chronological order
- **Events:** That you initiated or have RSVPd as attending, listed in reverse chronological order

Starting an Individual Account

The first thing you'll want to do when you set up your account is make sure your privacy settings are buttoned up. Stay on top of Facebook's frequent changes related to your privacy settings and remember that nothing on the Internet can ever be guaranteed private. Operate with this in mind, always.

As you approach privacy, keep in mind the purpose of social media is to let people "in" enough to learn who you really are (and you, them) in order to forge deeper relationships. If you lock "everything" down, this probably won't happen—we have to give to get. A lot of Facebook users are strictly business; they use Facebook as a way to push business content, not really to nurture relationships. That's not "wrong," but it is suboptimal because they miss the opportunity to get closer to people.

The best Facebook successes I know of are situations in which surprising bonds form as people get to know each other a lot better than they otherwise could have, especially as all of our time is limited. Facebook is an excellent relationship accelerant—and a highly time leverageable one in that you can converse with several people at once.

Because of the type of interaction that takes place on Facebook—a smaller, tighter circle than Twitter, and a more relaxed environment than LinkedIn—the opportunity to forge friendships with referral sources, clients, and prospects is notably greater with this tool than the others. When you let people into your life, even a little bit, they can glean insights about your good character, values, and sense of humor that they'd never otherwise know. And you can gain greater appreciation and respect for them, as well. This is how strong, long-lasting relationships form.

Before getting into "what" to share, I'll outline how friend lists work. Friend lists are the key to privacy controls—and they are also a way to prioritize content and to control your outbound volume, sharing certain posts only with people who will care about that specific content. It's a good idea, at a minimum, to set up a few lists into which you can categorize friends. Friends can be assigned to more than one list.

Creating Friend Lists

Select "Friends" in the top navigation, and from the left sidebar click on "All Connections" (or just about any other option) and you'll see, at the top of the center column, a "Create New List" button. Once you create your lists, to the right of each connection, a drop-down menu is available for you to select one or more of your list(s) to which you can assign the connection.

FIGURE 10.1 Create New List

What lists should you consider? I suggest having at least three or four categories with varying levels of privacy. Your lists might look something like this:

Access Level	Possible List Name (describes list members)
Least Private	Close Friends & Family
Less Private	Casual Personal Acquaintances
Somewhat Private	Business Colleagues
Most Private	Remote (hardly know)

Or you may not feel that all close family members, for instance, merit the same level of privacy, so you may not want to name your lists like this. Instead, you might prefer to name them something that equates more to the level of access list members will have (note: you then have to set the privacy levels for various Facebook features and photo albums, allowing or denying lists as you see fit. The default for all privacy settings is for everyone to see everything: not recommended.

Access Level	Possible List Names (describes content access levels)
Least Private	Everything
Less Private	Limited
Somewhat Private	More Limited
Most Private	Bare Minimum

Of course, you can name your lists anything you wish, and you may have as many as you like. And again, depending on how you'll use

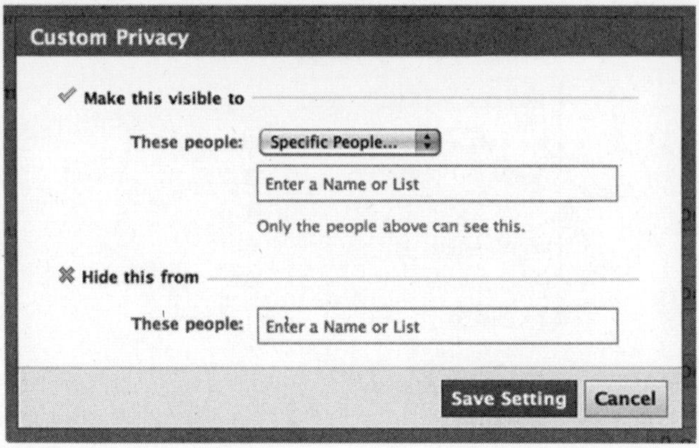

FIGURE 10.2 Custom Privacy Settings

Facebook, regardless of privacy needs, you may want lists to group people from different parts of your life or business world.

To choose a list instead of a person's name when you are editing your custom privacy settings (lists will not appear initially in the alphabetical drop-down choices in the fields shown in Figure 10.2), you merely start typing the list name and autocomplete prompts will appear containing the list name. To permit access to "Only Specific People" enter the list name in the Allow field, or enter the list name in the Hide From field to restrict access. You can assign your friends to as many lists as you like.

You can use these lists two ways: to restrict content from a group or to limit content to the group. Say you post something about a local event; if you have a list containing only people who live near you, you could post the link only to them. Or photos from a conference can be shared with attendees only. This is capitalizing on the relevance aspect of social media—courtesy to others is key. List types you might consider:

- People who attended a specific school with you
- Hometown people
- Current town people
- Members of an organization you belong to
- Coworkers
- Clients or customers
- Referral sources
- "The guys" or "the girls"
- Just attorney pals (or bankers or accountants or marketers, etc.)

FIGURE 10.3 Chat Settings with Lists

- Fellow parishioners
- Your kids and their friends

Other benefits of managing your contacts through lists are that you can filter the news feed to show just one group at a time—so if you want to see the postings of just family, you can. Then switch to view just coworkers, and so on.

It can also help to have a list you call "Chat" if you want to limit who can send you instant messages through Facebook's chat or instant messaging feature (Figure 10.3). After you set up friend lists, you can chose to suppress your "online visibility" by sliding the little indicator to the right of the list name, hiding all but a preferred "okay to chat with" list. If controlling your time and interruptions is a major consideration for you, this can be very helpful.

For more information on friend lists or chat settings, refer to "Settings" through your Facebook's top navigation.

Privacy Settings

For almost all areas of the site, Facebook offers a few standard privacy level choices and then gives you an opportunity to customize as discussed previously. In general, you'll probably want to set everything to be visible to "Only Friends" versus "Everyone." You may, for some things, choose "Friends of Friends" or "Everyone" if you think there will be pass-along value. This depends entirely on how you choose to use Facebook. If these settings still leave you too open, you are able to customize privacy settings for various features, such as each Photo Album, individually. Further, for every individual wall post or note you create, you can choose exactly who will or won't be able for view it, either by authorizing or restricting various friend lists, or choosing individual friends' names.

If you don't intend to house any personal content on Facebook, your privacy settings won't matter much, if at all. If you expect to mix business and personal, give some thought to how you might segregate the two.

For example, you may decide to dedicate the notes feature to the sharing of business-related content. In this case, go ahead and make notes visible to all because you would then want people to be able to see and share your content with others. You will always have the option of creating a particular note with locked-down privacy if you want to share it only with certain people or lists.

Unless your Facebook is 100 percent business, you are wise to adopt these few basic privacy settings to limit the chances of your data being seen and stored by individuals and businesses.

- In the category called "Privacy Settings > Search," there are currently two items:
  - Facebook Search Results: "Only friends" is best.
  - Public Search Results: Turn this off; make sure the "Allow" box is unchecked.
- In the category called "Privacy Settings > Applications and Websites" are settings for:
  - "What your friends can share about you." It is a good idea to edit these settings by deselecting all your personal information.
  - And within "Instant Personalization Pilot Program" make sure that "Allow select partners . . ." is deselected.

WALL SETTINGS When it comes to your wall settings, this is a little touchy. There is a particular setting: "Allow Friends to post on my Wall," which you can only turn on or turn off, across the board.

I strongly recommend keeping this feature on. It is somewhat unpleasant when someone friends you or accepts your friend request, and you visit their wall to say "Hello, thanks, nice to connect" and find you aren't allowed to post to their wall. This makes it obvious you are "in" but not all the way "in." It's really not a good feeling. Think how you would feel if others did this to you.

Allow the wall access, but if you're worried about what a person might see (such as controversial posts by friends) you can restrict them from seeing all "Posts by Friends" defined as "control who can see posts by your friends on your profile." To do this, either single the friend out in your Privacy settings or put them into a group that is restricted from seeing posts by friends.

Personally, I'm still hoping Facebook will modify this to: "control which friends' posts can be viewed on your profile." A setting that hides all posts by certain friends would probably be popular in helping to curb those who don't always seem to know when to curb themselves.

When you make individual posts to your wall, you'll use the publisher box. Whether it is a link, a photo or just a status update, if you're posting something you don't want everyone to see, you can select the little "lock" icon and change the privacy settings specific to that one item. Say you want to express a political view your friends will understand but don't want to alienate business contacts or family members. This is a great time to make use of the "Show to Friends Except:" "Remote," "Business," and "Family" lists.

YOUR PHOTOS AND VIDEOS Privacy settings for photo albums are excellent in Facebook. Create separate albums for sharing with different audiences.

Remember that while you do want to let people in, you can also control how "in" they get. For instance, it's a nice idea to have at least one "family" album where you feature some photos of your immediate family so that business contacts can see you as a parent, son/daughter, brother/sister, whatever. These should be photos you'd be comfortable having in your office, or in your wallet, readily shared with acquaintances.

It's up to you, but you may prefer to keep the vacation albums, high school reunion parties, and little Sammy smashing his first birthday cake up his nose separate for family and very close friends. Finally, when it comes to privacy, if you have children, I cannot stress enough how critical it is to refrain from divulging too much information about them, including their full names, where they attend school, and various other facts. Too many people have their privacy settings wide-open, exposing information about their children.

PHOTOS AND VIDEOS TAGGED OF YOU If you are mixing business and pleasure, it's a good idea to limit who can see photos or videos in which other people happen to tag you. This is a precautionary approach to content management. What Aunt Mary or crazy pal Bob thinks is a hysterical photo of you may not be something you want your business contacts to see. If you want people to see these photos, you can save them and load them into your own albums with your desired privacy settings.

TESTING PRIVACY SETTINGS After you've created your friend lists and established your privacy settings tailored to the levels acceptable to you for each friend list, you can and should test your settings; something you can easily do thanks to a Preview option in Facebook. To do this, from any privacy setting subscreen, choose the "Preview My Profile" button at the top right of the screen. You'll be able to enter various people's names to see your profile exactly as they see it. Test someone from each privacy level you have set to verify that settings are the way you want them.

Once your friend lists are established, when you invite a new friend or accept a friend request, you have the opportunity to immediately categorize that friend. It's a good idea to do so because when you send a friend request, while that request is pending, the person may have access to your profile.

Using an Individual Account

Once your privacy settings are complete, and you've got at least a skeleton profile established (the basics are fine) and a profile photo loaded, it's time to add some friends. Facebook will prompt you early and often to do this, and will suggest people you may know. Your profile being complete or detailed isn't nearly as important in Facebook as the interaction. Facebook differs from LinkedIn in this way.

Interacting

There are lots of reasons and ways to connect with your friends. Periodically, view your news feed and make a comment or "Like" (by clicking the thumbs up) people's items to show you are paying attention to them even if words don't come to you. Congratulate people's accomplishments and occasionally post a "hey, how are you doing?" message on friends' walls— or something more suited to the friend's personal interests. All of these "touches" equate to traditional ways of reaching out such as face-to-face time, a phoned "hello," or "thought you'd be interested in this" notes. It's a modern, more expeditious way to do some of this, and with more people, in the same amount of time.

TIP: Searching for Friends

To quickly go to the profile of one of your friends, simply start typing their name in the Search box at the top right of your Facebook pages.

Also, Facebook conveniently tracks all of your friends' birthdays for you. The list is found on the bottom bar within "Events" (icon that resembles a calendar) on a tab called Birthdays. Also, from your home page, you'll see a short list of upcoming birthdays on your right sidebar. Reaching out to people on or right before their birthday is a wonderful thing to do. If you think Facebook is shallow, wait until you have your first birthday with a flurry of great wishes—almost like being a kid again.

Status updates are the primary means of communication and help you stay current on people's lives. Status posts are just plain text entries in the publisher box atop your profile or home view. If you add a link in the box, what you've entered as text won't show up as your status, it will precede a "Link" addition.

People use the status updates differently, and some people don't use it at all, which is a mistake if you are using Facebook for business development. In general, be aware of the overall impression you create with frequent insights into your demeanor. Everyone has the occasional rough day, but if you tend to the negative (glass-half-empty view), watch out. See Chapter 14 for more on spotting and curbing excessive negativity.

If people perceive you as an Eeyore, it reduces their desire to be around you and their enjoyment in working with you. You don't have to be saccharine sweet either, but rather than posting mood-reflecting status updates, go with posts that are less personal.

Different approaches to status updates:

- Song lyric or line from a movie
- Something funny that a kid said
- Sage advice from grandpa or grandma
- Something you feel good about working on or completing (without naming client)

Making a conscious effort to frame things more positively can work wonders.

Friend Suggestions

As you add friends, or they add you, Facebook will prompt them to suggest friends for you as well. Beware because it is very easy to misread a friend "*suggestion*" (made either by Facebook or by a friend) as a friend "*request*." This can be a little embarrassing because with a too-quick click, thinking you are accepting someone else's request (perhaps skeptically)—pouf, you've suddenly initiated a friend request to a person you didn't intend to. It's happened to most of us. Pay close attention because the notifications for both are in the same general area and, at a glance, are easily misread.

Ignoring a friend suggestion made by an acquaintance is perfectly acceptable. The "suggestee" is unlikely to know unless the "suggestor" mentions it. How likely this is, and how consequential, is up to you to determine.

Declining Friend Requests

Facebook "friending" can become complicated in the same way that inviting people to a wedding is complicated—if you invite this person, should you invite that person, and so on. If you are friends with a particular person and an associated person requests that you friend, it is awkward to decline. Declining should be handled delicately. If you have pretty specific friend criteria (e.g., "we have to have met in person"), then it is okay to say so, very diplomatically. Just make sure you haven't made some exceptions they might spot. Unfortunately, you cannot suppress your friend list from others' views in Facebook, so anyone can see with whom you are connected. This is where that "wedding" dilemma comes in—they all have access to the guest list.

When to ignore a friend request is up to you. If you don't know the person, don't feel bad. If you're not sure whether you know them, before accepting the request, click on his or her name to see their info. You'll also see any mutual friends in the sidebar. If this doesn't trigger your recollection, I wouldn't feel too guilty about ignoring the request. If you do know them and don't want to connect, send them a message to explain. This is possible without your having to friend them.

Unfriending

Unfriending someone is a fairly serious thing. Don't unfriend a contact unless you have good reason to, such as their having done something to lose your confidence or respect—or otherwise demonstrate lack of trustworthiness. If you've become Facebook friends with someone whom you didn't know well and you regret becoming friends, you can hide them from your feed and they'll all but disappear from your sight. However, this doesn't preclude them from seeing what you publish, so if that is problematic for you, you might wish to change your settings so they no longer see your status updates and other published items.

If you do choose to unfriend someone, he or she is not usually notified unless they happen to use a third-party browser plug-in such as a Greasemonkey script called "Facebook Friend Checker," used with the Firefox browser.

Sometimes users deactivate their Facebook accounts and they disappear from their connections' friend lists and friend count. If they log back in, they reappear as friends. If you think someone unfriended you, it may just be that they completely exited the application.

Dealing with Annoyances

There will definitely be things about Facebook to annoy you. And it's possible you will do things on Facebook that annoy others. These suggestions can dramatically improve your Facebook experience, and help you improve the experiences of those to whom you are connected.

FREQUENT POSTERS   Frequent posters are especially noticeable when you don't have many Facebook contacts. If you have fewer than 50 and someone posts often, he or she can flood your news feed. You can suppress them from your feed if you really want to. Hover over one of their posts until you see a "Hide" button appear at the top right and you'll able to hide their future posts from your feed. This doesn't delete them as a friend, just hides them from the news feed.

Some people elect to have their Twitter posts (tweets) pour into their Facebook accounts. You can usually spot these because they have lots of "@" and "#" characters and unfamiliar abbreviations like "RT" in them. If someone is a frequent tweeter, or if you already subscribe to them in Twitter, this can be irritating. You may elect to hide the user from your news feed to remove the clutter.

Along these lines, if you use Twitter, I don't recommend that you have every tweet pour into Facebook. There are third-party apps for Twitter that let you feed some tweets in on a select basis—use one of those if you want to periodically cross-post.

As you accumulate more friends, you may want to go back and unhide some of these previously hidden friends because once you have more connections, their volume won't seem so out of proportion relative to the rest of the activity in your feed. To restore hidden items, go to the bottom of the news feed list to find the "Edit Options" link.

THIRD-PARTY APPLICATIONS   There are games on Facebook that are very popular—like Farmville, MafiaWars, quizzes—and various "gift" applications. These are not part of the native Facebook application but are built by third-party software providers. Some can be malicious, but most are harmless. The real annoyance is when the games post notifications to all the players' friends: quite annoying to those who do not play them, and they quickly drown out human interactions.

If you see other peoples' games or other application notices in your news feed, you can turn them off by hovering over the notice until you see a "Remove" button appear at the top right. You'll be presented with the option of removing the friend (doesn't delete them, just hides them from the news feed) or removing the application notices. The latter is usually the one you want.

In the event that you play games yourself, it's not a bad idea to let friends know how to hide your game notices from their feed. It acknowledges that you realize you're creating the noise in their feeds, but it also helps them have a more pleasant Facebook experience—and not curse your name every time they see you've fertilized your crops or found a cow. That may be a little extreme, but the point is, it would defeat your relationship-building purpose if friends chose to suppress you entirely from appearing in their news feed versus just hiding the offending application.

Certain applications send "invitations" and "gifts" to friends of those who use them. Whenever you receive these items, it is perfectly acceptable to choose "Ignore" to rid your inbox of them. People should, and generally do, understand if you tell them you "don't do apps"; however, most people will never notice if you decline these things. Often, users don't realize they are initiating the communication from the applications to their friends. You can avoid sending such things to your friends by avoiding applications altogether, or by being very careful about what you click when using an application.

Some of these application creators trick or mislead users into broadcasting invitations because their goal is to spread the application to as many users as possible in order to glean user demographics and provide eyes for their advertising. First, the applications often look like they are "part" of Facebook. Second, choices other than sending notices can be pretty obscured. If you find yourself in such a situation and just want out, you can exit the application at that point by clicking "Home" or "Profile," or closing Facebook in your browser window.

If you find that you unintentionally mass-broadcast a game, quiz, or invitation, a quick "mea culpa" status update goes a long way.

Making a Dynamic Company Page

The standard Facebook company page comes ready with info, wall, photos, and discussion tabs. As soon as you post a link or video, you'll have those tabs, as well. Other possibilities are documents, polls, reviews, and presentation slides such as an application like Slideshare.

You or your page administrator (you can designate anyone who "Likes" your page as a page administrator) can also create custom tabs to appear as your page's secondary navigation. With third-party applications, you can add blog feeds (yours or those of other authors and organizations). Tabs can be arranged in any order by dragging them.

Using unique, custom content is of growing importance as Facebook rolls out more improvements in their news feed algorithms to help bring users the most interesting, relevant content in the growing flood of information. Details shared by Facebook at their most recent f8 Developer Conference shed light on why some items surface before others. An article by Kbuzz reports "News Feed Optimization (NFO) has arguably become the new SEO (Search Engine Optimization),"[3] and in the competition for eyes and clicks in the largest, fastest-growing Web community, I can see why.

Like Google, Facebook will no doubt alter their algorithms as people learn how to game their systems, but for now, NFO (also called EdgeRank internally by Facebook) will rely on a combination of affinity score (relating to how, and how often, a user interacts with that page), weight (comments, likes, and tags), and time decay.

It's this first score, "affinity," that conveys just how significant it is going to be for a newly "liked" page to grab their newest liker with content lest they slip away from that user's news feed. As stated in the Kbuzz article, ". . . the more you interact with someone, the more likely you are to continue to receive their content. . . . It makes a stronger case for people to develop and create content that will elicit interaction and thus a higher affinity score and weight."

Aim high with content and engagement if you want to stay relevant and active with your Facebook company page audience.

Customizing Pages

Custom tabs can include a large variety of interactive technology, including forms, polls, and more—there is no limit to the creativity. Using Static FBML, you or a programmer can create unique tabs to suit your content and engagement needs. To obtain Static FBML, and make it available to your company's page, you or a page admin with appropriate permissions can follow the tutorial at http://highedwebtech.com/2009/06/19/how-to-add-a-custom-tab-to-your-facebook-fan-page/. (Note that in the comments of this blog post, some commenters clarify that more than one custom tab *can* exist per Facebook page.)

I haven't seen a lot of truly groundbreaking things on professional firms' Facebook pages yet, but definitely have on others. The winning "Facebook Top 40 Pages" from the Kbuzz survey mentioned earlier in this chapter are great examples of company pages with features that engage and impress.[4] Another neat example is blues musician Bob Margolin's personal and fan pages at facebook.com/BobMargolin and facebook.com/BobMargolinFan, respectively. In particular, check out the My Band, My Stuff, and My Music tabs.

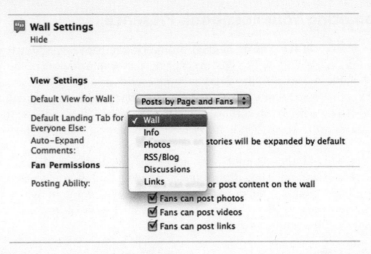

FIGURE 10.4 Page Wall and Tab Settings

It's also possible to insert full-fledged Hypertext Markup Language (HTML) pages onto a tab. Coca Cola (facebook.com/cocacola) made the Kbuzz Top 40 list, above, and has several neat tabs, including their Live Positively tab. Disneyland (facebook.com/Disneyland) did not make the list but has SoCal 2Fer and GiveADay tabs.

With FBML, you can create tables, boxes, and all sorts of other content formatting tools to organize your information. It's possible you would need to engage someone with the right technical skills to do this, though, so it doesn't end up looking amateur.

Despite the snazzy possibilities afforded through customizing a company page, never underestimate the power of a lively and interactive community through the core features Facebook offers. These include discussions on your wall and comments on links and photos that you share.

You can set any of your tabs to be the main "landing page" for new visitors. When you have interesting interactions, you might want to move beyond having your page visitors land on the wall or boring Info tab. If you have a custom tab that delivers a strong message about your firm, make that the first page nonfans will see.

The default landing tab can be changed anytime (click "Edit Page" under your company page profile picture), and in these settings (see Figure 10.4) you can also control how your wall appears to others, and whether fans' wall posts show on your wall (they don't by default). If they are hidden in the default view, your page doesn't look as interactive.

Promoting Your Facebook Presence

After you've set up your individual profile or company page, you'll want to get people to follow or "like" your page. The administrators of the page will be able to promote the page by "suggesting" it to all of their contacts. That's a first step. And you can ask people who like the page to tell their friends (they will, in effect, have done that because a little one-line notice will show up in their friends news feeds announcing that they like [your page].

You should also mention your Facebook page, with a link, on your firm's Web site, your LinkedIn profile, your blog, and in your email signature. Before you announce it, however, you will want to get a nice, easy-to-remember URL—a vanity URL—for your Facebook page.

Vanity URLs

It's a good idea to secure shorter "vanity" URLs for these pages. You only have one chance to name your page—once set, it cannot be changed. To get your custom URL, go to facebook.com/username. From this page, you are offered choices for your personal profile vanity URL (your first, most obvious choices may already be taken). Afterward, or if you already have one for your personal account, you will see an option under that, which says "Set a User Name for your Pages." Follow the instructions to secure your company page vanity URL.

If all reasonably good URL options through this official Facebook vehicle are taken, there is a third-party app (http://apps.facebook.com/webaddress) that you can access to set up a link. The official Facebook way is preferable, though.

The resulting links are what you should share with others.

Cross-Referencing Your Facebook Pages

After your company Facebook page is established, in the settings (edit page under the profile pic) you'll find options for creating "widgets" for other Web pages and blogs. Follow the instructions and place the generated "code" on your firm's Web site (career section if your Facebook page is for recruiting) and your blogs. You can do the same for your personal Facebook profile as well.

For company and personal Pages, share your vanity URLs on your Web site and blogs, Google profile, LinkedIn profile, and Twitter background pages, and include them in your email signature as well.

Advertising on Facebook

It's easy to advertise on Facebook, and very affordable, especially compared with traditional print ad costs. The demographic information that is available for advertisers to pick and choose from makes it easy to hone in on a certain locality, age group, and various other demographics such as political persuasion, religion, and marital status. Compared to the specificity this information provides for on-target messages, the idea of running ads in newspapers seems like shooting into an ocean to catch a fish. The community offers extraordinary potential to reach business decision makers and their tremendous buying power because Facebook has become the favorite social network for Boomers and they, as well as entrepreneurial Gen-Xers, are the fastest growing demographic on Facebook.[5]

Professional firms that have run ad campaigns on Facebook have been pleased with the overall results so far, although the firms that reported also said that it's very early to evaluate their campaigns' long-term effectiveness. Each reported that targeted ads did drive click-throughs. All the firms reporting said they intend to continue exploring Facebook ads and expect to get better at their messaging relative to their targeted audiences.

The price is right. And many firms have the types of goals in mind that Facebook ads would support perfectly, so experimenting along this avenue may be very worthwhile.

To explore advertising opportunities, go to "Settings" and "Help," under which you'll see a variety of help pages covering advertising. Or, from your company page, under the profile picture, you'll see a "Promote With an Ad" link that will introduce you to the concepts of advertising on Facebook, without initially requiring you to commit to running an ad until you get several steps deep—you can exit at that point, if you wish.

An interesting result of your advertising could be the further development of your audience personas (see Chapter 4). Paul Dunay, co-author of *Facebook Marketing for Dummies* (Wiley, 2009), discusses in his blog the ability to view aggregate public profile information (governed by users' profile settings) of people who have responded to your ads when more than 1,000 people have clicked through.[6] He says the resulting report "will tell you the most common Music, TV shows, Movies, Books, Age and Marital Status among the people who clicked on your ad." In the creation and evolution of your audience personas, the more you can know about people interested in you, the better. It enables stronger messaging both in advertising and content development, leading to better, longer-lasting engagement and, ultimately, prospect conversion.

CHAPTER 11

Self-Publishing with Blogs

Some say "blog" stands for Better Listing on Google and, while that is not the origin of the name (it comes from blending *Web* and *log* together), there is something to this. Sure, search engine rankings and listings can be bought, but they are useless if there is nothing of substance on your Web site once someone actually arrives there. Blogs are a solution to the problem of inadequate substance in the content of firm Web sites.

Further, taking advantage of the Really Simple Syndication (RSS) feed aspect of blog programming enables you to disseminate your news releases or other happenings much more broadly, less intrusively, and more cost effectively (even free!) than via print and emailings—quite powerful indeed.

Journalists and other representatives of the media increasingly rely on blogs because they are incredibly findable with search, the RSS feeds enable them to subscribe to relevant and credible sources, and blogs tend to be heavily linked to other sites and sources so users can get further information on related subjects. Not every blogger is a worthy and credible source, but from what we've seen with the media's use (including trade publications) of legal and accounting blogs thus far, the evidence is strong that professionals' blogs have huge potential for elevating the professional in his or her area of specialty. The bottom line is: blogs make journalists jobs easier—they will continue to use them.

Within the book *Inbound Marketing* is a statement that nicely summarizes what it is that a blog becomes for you: "Once you write that article, it gives you value forever. . . . A blog is a durable asset. . . ."[1]

In many ways, blogs are the holy grail of online marketing for professionals. But they aren't for everyone. This chapter will help you determine if blogging is right for your firm and, if so, who is most suited to blog, for whom (audience) they should write, what they should write about.

The Tools

Technically speaking, a blog is just a Web site built to certain Web standards that maximize the format of information so it's more readily categorized than old-fashioned Web site programming approaches. The consistent structure allows content to be easily found by users searching for timely, relevant information, partly because, unlike most other Web content, blog content is date-stamped, and newness matters. A blog-based Web site can look the same as any other site but boasts a few unique, defining elements. Particularly easy to maintain, blogs are Web-based content management systems with cushy back ends—no programming knowledge is necessary for the author of a blog, and creating new posts is akin to writing an email.

There are a number of blog platforms available. A leading tool for several years has been WordPress, an open-source platform with lots of professional-looking templates available for free or at very low cost (less than $100, usually). WordPress also has a hosted platform that is free and very easy to use. It is somewhat less flexible than the server version.

There is another freeware called Blogger (now owned by Google), but it is suboptimal for a number of reasons including limited flexibility with design and features. That said, Google is advancing Blogger all the time, and a lot of people like it. If you do choose Blogger, do be absolutely sure to remove the amateur-looking "Blogger" branding banner from the top. As a professional, your blog should brand you, not your software. My biggest concern with Blogger is that you don't own or control the platform (the same with any hosted platform) and since your content becomes an increasingly valuable asset, predictability is security.

Unless you are pretty comfortable teaching yourself new software, it may be worthwhile to invest a little money in initial programming and design (budget a few hundred to a few thousand dollars, depending on your desire for customization) for either WordPress or Blogger. An experienced programmer can set it up, customize the design and features for you, and show you how to use it.

Leading *purchasable* platforms that offer some templates or can be customized within the same approximate price range are products by Six Apart, and Expression Engine. Six Apart offers two products: Movable Type, which is purchased outright and is self-hosted (your Web sites and blogs are best hosted off-site rather than on your internal servers, where sensitive client data resides) and the company's hosted version, called TypePad, which lives on their servers and is purchased for a monthly or annual fee. In January 2010, Movable Type switched to an open-source model, also integrating full-fledged Web site features for an easier all-in-one (Web site + blogs) Web presence—too new to comment on, but promising as an integrated solution that should make Web maintenance easier for many marketing departments. Expression Engine is extremely powerful but not as user-friendly. It's also more difficult to find experienced programmers for this platform. Movable Type and Expression Engine will definitely require a programmer's skills to set up. A relative novice with an adventurous spirit and a little patience can set up Typepad blogs in a single day.

Another option is LexBlog, a company that designs, hosts, and supports blogs for thousands of lawyers, accountants, and other professionals. LexBlog is tailored for professionals, and the blogs are built on a custom version of Movable Type. You cannot compare Lexblog apples-to-apples with the other platforms described because their fixed annual fee covers consulting, design, development, training, search engine optimization, ongoing support and coaching, and access to a network of professionals who blog. If you expect to have numerous blog authors in your organization, and suspect they'll need ongoing support from people who understand professional firms, a full-service resource like this could be a wise choice.

There are other enterprise-blogging-solution providers that serve a range of industries. Two are Hubspot and Compendium Blogware. These are scalable services with setup charges and ongoing monthly fees.

If you elect to use a hosted version of any blog software, before you set up your blog or begin posting, be *sure* that you arrange for the blog URL to house your content on your own domain (one that your business owns the rights to) versus residing on the domain of the hosted platform. This is usually referred to as "domain mapping," and it is critical if you should ever desire to migrate your blog to another program. It also provides for a shorter, cleaner blog URL that brands only you, and not the hosting company, and it assures you would never lose followers as a result of relocating your blog platform. Relocating if you haven't mapped your domain could mean manually migrating thousands of blog posts to a new URL—a tedious, costly venture that can significantly disrupt your search engine standings and cause you to lose subscribers. Robert Scoble, one of America's best-known bloggers with a massive following, says: "Never change the URL of your weblog. I've done it once and I lost much of my readership and it took several months to build up the same reader patterns and trust."[2]

Blog Basics

RSS is the means through which Web-published content (blogs, video, audio, etc.) is delivered to Web sites or RSS feed "aggregators" that are programmed to fetch the "feeds." Many news-related sites and other online publishers syndicate their content as an RSS feed. RSS allows people to retrieve the latest content from the sites without the need to visit individual Web sites.

The RSS symbol in Figure 11.1 is usually bright orange (sometimes people substitute other colors), and it's the universal symbol for an RSS feed. Anytime you see this on a Web page, it means that at least some of that page's content may be "subscribed to" with an RSS feed reader or feed aggregator. Wise blog publishers also create a utility that can convert their RSS feed to email delivery format. I highly recommend this because it enables people to quickly and conveniently subscribe even when they don't know what RSS feeds are.

A blog's back end is very user friendly. Entering a blog post is much like writing an email. There are spell-checkers as well as the ability to format text in all the customary ways, insert pictures, upload and attach files, and embed links. Once you input your content, a title, and a category (the three minimum elements) and submit your post, RSS will "push" your new post out to feed readers (Figure 11.2), converters that turn it into emails (for those who subscribe that way), and stream ever-changing content into Web sites, yours or others that are set up to display your feeds.

Blogs, Blogging, and Posts

The term *blog* (n.) refers to the whole site (all pages together, comparable to "Web site") and each individual single entry is called a "post" (comparable to a single "Web page"). Some people mistakenly call the single entry a "blog" rather than a "post." This makes a person sound like an amateur, so you want to get the terminology right. The act of *blogging* (v.) is what you do when you write a post for your blog. To accurately describe your blogging activity, you would say that you "have a blog" and you "write a

FIGURE 11.1 RSS 2.0 Icon

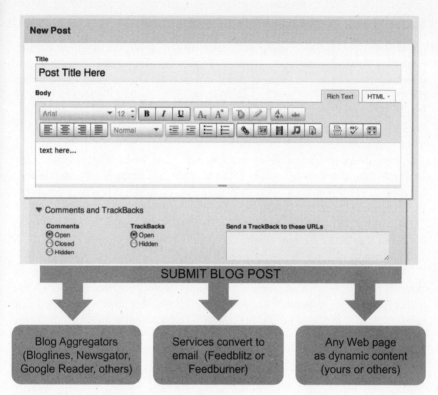

FIGURE 11.2 Blog Entry Screen and RSS Push

post." You didn't "write a blog today" or "post a blog today"; instead, you "blogged today," or "posted *on* your blog today."

You do, however, become the "author of a blog" (meaning the site in its entirety) or a "blogger," and once you have 10–12 posts live, you should promote the fact that you have a blog everywhere you can.

TIP: What Makes a Great Blog Post

The best blog posts are bite-sized snippets of information that people can absorb, consider, and act on. Think of a blog post as a single email answering a single question. Just as you'd write for a client, your email would address a certain issue and be specific to their unique circumstances. (Read more about this in Chapter 12.)

Subscribers, Feeds, and Feed Readers

Subscribers choose to receive your blog posts either via email or in their preferred feed reader (the subscriber opts in and controls receipt and unsubscribe options, so there is never any action needed on your part—no database management, and no worries about complying with the Canned Spam Act, ethics requirements for advertising, or IRC Section 7216 guidelines). This is easier for you, and appreciated by the subscriber who prefers to control the delivery of their news.

Some very common feed readers are Google Reader, Yahoo!, and Outlook. There are many others (search "RSS feed aggregator" on the Web for more). The feed reader gets notified (aka "pinged") whenever an author posts something to a subscribed site. The subscriber then needs only to check one place (their reader) to see if all his subscribed sites have new content. This is the easiest, most convenient way to receive and filter news and information.

Feeds are very easy to keep up with. Consider setting up feeds for yourself and your coworkers to stay abreast of your clients' industry news trends, happenings related to your areas of practice, and other technical news. Even a quick skim of headlines in your reader delivers far more information than most of us will take the time to seek out otherwise. Also, the articles and postings you'll receive will often contain the sort of information you'd want to forward to clients, prospects, or referral sources, so good "reasons" to keep in touch are literally landing in your inbox.

Advantages of Blogs over Print or Email

Web and print publishing can coexist beautifully, so it's not an either/or decision. There are distinct advantages to both, and readers of firm content (clients and referral sources) consistently report they like both mediums. Current readers' opinions merit consideration, but they are a very small group compared to the vast audience of prospects and future referrers you could reach via the Web. What you choose to do and how ultimately depends on your goals—your purpose. The following are some advantages to online publishing.

Unlike magazine or newsletter subscriptions, with a blog there is no waiting for an entire new issue to come out, and there is no manual thumbing through a large collection of articles to spot topics of interest. Subscribers receive posts one at a time and feeds can be easily forwarded, too, so there is good pass-along opportunity for your content. When people receive your content one item at a time, it is infinitely more readable.

A blog post is also much more convenient for a client or prospect to retrieve later, whether they bookmark it or not. Think of how many e-newsletters you subscribe to knowing how valuable they are and intending to read them but, alas, you don't. Same for other folks. We're all just too busy to read nonurgent emails right away, if ever. Unless they are *very short*. If it's not read now, one of two things happen: the delete key, or it gets filed away with our great intentions to read it later.

Perhaps that article your client missed is just what they're looking for information about, now. But how would they even remember which "quarterly issue" it came in? Classifying information by date instead of topic is a horribly ineffective way to archive information. Rather than trying to find an article in their email (if they even recollect keeping it), they can visit your blog to see it, along with any other articles you've written, when they are ready to actually absorb information on that topic. In the meantime, while they don't need it yet, others do, and instead of its being hidden in the email archives of the limited number of people you delivered it to, it is readily accessed by anyone, around the world, anytime. This is a distinct advantage—your blog markets for you 24/7/365 to a global audience instead of your content waiting, unread, in the inboxes of a few hundred.

If you replace the e-newsletters you distribute with blog content, you no longer have to deal with design and formatting, spam filters, spam laws, domain blacklist issues, e-newsletter services with monthly fees, and contact list maintenance. Instead, once a blog is set up, set up an account with a free service like Feedburner (a Google product) so that people can choose to subscribe by email in a manner that is completely self-administered. This helps you enormously because you don't have to try to educate people about RSS and feed-readers. If they are unfamiliar with those tools, they can fall back on their comfy email delivery. And if they use RSS, they will appreciate you even more.

Additionally, when you first set up Feedburner or a similar product, you can upload your mailing list and initiate a one-time opt-in request (it's recommended that you let people know this will be forthcoming) asking them to confirm if they'd still like to receive your information. At any time, you can check your Feedburner account to see how many subscribers you have, and depending on the service you use, you can typically export the list of subscribers (usually their email addresses only).

Both you and your readers benefit from the searchability of blog content. Most blog tools provide a "search this blog" utility—it's a must-have. As a blogger myself, I assure you that you will use your own blog content often in your follow-up contacts with people and for other reference purposes. Think of your blog as your own personal intellectual capital archive.

Anatomy of a Blog Post

To promote usability, blogs share a common format that includes the features cross-referenced in Figure 11.3. The following list explains each part of the figure:

- **About Page/Link:** Features name, bios, and contact info of contributing authors. Authors names may link to a list of the author's posts or may link to the author's full bio on the firm's Web site.
- **Archives:** All prior blog posts, searchable by keyword, category or chronology.
- **Author:** Indicates the person who wrote the post ("admin" isn't good). This tag may be omitted from individual posts on a single author blog if the author is identified elsewhere on each page of the blog (in the header or sidebar).
- **Blogroll:** List of links to other related blogs that readers would find of interest. Multiple lists can be featured. Without a blogroll, a blog comes across as anti-community.
- **Category:** Topic labels that inform readers of the breadth of the blog's content serve as the primary means of a blog's navigation, and are important keywords for the blog, so they should be well chosen. Good category names create "stickier" users; poor names confuse users. A blog post should be assigned to at least one category, but not more than two or three. A blog should have between 10 and 20 categories.
- **Comments:** Where readers leave their own reactions to the author's post. Opening the door to conversation is a critical component of a blog. Comments are usually monitored to prevent spam from appearing on the blog.
- **Date/Time Stamp:** The date and time the post is written. Posts are displayed in reverse chronological order (most recent first).
- **Links:** Every blog post should contain links to external resources. Link heavily and often, even to competitors. By linking to others, your site elevates in rankings. The words you highlight to "form the link" are called anchor text, and the more descriptive those words are, the better.
- **Permalink:** Each blog post has a unique Web address (aka URL or URI). This allows people to link directly to a post when referencing it on the Web, in email, or even in print.
- **Post:** One unique blog entry containing as little as a sentence and up to, usually not more than, 1,000 words. Posts may include supporting graphics or photos.
- **Post Title:** Each post has a unique title that can be a single word, a pithy phrase, or a news-y headline. The better your title, the better

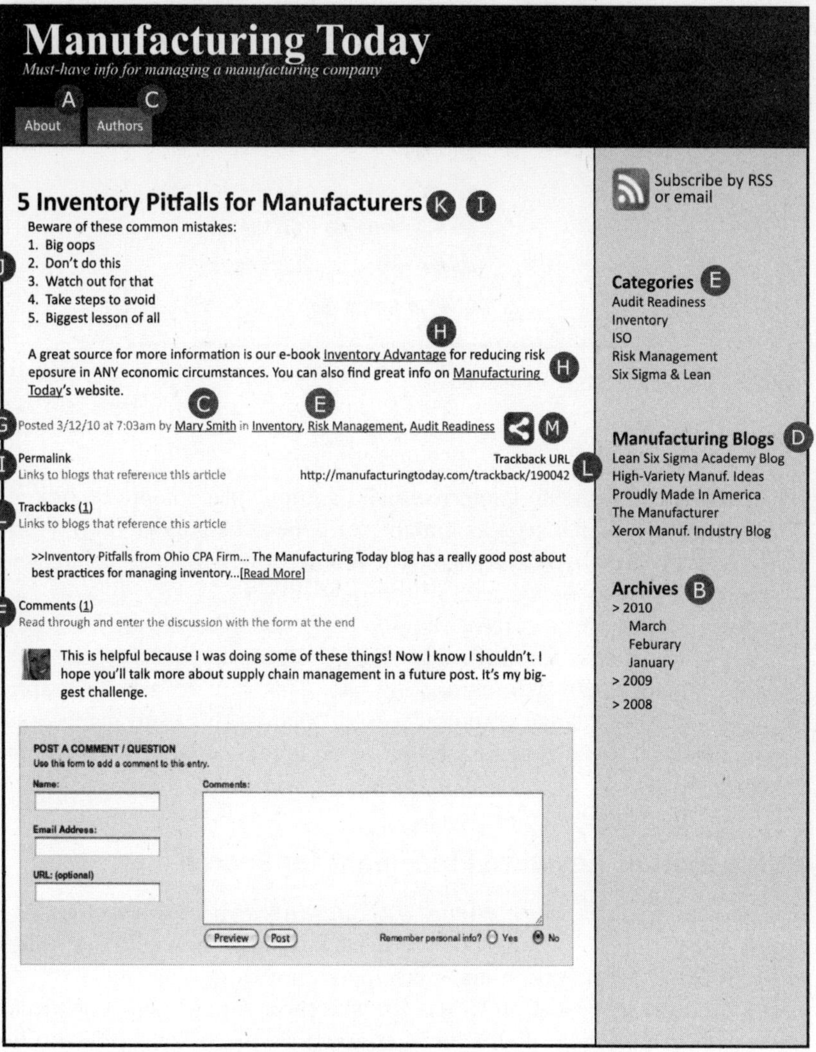

©2010 Golden Practices Inc

FIGURE 11.3 Anatomy of a Blog Post

Source: © 2010 Golden Practices Inc.

your readership. Compelling titles that hint to what's delivered within are best. Questions also work well as titles. The post title itself is a clickable link directly to the full post, the same as the post's permalink.

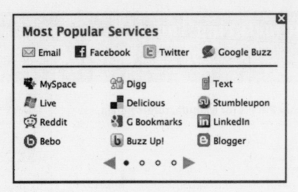

FIGURE 11.4 "Share This" Expanded

- **TrackBack:** A method automating an author's placement of a link and an excerpt (similar to a comment) of a new blog post onto a prior blog post (by anyone) to which it refers. This is usually done when the prior post is being cited in the new one.
- **Share Links:** Most current blogs have some type of add-on feature that makes it easy for readers to share the post on their favorite social media platform or a bookmarking site. This can be a large graphic, subtle text, or a small commonly-used "Share This" icon which opens a variety of social tool (as shown in Figure 11.4) from which a user can choose.

Words Matter: Keyword Placement for Search

You needn't spend a lot of energy catering to search engines in order to have a very successful blog, but some background knowledge may help you to make word-selection and placement choices that are more to your advantage than against it. Reviewing this section should help you decide how much or how little you want to consciously place keywords and key phrases as you write for your blog.

Keywords and phrases are the criteria that people enter into search engines to find relevant Web sites. The act of consciously selecting and placing these words and phrases to improve the volume of traffic delivered to your site or blog from searches is called search engine optimization (SEO). Search engine results based on your content—versus paid search placements—are known as "natural" or "organic" search results. To achieve organic search results, Web content authors increase a site's relevance by writing about what their desired readers care most about (hint: not brochure-type language).

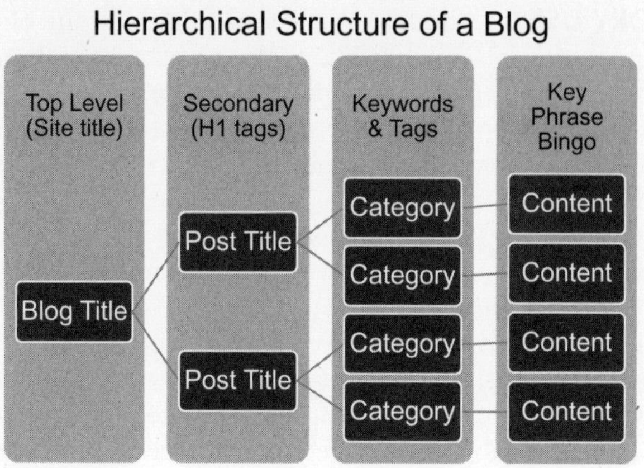

Hierarchical Structure of a Blog

FIGURE 11.5 Hierarchical Structure of a Blog

There are several different areas in your blog where keyword phrases are advantageously placed—and these locations are of varying degrees of importance to search engines (Figure 11.5).

The highest level of importance is the actual name of the blog and/or the URL or Web address of the blog. In addition to the title, search engines also give some search relevance advantage to the words placed in these elements:

- Post titles
- Categories to which posts are assigned (sometimes called tags)
- Subheadings used within posts
- Links, specifically the actual text comprising links (called "anchor text")
- Enhanced text such as bold and italics
- General text within the post
- Image file names and ALT tags

To help attract more visitors to your blog, you can consider which keywords or phrases your desired audience would most likely use when they search, and organize your blog posts to contain the most relevant keywords in the most advantageous places. This process is discussed more in-depth in Chapter 12.

You may also wish to consider what is known and generally understood about how search algorithms work, as well as real-time facts about terms that members of your audiences are actually searching. Bear in mind that gaming search engines that you will rank highly is nearly impossible and that what gets you ahead in one search engine may not help you at all in another.

CATEGORY USE   Aside from the overall title of your blog and the title of each post, the most significant indicator of your posts' subject matter, both for your readers and for search engines, are the one or more categories to which each particular post is assigned. Skimming the categories of your blog should provide visitors with an accurate contextual overview of your blog's content.

Category names should be descriptive key phrases, but should not be too micro in topic, either, because the ideal number of categories for a blog is between 10 and 20.

Categories, when clicked, serve as content filters for the reader, narrowing displayed posts to only those assigned to the chosen category. Some blogs have so many categories that it seems like a new one is set up every time the author posts. Others have so few categories that filtering by them doesn't help readers since it's too time consuming to scroll through any single category.

As a blog author, you will assign every post into one or more categories, but try not to assign it to more than two or three. If you are often tempted to put posts in several categories, this could indicate that you have too many duplicative categories or that your posts are complex enough to be broken up into multiple posts.

Strategically, your category names will often be fleshed out as key phrases are identified in the blog's planning stage, but do expect that some categories will need to be added or renamed later as the blog grows and changes.

Start-up Considerations

While it's sometimes easy to decide who, in your firm, should blog, or what they ought to write about, try to keep an open mind as you read the rest of this chapter. It may change your mind about both.

The following four-step process will help you approach choosing the best blog authors, bearing in mind exactly whom you'd like to attract as *loyal* readers, and the topics about which the authors might write to accomplish this. The four steps are to work through:

Step 1: Authors, desired readers, and subject matter
Step 2: Blog name and theme
Step 3: Blog author preparation
Step 4: Blog development and launch

This approach is based on experience watching lots of professional firm blogs fail to deliver results. Each and every instance was due to lack

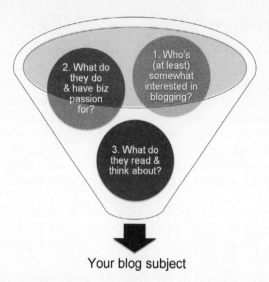

Your blog subject

FIGURE 11.6 Blog Subject Funnel

of forethought in establishing the right teams or lack of clarity about for whom the blog content was geared and the readers' level of sophistication. Making wise decisions in accordance with the following concepts will give you the best chance for success with your blog.

Remember (as per Chapter 4) that while I use the words *audience* and *desired readers* for the purposes of marketing specificity, the intent is that you will consistently view your readers as people you will engage *with*, not talk *at*.

Step 1: Authors, Desired Readers, and Subject Matter

The first step has three components that should be completed to help assure you have the right balance of success factors. These things are not mutually exclusive—they depend on one another and should be done simultaneously as shown in Figure 11.6. They are:

- **Locate passionate authors:** They must be at least somewhat interested in blogging, and at least one must be very interested or you are unlikely to have the enthusiasm and momentum to succeed.
- **Define desired readers:** What do the potential authors know and do? And for whom do they do it? This would be the most likely "audience."
- **Decide specific subject matter:** What do the potential authors read about? What do they care most about (passion) related to the audience?

What does the audience already read? What does the audience care about? Are these aligned?

As you work through the steps of author/reader/subject considerations, use each as a check point to make sure you have a good fit with energy, support, ideas, and passion behind each aspect. You may get reasonably far down a planning path thinking you have the right combination, but then discover one of the pieces is not strong enough. If you find that any aspect seems sluggish, this is a good time to do a gut check and think twice about launching a blog of that topic with those authors at the present time. Heed these feelings as a warning sign and consider a different direction.

FORMULA FOR SUCCESS Having witnessed several firms battle with author and topic selection mistakes or misalignments, it is fair to say that the success of a blog depends mainly on these two things:

- **Passion and interest of the author(s) in blogging:** Again, enthusiasm is absolutely requisite. This means the task of blogging cannot simply be "assigned" to your best subject matter expert as many firms are prone to do. There is nothing more certain to result in a boring blog than having authors who are forced to write for it. Bloggers need not be firm owners or partners, either. Look throughout the levels of your organization for good potential authors—this could be just the thing to empower and equip them to move to new levels in their careers.
- **Appropriateness of the content with regard to the desired outcome:** This should drive the topic. Whenever you write anything—a speech, an ad, a letter or email, a descriptive "blurb" when your firm sponsors an event, a proposal, or even your biography—the first question to ask yourself is: *Who is the audience?* The second question is: *What are we seeking to accomplish with the audience?* The third is: *What does the reader care about?* The purpose of the blog needs to be crystal clear. And you need to be sure the authors are able to accomplish the goal (see A Story of Misalignment).

A Story of Misalignment

This is a true story of an unfortunate misalignment between goals and content. A mid-sized firm created an industry niche blog to promote their complex audit and consulting services and to attract new clients. The target audiences were top executives in the organizations and referral sources, primarily lawyers. Great concept. However, they had problems with execution.

Situation

The blog authors were partners and managers with knowledge and passion to cover interesting, rich topics. Other partners (with rank) initially supported the blog, in concept, but soon proved to be skittish about subject matter. Consulting-related topics—discussing situations where judgments are applied—didn't often make the cut leaving simple tax- and accounting-related posts. Unfortunately, "simple tax" was not what the service the firm sought to sell, nor was it interesting enough to sustain the initial exact-target readers that a good promotional campaign had attracted. These were initial problems but the situation got worse.

Significant news broke in the sector about an inquiry into the financial practices of some industry organizations. While the situation was extremely touchy, the topic could have been approached with neutrality, delicacy, and professionalism—the same way the organizations in question approached it—but the firm remained silent on it for months.

Initial reluctance to cover complex topics evolved into failure to acknowledge major breaking news in the sector in which they were attempting to position themselves as thought leaders.

Missed Opportunity Cost

The firm's absence in the discussion of such significant news and activities cost them credibility. An "industry thought leader" finds an appropriate way to participate in the conversation, perhaps consulting with a PR firm specializing in crisis management to advise on approach. It could be worth the investment if concerns are high, yet thought leader status is a serious quest.

In addition to the blog's diminished credibility, the firm missed an enormous opportunity to dominate in online searches related to that news at a time when a compilation of external news or a couple short articles could have sufficed in bringing a high level of visibility among the high-ranking executives in their prospects' organizations. The firm instead posted on innocuous topics during this crucial time.

Result

The blog no longer supported the firm's marketing objectives. The safe topics (of low intellectual value) were far below the quality of content needed to attract and hold the attention of the C-suite. The firm also missed the chance to secure its position as a strong resource for trade organizations and media representatives who could have bolstered the blog's readership and the firm's standing in the industry, which it was initially poised to achieve.

When you meet to discuss a potential blog topic and audience in the steps below, be thoughtful about the degree of substantive information to offer your audience. During these discussions, start listing article ideas—this is the beginning of your editorial calendar. If, in this process, you suspect that you cannot make it spicy enough to attract or sustain the attention of your desired audience over time, then consider moving on to another topic and audience idea. Without appealing content, the blog will not do its job.

As content expert Joe Pulizzi says, "Two ingredients that make content marketing go are passion and consistency. If you can't find the passion, it might be the wrong niche."[3]

Make sure your firm is really willing and able to do what it takes to achieve your goals.

LOCATE PASSIONATE AUTHORS   Enthusiastic, passionate blog authors are a must. But a lot of firms start with a topic and try to back into finding bloggers for the topic.

When approached, people may feel pressured to say yes or may be told straight out that they are expected to blog. This is not the best approach for the reasons just described. If you have a great topic idea—but no one is fired up to write about it, then pass. Do not start a blog, especially your first blog, without a lot of enthusiasm. In a larger organization, especially a skeptical or highly political one, if the "first" blog fails, it may be very difficult to get the firm to support a second attempt.

It is always advantageous to have two or more authors sharing the job of creating blog content. More than just spreading the workload, the authors will encourage and inspire each other by feeding off of each other's energy. They may even gently guilt each other into posting more frequently than they otherwise would.

Some firms discover that a slow start or tentative support can elevate, even resulting in a marketing culture shift within a firm. One such firm is Mohler Nixon, a Top 100 CPA firm in Silicon Valley, Palo Alto, and Sacramento, California. Their blog, *MNW Informed* (www.mohlernixon.com/informed) started off a bit slowly and wasn't publicly launched until a year after some team members had started posting. It received an infusion of enthusiasm in late 2009 and formally launched shortly thereafter. While it's too early to expect measurable business development results, other meaningful results can already be observed. Michael Louie, the firm's marketing associate reported,

> *We launched the blog five months ago and it's been a transformative experience throughout the entire firm. Every week it seems as if more partners and managers are "buying into" the powerful benefits of displaying our expertise online. Our content is increasing our online traffic*

steadily and we've even had several clients and prospects call our blog's authors for more information.

Look beyond your firm's partner or owner group to find your blog authors. Nonpartners are often better, more committed bloggers and may be more comfortable with social media so the learning curve could be lower. Something to keep in mind is that anyone employed by the firm who writes for the blog should write under his or her own name. It might be new territory for your firm to have "nonpartners" through whom the firm is findable on the Web. Without intending to sound rude, it's time to get over it. Team members are probably already on LinkedIn, Facebook, or MySpace and are probably associated with the firm in one or more of these places. Harness and leverage the multiple marketers you have.

Whether bloggers are owners or employees, another question might also arise: When someone leaves the firm, who owns the content? What do we do with content posted under the name of a former team member?

Because blogging is so tremendously valuable for the firm and simultaneously elevates authors to expert status as individuals, both the author and the business benefit equally. Enthusiasm of an author is requisite for a great blog, therefore it's counterproductive to discourage would-be bloggers by expecting them to create content to which they'll have no future rights. Instead, incentivize authors by offering that content they create remains their intellectual property—it will belong to both the firm *and* the author—in other words, it's a nonrival asset. From a policy perspective, what this might look like is:

In the event the author departs the firm, s/he may use the original work and/or edit and republish as desired. Simultaneously, the firm may continue to list or edit the work and reserves the right to change the author to "firm" upon the author's departure.

With the potential blogger pool wide open, a good approach is to announce within the firm (without scaring people) that you'd like to start a blog or two and that you have some topic ideas, but that you understand the most critical success factor is heartfelt interest in blogging so you are seeking to discover who has an interest in writing some posts for a blog that prospects, referral sources, and clients would read. You might be surprised to see who steps forward.

People may require some education as to what blogs are before they are willing to entertain the opportunity to write one. Sometimes the best way to convey this is to show them what you are talking about. There are some compilations of accounting and legal blogs out there. And there are several "types" of blog post formats. Some blogs adhere to one style and others mix it up for variety:

- Very short posts of a sentence or two (context or opinion) and a link to another source
- Short articles of 100–400 words, more like a newspaper or magazine feature—think *USA Today* snippets
- Longer pieces that would break, with a "click to read more" link

For inspiration, you might want to review some existing blogs to get ideas about how you might approach yours. An evolving list of CPA blogs is found at www.accountingbloglist.com. And lists of legal blogs are found on the American Bar Association's *ABAJournal* Website at www.abajournal.com/blawgs/, and another by Ian Best as his third-year law student class project at http://3lepiphany.typepad.com/. Due to the tough, but not impossible, to navigate regulatory requirements, there are very few wealth management blogs—a short list is found on the MoneySmartLife.com site at: http://moneysmartlife.com/financial-advisor-websites-with-blogs/.

To help people determine if they are likely to enjoy or excel at blogging, have them review some of the accounting blogs that are out there, and then consider the questions in Figure 11.7.

Once you have identified your passionate bloggers, or at least passionate subject-matter experts willing to be interviewed regularly by your marketing department or an outsourced writer for postings, let their interests help drive the subject matter of your blog. Even if the resulting topic ideas aren't the ones the firm, as a whole, is most eager to feature, that's okay, because when the passion-inspired blog starts working well for the firm, others are likely to better understand what it takes to succeed and how effective it can be, and may be interested in starting one of their own. One such firm—where a passion-inspired first blog led to the motivation to launch subsequent blogs—is McKonly & Asbury in Pennsylvania. Scott Heintzelman needed no prodding to start his Exuberant Accountant blog, and, a year later, other practice areas were eager to emulate some of the success Scott was having. Read more about this in McKonly & Asbury's case study in Chapter 7.

DEFINE DESIRED READERS   With passionate authors identified, you can begin to think about what you'll blog about, but first, think about exactly who your readers ought to be. If you're going to blog with an end goal of growing your practice, you would want your readers to be people who either make the buying decision for your services or who influence the buyers.

More often than not, a sector-specific blog will be more compelling, therefore more fruitful, for a professional firm targeting business owners,

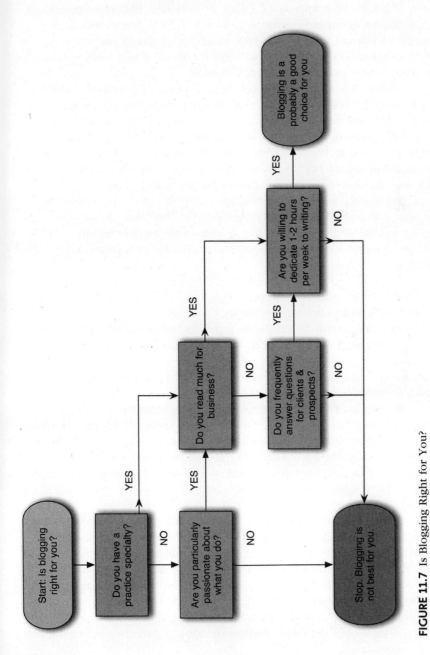

FIGURE 11.7 Is Blogging Right for You?

Source: © 2010 Golden Practices Inc.

than a service-specific blog. In other words, blogs posting once or twice a week about just tax and tax law are probably not going to continue to interest a chief executive officer or even a chief financial officer week after week. Who might it appeal to? Other practitioners like you, most likely. But you aren't writing for yourself. Unless fellow practitioners are your intended audience, it's better to take an approach that is not limited to the topic boundaries of your particular service offering if you wish to hold the continued attention of the readers you seek.

To define your audiences and their respective "personas," start with the Persona Profile Process outlined in Chapter 5. Through the process, you'll create profiles to identify the unique needs and situations of the people you seek to appeal to with your blog's content. The concept here is that you have to know exactly who your audience of buyers and influencers are in order to expand your business, and only after you know who they are can you begin to anticipate what they care about.

I mentioned sector-specific blogs often because they tend to be the most successful for business development. They also provide flexibility for the author and variety for the reader, while supporting the author's industry expertise. Consider these sector-specific accounting blogs, for example:

Dental CPAs: http://dentalcpas.blogspot.com
FarmCPAToday: www.farmcpatoday.com
Driving Successful Dealerships: http://dealership.somersetblogs.com
Reed Tinsley Healthcare Blog: http://rtacpa.blogs.com

These blogs have differing tones and styles, but a common element is each author's ability to discuss *any* topic under the sun that decision makers in the respective industries will care about. This benefits the authors because they don't have to stay within the confines of financial topics. Instead, they can showcase their depth of knowledge on business operations as a whole by talking about any aspect of the readers' world, while all the while remaining on topic. This also makes the blog more interesting for the subscribers (C-suite readers' interests are much broader than matters of finance and law).

Focused on health care-related topics, Reed Tinsley will never bore his physician group readers with off-topic year-end inventory discussions, and Somerset will never burden their auto dealers with Medicare reimbursement best practices. Relevance is essential—especially in our busy, information-flooded culture. Anytime a blog posts something that is not applicable to a subscriber, the authors risk losing future readership.

Seek to be the resource that filters well and provides your desired audience with only the most worthwhile content that they won't want to miss. The preceding blogs effectively position these firms as experts in their respective fields and they become must-read resources for people in the industries for which they are geared.

Service-specific blogs can be effective, too, especially where the service is urgent or need driven and in which highly specialized skills are an obvious advantage to the customer. The most successful blogs in this category also tend to be in areas where good persona definition work takes place. Accounting examples are business valuation services and fraud investigation. Law examples are underfunded public pension litigation and divorce. Note that all of these are situation-based topics.

Steer clear of "general practice" blogs unless it's absolutely the only way you can get your folks to blog. If you take this approach, it's a good idea to have a "category" identifying each audience (e.g., "construction" and "not-for-profit") so that you can categorize each post into only the categories to which it is applicable. It is possible to offer RSS feeds by category, so this is a way to let readers pick only what they want to read. Also, if one practice area seems to have more enthusiastic bloggers than others once you get started, you can always "spin it off" as a blog on its own—the way *Frasier* spun off from *Cheers.*

In the accounting sector, firms are often tempted to create a "tax" blog or a general accounting blog. As indicated on the Accounting Blog List (www.accountingbloglist.com), there are many "tax" blogs and many "general accounting" blogs. Who is more likely to regularly read a blog that covers only tax or accounting methods, a C-suite exec or a fellow practitioner?

In law, practice-specific blogs are the most common. Even if they attract other lawyers as readers more so than prospective clients, it's not as problematic for the success of the blog because of two things: lawyers cross-refer much more than accountants do, and in-house counsel are quite often the legal service buyers they are targeting—lawyers rely heavily on one another for networking through reputation and word-of-mouth, and blogs help them achieve this.

CONSIDER SPECIFIC SUBJECT MATTER   Early on, brainstorm with your blog authors to create a list of posting ideas or even an editorial calendar, if you enjoy that level of structure and especially if your audience and topic has "seasonal" issues you could plan ideal timing of content around.

While calendaring blog posts is a good idea, be sure to remain flexible because inspiration may hit at any time. Flexibility is crucial because posting on emerging issues can attract highly desirable media attention. As to frequency of posting, when starting a new blog, it's best if you can post twice per week. Even weekly or biweekly is acceptable over time, but twice per week in the first year will help get your blog some good activity and traction in its early days.

As you think about what the blog's content might be, there are a few key considerations.

What do your authors know relative to the audience?   The obvious starting point as it pertains to your subject matter is covering what your bloggers know about and "do" in their day-to-day work. When you think about individual posts, think about the most common questions you can discuss and misconceptions you can clear up. With each post, get micro. Don't stay too general. Each blog post should talk about one small aspect of your reader's world or concerns. Answer one question. Clarify one point. Provide one bit of news. Always strive to keep the level high. Remember, it's not good to talk down to your readers.

In addition to what you already know, as a blogger you will be continuously learning and enriching your own knowledge. You will learn as you look around Google, Twitter, or the Web for content ideas. Share-as-you-learn content opportunities are also very strong for younger practitioners: career building associates or newer staff-level people are often tasked with researching and applying concepts and rules. Leverage learned information while reinforcing the content. Steven Covey says[4]:

> . . . you learn best when you teach another because you internalize and conceptualize more fully when you know you will be teaching—that those who teach what they are learning are, by far, the greatest students.

You and your team members can reinforce and improve your learning while creating and sharing credibility-building knowledge with your marketplace. Do watch out for too-simplistic content when doing this, though. Try having the junior person co-author with a more senior person who can add more context or real-life examples.

What's already out there? What's not?   If you didn't do the following items in the persona development phase (Chapter 4), get your authors together to brainstorm lists that answer these questions relative to each of your prospective audiences:

- What does the audience read (online and offline)?
- Where are they already congregating online (other blogs, Web sites, or forums; trade or other associations; local networking groups and LinkedIn groups; etc.)?
- What type of information is already in abundance?

When you find abundant information, you want to refrain from merely repeating it. This won't set you apart. However, you might refer to that information while building on it. You are also looking at what content is already out there in order to determine what information gaps seem to exist that the firm could fill. Capture your ideas about what you are *not* finding enough of. Put yourself in your desired reader's mind and imagine questions you might ask. Through your posts, seek to answer *those*.

As you peruse sites looking at current resources and gathering content ideas, follow links within the content and in blogrolls to find additional resources. Bookmark any resources that look promising or that you'd like to come back to again. Also note the highest-quality (and trafficked, thus influential) blogs you find because you will want to list them in your blogroll as well as refer to them from time to time in your content.

Another audience and topic consideration should be saturation. If there are already dozens (or hundreds) of blogs for an audience with content similar to what you'd be writing about, it is a lot tougher to stand out. But don't get stuck thinking you have to be the lone blog on a topic, either. While it's an opportunity to stand apart as the "first" thought leader on the topic or for that sector, it can also be lonely. When there are a few or more blogs on a topic, the authors, collectively, can cross-reference one another and form a community around that topic. This is healthy and rewarding for all the blogs that participate in that community.

A common misconception by those new to social media is in thinking that your blog will become *the* place where a group will hang out. It's not like that. Consider your blog as one branch of a tree, or one intersection of threads on a spider web. When there are a lot of blogs on a particular subject, that tree or web is gigantic, and when there are few it is small. But your blog isn't the tree trunk nor is it the web's center. When you are part of a community, you are one among many. If you want a lot of people connecting to you (and I suggest that you do), you need to connect to others.

What big "buckets" do your content ideas fall into?   As you work through content ideas in the preceding steps, you'll begin to observe that your topics are either "big buckets" that can be broken up into several specific (micro) post ideas, or that they are micro ideas that can be nicely grouped into bigger buckets. These buckets become possible "categories" within your blog.

When someone visits your blog, they should see the category list in a sidebar near the top of your blog. A blog should have between 10 and 20 categories at most. Skimming the category list should help the viewer gain context of your blog, so they should be well chosen. Good category names create "stickier" users. Bad category names confuse or fail to interest users. Categories are the primary navigation for users who land on your blog.

From a goal perspective, to ensure you can deliver the right level of content relative to the goals you have with your desired readership, do the categories make sense? Is the sophistication level appropriate? Can you fill the categories with at least several rich postings each?

If you take the general or one-blog-for-the-whole-firm approach, you will definitely want categories for various industries (that you could break out later if you discover they can stand alone) as well as topical categories. As you create each post, you will categorize it in the appropriate industry *and* topic. This allows readers to filter content in a reader-centric manner, quickly identifying what postings are most relevant to them. As mentioned above, do be sure to offer RSS feeds by sector if you do this.

Step 2: Blog Name, Theme, and Design

When you've successfully worked through Step 1, you have a strong sense of whom you're writing for and what your blog will be about. The next step is to name your blog and think about possible themes. In naming your blog, there are three components:

1. Actual blog title (short, sweet, and interesting—even a "pun" is good; "FIRM blog" is very, very dull)
2. Blog "subtitle" or descriptive line indicating whom the blog is for and what is to be found upon reading it
3. Blog URL (Web address)

BLOG TITLE AND SUBTITLE   Optimally, the title of the blog should help people understand the nature of the blog, its content, or its audience. In other words, it shouldn't be about *you*, it should be about the *reader*. Names that are plays on words, or otherwise funny or creative, show personality and are generally well received. Descriptive names guide readers, setting their expectations. Boring names don't help break unfortunate "dull" or "too serious" stereotypes of the professions.

Some good title and subtitle examples:

Title	Subtitle
FarmCPAToday	"A blog for farmers & others interested in the ag industry"
Gray Matters	"Resources for public company CFOs and Controllers"
Renewable and Clean Energy Source	"Covering EPA regulations and other compliance driven programs"

Title	Subtitle
Fraud Files	"Daily commentary on fraud, scandals, scams and court cases"
Washington Construction Law	"New developments, resources & commentary of interest to owners, builders & design professionals"
Dick Price's Family Law blog	". . . information about divorce and other family law issues for Tarrant County and Texas . . . emphasis on practical information to get better results and lessen the pain often experienced as people work through the court/legal system"
Protecting Public Pensions	"A blog about public pension under-funding, qualification compliance, and trustee fiduciary duty"

Wherever possible, the subtitle should include the audience (industry and role of the reader) as well as keywords.

BLOG URL   The blog can be housed within your firm's Web site as a subdomain (sample: www.BLOGNAME.FIRM.com) or as a folder (sample: www.FIRM.com/BLOGNAME) or it can reside apart from your Web site on its own URL (e.g., www.farmcpatoday.com).

No matter which way you host the blog, be sure to purchase the URL that matches your blog's name (sample: www.BLOGNAME.com) in order to protect the brand of your blog. You would also redirect this link to where the blog resides if you don't house the blog at the name-specific URL. Also be sure to buy obvious variations of the blog URL (i.e., plural, common misspellings, etc.) just as you would for your firm's regular URL. If the URL that matches your proposed blog name is already taken, you should seriously consider passing up that name as branding confusion could develop.

An example of such branding confusion is *Gray Matters*, created in December 2008 and housed at http://cfo.markbaileyco.com and www.graymattersblog.com. In retrospect, Mark Bailey & Co (MBC) wishes they had purchased the nonplural version to protect it, too, because another CPA firm, created a blog called *Gray Matter* (not plural) housing it at http://graymatterblog.com, a domain purchased in April 2009. Though the firms are not direct competitors, the potential for brand confusion among visitors is high. And, unfortunately for MBC, the other firm could benefit more from this confusion since *Gray Matters* was already a popular blog and the omission of just one letter from the URL, a common mistake, allows the second firm to potentially leverage MBC's branding dollars and time.

Choose your name carefully and protect it as best you can. If another blog exists that is similarly named, whether by someone in your profession or not, do not choose that name, as there can be legal ramifications. A helpful article on this topic by Charles Runyan that contains several steps and resources for due diligence is found at www.keytlaw.com/urls/howtoobtain.htm.

BLOG THEME   While choosing your blog's name, begin visualizing how you might tie the name into a theme for your blog. Blogs typically have a banner that is static at the top of every page. If you have an industry-specific blog, the imagery on the blog should be geared toward your audience, to emphasize the reader, not just the firm's branding. One of my favorite examples of this (Figure 11.8) is the *Washington Construction Law* blog—it visually underscores the purpose of this blog in a way that just showing the firm's logo could never accomplish.

If you have a play on words title or a conceptual title, illustrate it with your theme. For example, *Gray Matters* is geared toward CFOs of public companies, and its content is intended to shed light and perspective on

FIGURE 11.8 Blog Banner Examples

complex regulations that are definitely not black and white. Using good design, the firm made that point visually.

Blog banners are also an excellent place to humanize your blog and reflect your geographic ties. Paul Neiffer, author of FarmCPAToday.com, actually accomplishes four things with his banner: he humanizes himself as a practitioner, he reinforces the blog's audience (farmers), he features local geography recognizable to those in Washington state, and he helps promote the artwork of an area photographer—a friend of the firm—via a link in his blog's footer.

Step 3: Blog Author Preparation

Before or during the blog's design phase, blog authors have some homework:

- Read Chapter 12, "Writing for the Web."
- Read Chapter 13, "Social Media Etiquette."
- Read Chapter 14, "Best Practices."
- Read and study other blogs on similar topics: at least one to two hours per week.
- Post comments on some other blogs and begin to develop online relationships with other blog authors.
- Develop ten "starter" posts (each author).
- Have someone review starter posts.
- Learn blog software (probably after blog design and programming are complete).
- Tighten up LinkedIn profile and set up a Google profile in preparation of increased traffic.

READ BLOGS It is vital that blog authors read some other blogs regularly. This is the fastest way to learn what works and what doesn't. Visit several blogs and keep looking until you find some you like. Look down the left and right sidebars of the blogs you visit to see other blogs in their blogrolls, as they are usually related in subject. This is how you find good blogs. As discussed earlier, add the most applicable ones—those you think your readers would like—to your own blogroll. Be sure to capture them by bookmarking or whatever means you prefer. You can also search for blogs of interest to you using blog-only search tools: http:// blogsearch.google.com and technorati.com among others.

When you read these other blogs, you'll gain a lot of ideas for posts of your own. If you are inspired by what you read, it is perfectly acceptable (and highly encouraged) to use excerpts of other blog posts or articles (with proper citing and linking) and add your thoughts, as well.

This practice is known as "continuing the conversation," which is a big part of the experience of blogging, a part that attracts significant readership.

CREATING INITIAL CONTENT   There are a few reasons behind the recommendation to create a handful of starter posts.

One reason is that you'll want to have at least ten posts live on your blog before you promote it to anyone. This is so that new visitors can have enough items to skim through that they can ascertain the value of your blog and feel compelled to subscribe to it so they don't miss your future posts. Clearly, you need to trigger the "WIIFM" (What's In It For Me) for them to do this. If all you feature at the time of this critical initial visit is a "welcome to our blog" post (don't post one of these, by the way), few will subscribe. The most well-meaning visitors might think, "I'll check back later," but given how busy people are, this is unlikely—make the most of this opportunity to hook them. Having a solid base of posts lets people get a flavor of what you are going to continue to deliver as to quality, depth, and breadth of content.

Another reason to work on these sample posts before launch is that it takes a while for a new author to find his or her voice. It's typical that the first posts will seem more contrived and later posts more relaxed and free flowing. This is a normal part of the acclimation process. Writing several early provides a less pressured environment to help you work out any kinks and begin to find your voice.

It's wise to ask someone seasoned in the art of blogging to review your first posts. They are not doing this as a grammar editor, but to help you in a more strategic way. Are you making good use of your title, headings, and subheadings? Have you linked to all the resources you can, and did you choose good anchor text? Have you properly cited your resources? How is the tone of the post: do you sound like a person and not like a company?

It's best for authors to be conversational in their tone. Whatever you do, don't allow your blog to go through, or appear to have gone through, a PR-department-type sanitization process. Blogs actually lose credibility from that. Readers seek authenticity—the polar opposite of the corporate approach.

TRAINING ON BLOG SOFTWARE   Make sure that all blog authors have a working knowledge of how to accomplish the following tasks (and best practices for each of these) via the blog software they will be using:

- Typing a new post from scratch and all basic text formatting functions (bold, italics, strike through, bullets, numbering, and larger text for headings and subheadings)
- Pasting text from other sources, especially how to deal with nuances pertaining to stripping out other programs' Hypertext Markup Language (HTML) formatting
- Inserting links and using anchor text to most effectively reference the linked location
- Inserting images including sizing, left/right placement, and assigning Alt-tags
- Uploading and referencing documents
- Performing spell-check
- Assigning a post to categories
- Assigning tags (if applicable)
- Back-dating and future-dating posts
- Creating a TrackBack
- Accepting comments and TrackBacks

COMMUNITY PARTICIPATION STARTS HERE Building blog readership is primarily accomplished through participation in online communities that will care about your content. For best results, this should begin before your blog launches and continue through the life of your blog.

Follow the blogs of those who write for the audiences for whom you will write—the ones you identified as worthy of inclusion in your blogroll—and comment on those blogs even before you launch your blog. This way, when you launch, you'll have some established bloggers (who have already seen your name as a legitimate contributor) to mention it to and, after you have a nice little collection of relevant posts, they may be willing to mention your new blog as a new resource to your mutual audience.

Coming to the attention of the authors and readers of established blogs is your goal. Being taken under the wings of authors with strong followings among your desired audiences is publicity you simply cannot buy—but this honor must be earned. To what degree does this help? Ask Paul Neiffer, author of FarmCPAToday.com, who was quickly picked up by Legacy By Design—a well-known and respected resource in the agriculture community.[5] Because Paul reached out to Legacy By Design as he was preparing to blog, they referenced him early and often. This was a big part of his rapid success as a blogger (see his case study in Chapter 7).

Whatever you do, refrain from soliciting blog authors or Web sites to link to you or to "trade links." This is very tacky—you have to earn mentions by being a good content source, whether in your comments on their blogs, or within your own blog posts once it's live.

Step 4: Blog Development and Launch

Most firms will work with a designer or developer to set up their blog. A money-saving tip: before retaining someone, know what you are aiming for with regard to steps 1 and 2 so you can provide clear direction from the start. The developer should be made aware of all the decisions you've made about audience, subject matter, name, and theme. Also be prepared to discuss the number of blogs and blog authors you anticipate having, and be thinking about future scalability with regard to both. Together, you and your developer can choose the most appropriate tool for your needs.

Your developer will most likely create the artwork for the "appearance" of your blog, set up the tool for your unique needs with any pages you want included (legal terms, author pages, about, etc.), plus create, format, and place all the other blog elements discussed in the Anatomy of a Blog Post (Figure 11.3).

LAUNCH PREPARATION　While the developer is under way with programming, you can be strategizing your blog's launch promotion. To market your new blog, you may want to undertake some or all of the following:

- Postcard mailing to all prospects, referral sources, trade groups, and other contacts related to the blog and the firm
- Email promotion—one or two times to all of the above, with periodic subsequent mentions in your firm's email newsletters
- Links in the email signature blocks of all personnel who interact with the blog's desired readers
- Web site links everywhere relevant (every author's bio, every related service page, every article, etc.) and links from all authors' social media profiles (LinkedIn, Facebook, Twitter, etc.)
- Print references everywhere relevant (articles, newsletters, announcements, bios, proposals, sponsorships and speaker "blurbs," etc.)
- News release announcing the new blog, spinning it (if applicable) as an industry-specific resource (send to all industry associations and publications) and deliver to all your typical recipients, peer publications, and place on your firm's Web site

Blog Tips

Once your blog is up and running, there are a few things bloggers should know or do in order to be most effective. These tips are here to help fast-track you to blogging success.

Spotting Blog Comment Spam

Comments should always be moderated before posting. They'll sit in a queue for you to review. Be careful before "approving" because it's easy to fall for blog comment spammers. They are trying to gain clicks and inbound links from your readers. Some are very difficult to spot. Spammers aren't above employing extreme flattery tactics, either.

If you're not sure if a comment is a ploy, check the link they've provided and their email address. The link will usually go to a product page that has nothing to do with what you are writing about. However, sometimes it's that of a competitor or related service provider—for instance, many law firm blogs are being spammed by a company acting on behalf of the once "venerable" Martindale-Hubbell legal directory, as discussed on the New York Personal Injury Law Blog.[6]

Often, the comments are ridiculous. Here are some examples of some spammy comments I've received:

"This is a wonderful opinion. The things mentioned are unanimous and needs to be appreciated by everyone."

"Easily, the post is really the freshest on this noteworthy topic. I concur with your conclusions and will thirstily look forward to your approaching updates. Just saying thanks will not just be adequate, for the extraordinary lucidity in your writing."

And about this brilliant one, I'm not sure what kind of machine made *this* up:

"Quality process—I have positioned the script along my Christmas wish heel and brought it to my web logs situation. Give Thanks you for alarming me to your locating—I don't read every post altogether, I experience, and this great slipped last my microwave radar."

These examples aside, some spam is actually difficult to spot. If in doubt, don't approve the comment—doing so can alert the sender that you are prone to accepting spam and you can find yourself bombarded, very much the same way that alerting an email spammer to the fact that your email address is valid can invite more email spam.

Also, always be far more careful than MartindaleHubble apparently was in the event that your firm hires a company to handle search engine optimization. Be sure that they do not resort to similar unscrupulous tactics to get inbound links for you—it does happen to reputable firms, and it's very embarrassing.

Telltale Signs of an Amateur Blog

To help you avoid embarrassment in a well-established community (blogs have been around for a decade), here are some signs that a blogger doesn't "get" the blogging community or spend much time in it:

- Comments are disabled (in my opinion, this disqualifies it from being a true blog)
- No outbound links in the posts
- No blogroll in the sidebar
- No indication of who the author is or about the author link/page
- Too many or duplicative category names, or no categories set up
- Underlining of text that isn't a link
- Walls of text with no subheadings and paragraph breaks
- Corporate speak
- Lots of approved comments that are obvious spam
- Calling their blog post a "blog" (e.g., "in the blog I wrote yesterday")
- White text on a black background—it's hard to read and hurts the eyes.
- Using Blogger.com but not removing the Blogger logo at the top of the professional firm's blog
- Ending posts with "For more information call or email me" or similar pitch. They won't. That's not how blogs work.

And when I asked my Twitter and Facebook friends to chime in, they contributed these "signs" that a blog is amateur:

- Infrequent updates (Ginger Lewis @Ginger_Lewis, Andrew Rose @NadenLean, and Jason Blumer @JasonMBlumer)
- Internal focus versus external focus (Ed Kless @edkless)
- Relying on memes instead of creating original content (Robin Wheeler @pvoppymom)
- No clear relationship/brand beyond the blog itself (Langston Richardson @matsnl)
- There's no RSS feed (Ginger Lewis @Ginger_Lewis)
- Links are broken links and typos (Susan Gorham @susangorham)
- Consistently poor grammar and spelling (Debra Helwig @dhelwig, who elaborates: "If you can't take the time to proofread, or have someone check you, how can I believe you'll be careful when you do work for ME?")
- Asking to swap links—gotta earn that (Robin Wheeler @poppymom)

Promoting Your Blog

Promoting your blog as part of your business identity should become habit for any blog author. The blog name and URL should be part of your automatic email signature, added to your business card, on the bottom or end slide when you do presentations, and incorporated in all your online bios and profiles.

If you have a blog, simultaneously being on Twitter—and using it in accordance with this guide—can be extremely helpful in building your reader base. See "Repurposing Your Content" in Chapter 12.

Get listed! For instance, lawyers should get listed on ABA's Blawg list, and accountants should contact me to get added to AccountingBlogList. com. There are many other lists and "hubs" for readers who share common interests. As your blog grows to include more content, be thinking about additional strategies to broaden your readership.

Bill Kennedy, a CPA focused largely in technology, has a significant presence in social media that started with his blog. He advised[7]:

To promote my blog I looked for existing communities where potential readers were already going. That's what led me to approach AccountingWEB. Since I work with Microsoft products, I approached them as well. Microsoft added my blog to their user community site. It is also fed automatically to my Facebook and Twitter pages as well as to the LinkedIn Group I started (which has grown to 4,000 members). I don't say this to boast. There are a bunch of other things I tried that did not work for me. The point is that you can't just rely on your writing. You have to be constantly promoting your work if you want it to be read. One other thing I try to do is read other people's blogs, for both content and ideas. I also leave comments, partly to encourage others to leave comments on my blog.

Bill's last point is essential. To really be successful, you cannot ignore others. Keep reading other blogs and commenting on them. Be sure to view your blog visitor stats to identify which sites are referring them and follow those sites. Thank the people (via a comment) who mention or link to you or your blog in their posts. Also use WebsiteGrader.com and similar tools to target high-influence sites (those with "authority") in your niche areas on which you can comment to become known to more of the right ki nds of readers.

The content in your blog can also be very strategic. Much the way leaving comments on other blogs helps you, so does linking liberally within your posts to other resources and writings. This is called "link love" and you want to give lots. The authors of the sites you link to can see that click-throughs come from your blog (as the referring site) and they are likely to visit to check out what you said about them. These people are potential new followers and promoters.

It's not just about bloggers, though. Lacing your content with the names of people and companies whose attention you want to get, as pointed out in *Socialnomics*, is a tried-and-true approach, "Local newspapers have used this principal (sic) for years. The content of the story wasn't half as important as ensuring that it was crammed with local names."[8] I don't endorse the concept of content not being as important as naming others, though. Perhaps they got away with that in a small town where the available papers were few, but online, you are literally competing with everyone and mediocre content will not do if you have high aspirations.

Summary of Part III

These four tools are very different from one another, each with strengths depending on how you plan to use them and what your needs are (refer to the comparison chart in Chapter 3). Now that you have much more detailed understanding of the tools, it should be clearer which is the best, most appropriate starting point for you. Long-term, blogging is ideal, but with blogging comes the greatest time commitment. If I had to hedge my bets, I'd say that blogs and LinkedIn will outlive Twitter and Facebook, but nothing is certain.

If you're still not sure, my recommendation is that LinkedIn is the best starting point for most professionals.

PART IV

TIPS
Tips to Being Effective Online

CHAPTER 12

Writing for the Web

This chapter is geared for blog writing, but the concepts apply to any online text, including Web sites and e-books.

Online writing is much different than writing for print. For starters, people don't read vast amounts of on-screen text word for word. Instead, online readers scan text. This is why, although the Web offers limitless "space" for content, brevity is essential. Visual aids like headings, subheadings, bolded text, bullet points, and links are especially effective at helping readers find what they'll consider to be the most important parts of your content.

Good, credible Web content generously links to additional information. Remember early Web sites that tried to keep visitors captive disabling the "back" button, limiting the number of outside links, and forcing any links to open in a "new window"? Trapping people to keep them on a Web site was old-school thinking and, actually, kind of shameful. We should have acknowledged then what we admit now—that without great content, we have no right to expect people to linger or return. Interesting content and useful outbound links enrich the readers' experience leading to return visits, subscribers, and organic promotion through sharing links with friends. Thus begins the social Web. Good content is at the core.

As discussed in Chapter 1, positioning yourself and your firm as hire- and referral-worthy is achieved best through substantiating your claims of expertise—demonstrating knowledge, capabilities, and thought leadership with evidence. Generously share ideas, tips, and opinions in articles, e-books, or white papers; illustrate approaches to solving problems through (sanitized) case studies; and name and link to organizations or publications to which you or the firm have contributed to the advancement of ideas or practices.

At the same time, be cognizant of appearing too self-centered or firm-centric in the presentation. Make your content centered on the reader. You'll gain the recognition you seek by being the source of the information without having to remind readers continuously that you are the source.

Most importantly, know the reader well so your content is right on target. In the words of David Meerman Scott[1]:

> *Truly understanding the market problems that your . . . services solve for your buyer personas, you transform your marketing from mere product-specific, ego-centric gobbledygook that only you understand and care about into valuable information people are eager to consume and that they use to make the choice to do business with your organization. Instead of creating jargon-filled, hype-based advertising, you can create the kind of online content that your buyers naturally gravitate to—if you take the time to listen to them . . . [t]hen you'll be able to use their words, not your own.*

- The added benefit of today's Web is that conveying personality in your writing is appropriate online. As a practicing professional with many competent competitors and a buyer who struggles to distinguish one practitioner from another, your demeanor and who you are as a person are what truly set you apart. Chemistry matters.

Now people can get a flavor of it before they meet you. I know it sounds questionable to someone unfamiliar with blogs, but remember what Scott Heintzelman said in his (Chapter 7) case study: "I had never met this gentleman prior to our meeting, but his quote to me at breakfast was that he felt like he knew me and what I stood for because of the blog." I've heard this numerous times myself in the five years that I've been blogging.

Before you create your content, remember this: social media (with the exception of LinkedIn) weren't created for marketing, they were developed for communicating—and *that* is precisely why they are so effective for marketing.

- Communication = stronger relationships = more business.

Don't be tempted to write in the older, fluff-laden way. Adding old-style "marketing" noise and behaviors into these new communications *undermines* the whole purpose and negates the benefits of using social media.

Common Blog Posting Formats

There are lots of ways to blog, but there are four styles of posts that most bloggers use:

1. **Original content:** Long or short articles, opinions and commentary, or stream of consciousness
2. **Outside content with your brief commentary:** Short introductions (one or two sentences) follow by referencing an external source Web page or blog post (via excerpt and link)
3. **All nonoriginal content:** More of a news aggregator with quick references of current or breaking news or items of interest to your sector (headline with or without lead sentence or two and link)
4. **Nonwritten content:** Multimedia

Some blogs feature a mix of these posting types and others maintain a single format. Either is fine. If you have a multiauthor blog, your authors will likely have different writing styles, tones, and post types. One author may be analytical, another may be more philosophical, and another might project humor. When tones vary, it creates variety your readers will enjoy. Humanizing yourself and your firm is a core purpose of blogging and social media participation, so a blend of styles will support the goal beautifully.

Many authors enjoy introducing multimedia into their blogs. Current technology makes it very easy and inexpensive to create audio (podcast) or video (videocast) content instead of or in addition to written blog posts. If you're a person who'd rather talk about a subject than write about it, these could be great alternatives for you.

Resonating with Readers

When you start exploring social media, you might suddenly realize that you can communicate with *everyone*. But that doesn't mean everyone will care about what you have to say. How can you get them to care? You need to write what *they* care about—hopefully that correlates with what *you* care about. First and foremost, decide for whom you are writing (see Chapter 5). Only then are you poised to attract and hold the attention of specific desired readers.

Subject decided, the depth, originality, and usefulness of your content will determine the loyalty of your readership. In blogs and other forms of content (e.g., proposals, Web site, brochures), to write in ways that will keep readers' attention, focus on producing content that will inform in ways other people do not and resonate with them at an emotional level as it pertains to business (usually) such as getting to the heart of "what keeps you up at night?" without, of course, using that cliché phrase.

Most professionals sell problem resolution or problem prevention, or both. When you present what you do, resist the urge to simply *list* your services without further information. People need more than the list, they need context and answers: why do the problems occur, are they common or rare, what are the implications if they go unfixed? To encourage buying, ultimately seek to provide reassurance that you can ascertain what is wrong and are qualified to resolve it.

Another purpose behind providing the contextual information is to aid people in finding you via search. The average person probably won't search for the labels you've chosen for your services, especially if the labels are technical or obscure. Highly findable content contains discussion of the situations that trigger the need for the services, provides ideas about how to diagnose or verify the problem, and perhaps offers initial suggestions or steps to remedy the problem. If you've done the persona work discussed in Chapter 5, you have begun to identify the situational triggers that influence buyers. Buyers don't necessarily have the knowledge, insight, or context to bridge from their current view of their situation to your offered solutions. You may need to help them bridge.

Great content will contain a mix of five aspects of a situation (Figure 12.1), focusing mostly on describing problems and symptoms. As a starting point, to develop good content, think through and address the five aspects of several situations you can identify for each persona.

To explain the five aspects—from root cause to problem, symptom, solution, and prevention—imagine you're walking through your dark living room barefoot in the wee hours and your foot painfully greets a heavy object—expressing your discomfort, you hobble to bed. When you awaken, your toe is swollen and badly bruised. You think it might be broken and aren't sure if you need medical treatment. You turn to the Internet.

We humans don't all use search engines the same way. Some would search "swollen bruised toe" (symptoms). Others might search "is my toe

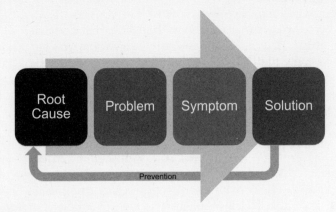

FIGURE 12.1 Five Aspects of a Situation

Source: © 2010 Golden Practices Inc.

broken?" (possible problem), and still others may search "symptoms and treatment for a broken toe" (symptom list for possible problem). However, few will search "splint," "bandage," or "ibuprofen" (solutions) to find the detailed information and validation that they need. Nor are people likely to search "kicked the coffee table in the dark" (root cause) or "turn on a light" (prevention).

Professional firms typically focus on presenting their solutions with little or no discussion of symptoms, the problems generating the symptoms, and the root causes behind the problems. Venturing down the extremely valuable path of those middle areas—symptoms and problems—are what blogs usually accomplish very well, rather organically. The sort of content that goes into detail reassures people that you know what you're talking about, and can begin to create a sense of confidence in the reader that, because you "get" them, you could also be the one who knows how to help them.

It's perfectly all right if what you discuss is complex because, though people like to self-diagnose, we don't always know what we need, even as we're staring at that shelf of solutions (prescriptions). When problems are big, we rely on experts to diagnose the problem, identify the root cause, and prescribe treatment. It's human nature that we almost always think our problems are bigger than they are. But you know your specific audience, so you need to judge the appropriate level of complexity. Just don't confuse my statement that "it's okay to discuss complex problems" with a recommendation to be extremely technical unless, of course, your audience is your peer group. I'm referring to *situational* complexity, not technical know-how.

Going back to the medical example, when a medical site tells you that your symptoms could be evidence of several potential problems, and that the root cause of the problems could be complex—and how—this is done in layperson terms. Technical names for things are certainly given (with links to more information), but the sites don't go into detailed medical descriptions and terminology (as found in medical journals) that would be equivalent to your legalese, tax section code references, or generally accepted accounting principles (GAAP) requirements. The goal is for you, the professional, to make a complicated situation more understandable to other smart people who don't share your specialty. This doesn't require dumbing down the information; it requires looking at it from an outside perspective.

If you're thorough in identifying your audience when you strategize your blog's purpose, you can actually picture a person you know in the role of your audience member and write just for him. How would you describe it in conversation over lunch? Writing with one reader in mind helps with this process, as does picturing your audience as peers, as if you're literally conversing with a friend.

As you write for a blog, don't get bogged down by thinking you are writing to the world. You're not. You are writing for an individual reader. Every single time.

Writing Quality Blog Content

If you're targeting business clientele and trying to set yourself apart as a thought leader, aim your content to the highest level of your intended audience. Often, these are business owners, executives, or upper-management persons so posting factual updates on new legislation usually won't cut it.

Business leaders want to read original thought or well-summarized facts that matter to them. If your audience may not know something matters to them, yet you are *sure* that it does, it is your job to make sure they can tell quickly from the title (think effective newspaper headline) that it does. And it's a wise idea, in the first sentence or two, to tell them exactly why it matters.

Sometimes when we think of "quality" of content, we think "error free." However, almost perfect is okay in blogs. Carefully check spelling and grammar before posting because, even though it's "easy" to edit a blog post, after a post is live, "resaving" resends the blog post to RSS subscribers. It's this author courtesy that explains why you find more minor errors or typos on blogs than other types of Web pages—you should correct errors only if they are major. It's understood that blog posts will contain the occasional error, but if this will make you crazy, just be extra careful and a little more comfortable with "almost perfect." It's actually a bit liberating!

TIP: Writing Stronger Blog Posts

- Great titles inspire people to read. People seem especially attracted to lists (e.g., "Top 5 things to know about . . ."), questions (e.g., "Wondering how to avoid . . . ?") and "how-to" phrases.
- Write in the present tense.
- Include links to promote other people and provide readers with the option of further information.
- Include relevant graphics, photos, or illustrations. It helps guide readers through text and adds personality to your posts (think of how *USA Today* does this).
- Limit yourself to one point per post. It's okay to relate two things together (making one point). If you want to go much deeper, it's probably a second post.

Continued

- Try not to use the word *client(s)* when you refer to people you serve. It sounds impersonal and, worse, it distinguishes your current reader (prospect) from your past buyer, which is counter to your intent. When referring to a scenario where you've helped someone, allow the reader to see herself as the beneficiary in the same situation.
- Say "you" when referring to the reader—not something impersonal like "readers" or "clients". It's more engaging and makes the reader feel like you wrote for them.
- Don't invite comments or feedback in the body of every post—at least not at the beginning. It takes time to earn participatory readership—no need to draw attention to the early "quietness" by asking questions that may go eternally unanswered.

Be Smart and Opinionated

When I read accounting and legal blogs, I see many that write for a reader that is less savvy than most business owners and high-level executives or managers. I see far too many watered-down posts with 101-type content. This could be a result of the firm trying to keep things generic, or it could be due to underestimating the reader's ability to understand. If the content doesn't help the reader, it doesn't help you. Ardath Albee counsels, "The traditional approach of one-size-fits-all content is the basis of ineffective nurturing."[2]

Don't be tempted to write your content geared to a novice level or it can seem condescending or out of touch with the needs of the highest-level people you are targeting—the final decision makers. Either way, they won't continue to read you. When thinking of posting basic information, ask yourself (or search to confirm) if you are likely to find similar content elsewhere on the Web. If so, don't bother with it unless you have editorial value to add to the conversation.

Aim to illustrate your intellectual depth. This is requisite if you seek to be perceived as a thought leader. If your content ends up over your readers' heads, readers won't think *less* of you, they'll think *more* of you. This is far safer than dumbing down the content so much that it's insulting or—just as bad—dull.

To help circumvent dullness, don't be afraid to be opinionated. Being opinionated doesn't mean being obnoxious or offensive. Being willing to take a position on some things allows people to see who you are. Somebody who never takes a stance can seem wishy-washy. We've all heard about the frustrated client who complains that their advisor lists all the options but is hard-pressed to tell the client what he or she would do in the client's shoes—even when the client begs their opinion. People don't want a reluctant advisor, so try to convey that you are someone who can see the big picture, identify options, and aren't hesitant to make specific recommendations.

Aspire to *move* people. Give them something to applaud. Stand out! Don't dumb it down. And then watch for readership trends to help you gauge how you're doing (much more in "Monitoring Content Effectiveness" in Chapter 6). Are people subscribing? Is anyone commenting? Are people cross-referencing or sharing your posts on Twitter or bookmarking sites? If so, you are hitting the mark with quality content.

Posts that Teach

When it comes to teaching, professionals confide they are worried that they'll educate people so much that they'll tackle their own challenges. Or they fear they will educate competitors about their unique strategies or ideas. Unless your processes are completely groundbreaking, it's likely your competitors already do what you do or could figure it out fairly easily. If your processes are particularly unique, it's not necessary to convey detailed processes and strategies to accomplish most content goals that I've seen.

If you're concerned that readers will become do-it-yourselfers with your shared insights, don't give it too much thought. First, all of the knowledge you possess certainly can't be conveyed in your blog. Second, FTI or "failure to implement" is a condition almost all business owners suffer from. In most cases, you could give step-by-step instructions and people will still need help to implement.

Storytelling is a brilliant way to illustrate your expertise as you share real-life examples of issues and how they might be handled. People love stories, and stories are memorable, so you will be memorable. Recall what blogger Paul Neiffer said in his case study: "My main piece of advice to others is to be a storyteller. I think back on who my best teachers were in school and they were always the storytellers—they just made you want to hear more."

In sharing samplings of your experiences and advice, you allow readers some insight into the complexity of your practice. This builds trust and confidence. Do everything you can to position yourself as a resource for information they can't get elsewhere so they'll continue to read you.

Content Clarity

Whatever it is that you're writing—your blog; a tweet; an article; a book; a newsletter; Web content; or even a good, old-fashioned letter, memo, or email—you want the reader to easily follow what you are saying. To accomplish this, your communication needs to be clear and concise.

One of my favorite bloggers, Dianna Huff, has a terrific blog post called "Pruning Deadwood from Your Copy" that offers up this tip[3]:

> *Hunt down redundancies. When I write fast and without effort, I find my copy is full of useless words that I use over and over and ideas that I communicate two or three or four times (just like this sentence, ha!). Here is how I can edit this sentence: When writing fast and without effort, my copy becomes bloated with useless words and repeated ideas.*

Try to step away from your work and come back to it a short time later to see it with fresh eyes. Dianna also recommends looking at it in print to spot extraneous text.

A few formatting tips for clarity and ease of reading are:

- Be concise. Less is more.
- Keep sentence structure simple and short. Break up your text. A lot.
- Use well-chosen headings and subheadings so readers can quickly skim your content, and for search optimization.
- Keep paragraphs to between one and three sentences, maximum, for easier skimming—never more than a four- or five-line block of text in your blog's display. This makes it much easier to read and is less imposing than a giant "wall" of text.

Fluff Removal

There is no place for fluff on the Web. Fluff is different from redundancy; it is the opposite of substance—it is the useless filler and corporate-speak that often plagues business content. To spot fluff, look first for the gobble-dygook (discussed in Chapter 1). It's the stuff that might sound smart at first until you look closer and realize it says nothing at all. It's often the stuff that "everyone else" says. Fluff gives the impression your content was run through the corporate PR department—the antithesis of authenticity because it's all about "spin" and nobody wants to be spun "to."

Conduct a fluff removal exercise of your content by striking every word that isn't essential and words that sound ridiculous or odd if spoken aloud. Stick to using words that humans actually speak (such as "use" instead of "utilize") in regular conversations. Ban phrases like leading-edge, turnkey, world-class, or enterprise-wide solutions that you expect to see in a press release or hear uttered in a sales pitch. Today, online and off, people want useful information that doesn't waste their time—unless, of course, it provides brief amusement.

Content Idea Starters

Great blog fodder is everywhere. Reading is essential for blog authors and a key reason is to find continuous inspiration. A common trait among the most successful bloggers is that they are heavy readers. My accounting industry colleague Jessica Levin recommends, "Read more than you write and read outside of your industry." I agree wholeheartedly. Bring information from many sources to your readers, and bridge the connection by telling the reader why it's relevant to him or her.

Even if you're not a heavy reader, there are many ways to find good things to write about in a blog. Three great ways to find original content are to go back through your outbound emails, search online, or feature guest authors.

One note of caution: Reusing content that was written for non-Web audiences such as print newsletters doesn't always work. This type of content probably has an impersonal tone that will seem out of place on a blog. Either edit it to make it more personal and casual, or link to it as a supporting document (paste in some excerpts if you like) and be sure to explain why your audience would want to read it.

Previously Sent Email

Just think about how many questions you've already answered for people. Comb through "sent items" in your email to find advice you've given or answers you've provided to the questions of clients, prospects, and your coworkers. You can sanitize these emails by stripping out any client identifiers. Then add a sentence or two framing the context of the advice and voila! You have an instant blog post that exactly aligns with an objective of answering "one question at a time" in your blog postings.

When giving context, it's best to be as specific about the situation as you can be: "When a 45-employee manufacturer faced layoffs from the economic downturn, three concerns arose. . . ." or "A government concrete contractor who leases most of his equipment asked . . ." This helps readers (your personas) relate themselves to the situation and better understand how what you're talking about can be applicable to them.

Searching Online

Material related to your topics can most certainly be located through Twitter and Google search on an ongoing basis. To minimize search time in the future, once you run a single search that generates the kind of search results you're seeking, you can "subscribe" to that search so new matching results will automatically be delivered to you.

If you need a tool to read subscriptions, I recommend Google Reader (free) to view these search results daily or a couple of times per week. To capture Web-searched terms, set up "Google Alerts"—one for each search term—and designate each alert to be delivered to Google Reader where, if you like, you can create separate folders to categorize these feeds.

Within Twitter, you can search for any term or hashtag, and when you do so, each Twitter search generates a unique search feed. You can find this designated as an RSS icon at the lower right-hand side of the page after searching (see Figure 12.2).

Right click on the RSS icon and copy the feed URL so you can go to Google Reader, click "Add a Subscription" (see Figure 12.3), and paste the Twitter search feed URL into the box.

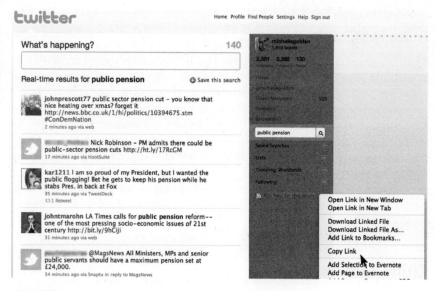

FIGURE 12.2 Grabbing a Twitter Search Feed

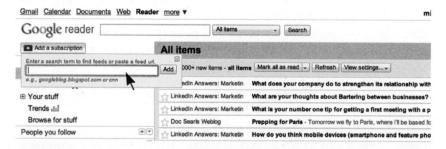

FIGURE 12.3 Subscribing to Feeds Using Google Reader

That's all there is to it. You'll now receive any search results as they occur. You can delete any of these searches at any time. Searches you might wish to subscribe to are:

- Search for articles/news in your topic areas using various keywords and phrases (experiment and adjust them to refine your results for greatest relevance).
- Subscribe to all persona-related industry or topic blogs (in Google Reader).
- Search your top keywords on YouTube, Slideshare, and Social Mention to see what shows up in the search results. You may discover great new resources.

Featuring Guests

Seek out guest authors to mix things up, help establish your credibility as a well-connected person, and to simultaneously promote someone else. Look for people who are experts in the field you write about.

Don't overlook the opportunity to feature clients, prospects, and referral sources. Scott Heintzelman, the Exuberant Accountant, does this—he invites them to write or he interviews them, giving them an opportunity to discuss the neat things they are doing. They love this and appreciate Scott for the visibility.

Experts who don't have their own blog yet, or who are new to blogging and are seeking to build an audience, might be particularly willing to do this.

Citing Others

Whenever you reference another person's work, name the person, name the site or publication, and link to both. Point the text of the name to the persons' "about," "author," or "bio" page. Point the text of the company name to the company's home page, and point the text containing the title of their article or blog post directly to the URL (aka Permalink if it's a blog) you are referencing. Most of the time, it is acceptable to include excerpts of the person's work. You are doing them a favor by pointing your readers to them and their site; they won't mind as long as you give them full credit for their work.

Including an *entire* post within yours is not usually okay unless the post is extremely short. If you do this, you should still encourage your readers to visit the source's site. It's worth noting that people whom you cite often reciprocate if your content is relevant to their readers, too.

Creative Commons (CC) is a nonprofit organization (creativecommons. org) that provides easy-to-use legal tools that work alongside copyright laws to designate permissions for the use of Web and creative content. Using CC, the average person can designate "some rights reserved" (and exactly which ones) instead of the default "all rights reserved." Being generous with content sharing is part of the social Web, where you *want* to invite people to spread your content—with proper attribution, of course.

Many major media use CC, as does the White House and Public Library of Science—basically, people and companies interested in sharing and collaborating use CC licenses.

CC license types or "conditions" include Share Alike (sa), Attribution (by), Noncommercial (nc), and No Derivative Works (nd)—you can learn more about them at http://creativecommons.org/about/licenses/. License terms are often combined (e.g., cc-by-sa) so you may specify exactly how people can use or refer to your work. Understand what the terms mean so that you know how to refer to the work of others if you want to cite them, use their images on your blog, and so forth.

Creating E-books

A great idea for drawing readers and underscoring your expertise in an area is creating an e-book. E-books are PDF or digital magazine files created in landscape format for easier online reading. They can be freestanding books or parts in a series. E-books are highly sharable and they are perfect for professionals to use to share what they know in a helpful way.

E-books are a good alternative to the stale "white paper." White papers are more technical and formal, while e-books are more pleasant to read. While an e-book might be the same length as a white paper, it is designed with more white space, fewer words per page, and more graphical interest—pictures, charts, and bullets. Because they appear much lighter in text than a white paper, they are more visually inviting to read. David Meerman Scott calls the e-books the "stylish younger sister to the nerdy white paper."[5]

Design matters, so have a professional handle the layout or create a template you can place text into, following the designer's guidelines.

- About 5,000 words
- About 25 pages (20 minimum to 50 maximum)
- Roughly 200 words per page

The content of an e-book should be optimized for Web search. It should also have a dynamic table of contents so people can navigate easily within the book. For e-book samples, visit www.changethis.com.

In his e-book *The New Rules of Viral Marketing: How Word-of-Mouse Spreads Your Ideas for Free* (download at www.davidmeermanscott.com/ documents/Viral_Marketing.pdf), David Meerman Scott provides several useful tips such as:

- Don't charge for e-books or lock them up behind a registration-required wall. This reduces sharing.
- Put a Creative Commons license on the content so people know they can freely share the work.
- Create a custom landing page from which people download the book.
- Promote it "like crazy," including having links everywhere and alert others (bloggers, analysts, media, and I'll add industry associations) about the resources, but don't email them the PDF (unless they directly ask); instead, send them the link (so you can track downloads).

David cautions that there are no guarantees that your e-book or other marketing will, in fact, go "viral." But he offers several tips to increase your odds.

Creating Podcasts and Videocasts

Podcasts and videocasts are other excellent ways to bring your humanness to the Web. Hearing and seeing someone is entirely different than reading words on a page. These are excellent vehicles for professionals to use, though it's normal to require practice to feel comfortable on microphone or on camera. If you think you might be interested, practice several times to become more comfortable before you decide to ditch the idea. Few people feel good about their 'casts right away.

Productions are generally best when they are no more than three to five minutes in length. Three to four minutes is a actually a pretty long time to hold someone's attention—five to seven minutes can feel like an eternity for a listener or a viewer. However, some "casters" are very successful with longer segments. Start small and you can build in length if your audience supports it.

Make just one major point per podcast or videocast. If they are short and well done, people may click on a second or third one. Look at click trends to see if you are succeeding at hitting the right length. If you have a few and people (aside from team members or your family) don't click on a second one after viewing the first, it is an indicator that the delivery needs improvement or the message wasn't worthwhile. Heed these signs.

Both podcasts and video files are easily embedded in your blog site as well as referenced in your regular Web site. If you prepare your files correctly, you can use the searching and storing advantages of YouTube and iTunes by housing your content there and offering your media files by RSS feed. Both sites have the ability to let subscribers know when you've added new content, and iTunes subscribers will have your content automatically downloaded for them in the event you choose to do a "regular" program.

There's not much stopping you from producing your own podcast or videocast. And the necessary equipment is inexpensive. The chief concerns are sound, lighting, and content:

- **Sound quality:** Must be good—free of fades, "brushing" Ps and Bs, nose breathing (often found with headset mics), background noise, or other such annoyances. Also, practice introducing some inflection in your voice so it's not monotone or boring—ask someone who will be very honest with you if you sound dull and/or unnatural. If so, keep practicing.
- **Lighting:** Must be good—especially for financial professionals and lawyers. "Shady" is not something you want to be, nor is looking like you're under bright interrogation lights. Medium, warm lighting or daylight is best.
- **Content or Script:** Your message should sound conversational, not "read aloud." Prepare a script and practice it, but when you deliver, go from memory. A one-page reference with a couple of key points will be okay, but don't have any paper-shuffling sounds in the background.

If you're interested in producing podcasts, a great read is a *How to Do Everything with Podcasting* by Shel Holtz and Neville Hobson (McGraw-Hill, 2007). Or for a resource on both video- and podcasting, try *Podcast Solutions: The Complete Guide to Audio and Video Podcasting* by Michael Geoghegan and Dan Klass (Berkeley, CA: Apress).

From a strategic standpoint, approach podcast or videocast content much the way you plan blog content. Know your intended audience and discuss what they will care about. With audio and video, however, you'll find you have a heightened level of interaction over written blogs. This means it's likely you'll have more interaction with your viewers and listeners. Enjoy the opportunity to involve listeners: ask questions and seek out their input. Let them contribute to and guide the direction of future content. Recognize them, like you do in a blog, by naming them. Also feature guests to offer a broader variety of faces or voices. Promote upcoming shows and take "real-time" questions through Twitter or email.

If you try podcasts and videocasts and decide you enjoy it, invest in creating a themed musical intro as well as branded visuals if you're doing video.

Writing for Search Engines

Studies show that most search engine users don't look past the first page of returned search results, and rarely go deeper than the third page. With 10 results per page, there is a lot of competition for the first 10 spots, and less for the next 20.

Search engine optimization (SEO) is the act of improving the position of a site when searches for certain words are performed in order to increase the volume and quality of Web site traffic. SEO efforts generally involve a site's content and coding.

The perfect SEO recipe is kept secret. Webmasters aspire to understand major search engines' ranking methodologies, but search engine developers don't release the details of their algorithms because they don't want programmers to be able to game the system. For instance, there are over 200 factors in Google's ranking algorithms, they share only loose guidelines as to what will increase or decrease rankings, and they change back-end details often.[6]

What remains consistent is that search engines seek to ensure that users find the Web sites with the most useful content, so the typical model for algorithms gives heavy preference to sites that appear to contain a great deal of content about the searched topic. The best organic (unpaid) SEO strategy is rich, focused, authentic content. Search engines are designed to detect quality content; if you make sure to have that, you have optimized your blog or Web site for search.

What Keywords Should I Use?

Keywords are the terms or phrases that people enter into search engines to find information they seek. In performing the exercise described earlier in this chapter in the "Resonating with Readers" section, you will have identified many pertinent keywords to start weaving into your content in order to attract your targeted personas to your blog. Search engines place heavy emphasis on the text of a Web page, with varying priorities for different "types" of text.

Where possible, use your identified keywords in the most advantageous places: links, titles, and subtitles—the same strategies that make it easier for a reader to skim your content (good headings and subheadings) also positively affect search engine rankings. This is not by accident.

Determining additional keywords requires observation. You'll learn more from viewing your own traffic sources than from anything you could read here about "best terms" to use. In your monitoring efforts described in Chapter 6, you'll see that when it comes to searches, people seldom search for the terms you think they might. People often use layperson terms or terms that are sometimes not politically correct (e.g., *nursing home* versus *long-term care facility*)—be willing to use both. Avoid fancy and technical terms when simple ones will do because that's how people actually talk, thus it's how they search. Learning from visitor trends over time helps you discover ways to adjust your writing to draw more of the visitors you want.

If you have a series of terms you know you want to appear high within search results, develop a blog content strategy around those words. To aid you in appearing in the results for a certain phrase, write a few different posts on the subject. Search engines are apt to see that your blog focuses on that topic. Note that if key phrases you choose are especially common (e.g., construction + Chicago), good rankings will be much harder to achieve than if the key phrases are more distinctive (e.g., "job costing methods" or "construction site liability Illinois").

TIP: Preparing Keywords

Keywords are the terms or phrases used to find information online. Here are some tips for perfecting your use of keywords in your writing:

- Put yourself in the shoes of your audience. Ask yourself, "What would *they* call it?"
- Refer to your audience's industry "buzzwords." Using technical words and nontechnical words are two different strategies—try both. For example, Reed Tinsley talks about "National Provider Identifier (NPI) of the performing physician in Item 32 of the CMS-1500 claim form" and "Medicare Claims Processing Manual to implement changes to 42 CFR section 414.50." These are terms that physician groups (his audience) absolutely search.
- Ask clients what topics they search online.
- Increase your chances of a higher ranking in the results pages by focusing on three- and four-word phrases (versus one or two words). For example, Reed Tinsley appearing on page one search results for "Medicare" is unlikely due to extremely high competition,

Continued

but achieving page one results with his longer terms is more feasible.

- Consider how a variation of a word or words within words will be "seen" by search bots (e.g., *sit* is within *sitting,* but *sat* is not within *seated*).
- Mention geographic locations (e.g., Arlington, Highway 40).
- Mention competitors (always in a favorable light) and industry experts. You can get some search engine mileage out of people who are looking for them.
- See how people tag you and your content in social media book-marking sites as well as in Twitter lists. These might be good new keywords for you.

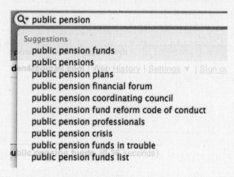

FIGURE 12.4 Note Google Search Prompts

An extremely easy way to find ideas of similar search terms is through prompts that search engines give users. When you use Google to search a topic, as you enter your desired search term, prompts will appear (see Figure 12.4) to help you "finish the term." These are valuable because they are provided based on words others most often search—terms whose popularity becomes self-perpetuating because others may click on the prompt rather than typing more.

Also, search results pages can include references at the bottom of the page to "related searches" (see Figure 12.5). These are also helpful in guiding you toward most-used terms.

There are some online resources (see feature box Keyword Identification Tools) you can use to test search volume and similar terms for phrases you suspect might be good. The "suggested" phrases can be enlightening. You may find that a small tweak such as replacing a single word in the phrase you were considering can exponentially increase your traffic.

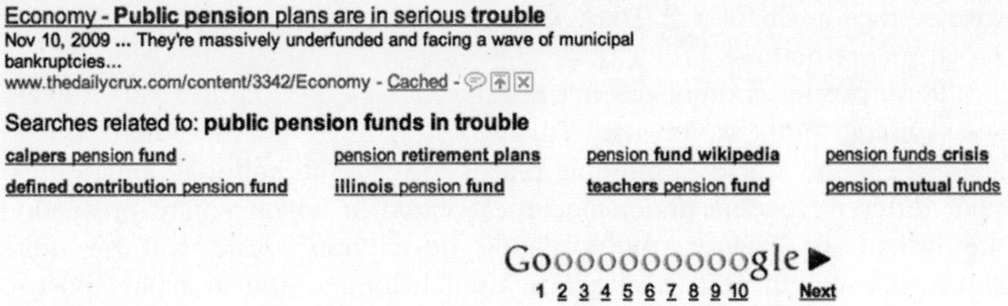

<u>Economy</u> - **Public pension** plans are in serious **trouble**
Nov 10, 2009 ... They're massively underfunded and facing a wave of municipal
bankruptcies...
www.thedailycrux.com/content/3342/Economy - <u>Cached</u> - ⌖ ⊞ ⊠

Searches related to: **public pension funds in trouble**

calpers pension **fund**	**pension retirement plans**	pension **fund wikipedia**	pension **funds crisis**
defined contribution pension **fund**	**illinois** pension **fund**	**teachers** pension **fund**	pension **mutual** funds

Goooooooooogle ▶
1 2 3 4 5 6 7 8 9 10 **Next**

FIGURE 12.5 Refer to Google's Related Search Terms at the Bottom

---

Keyword Identification Tools

Use these tools to test search volume for keywords you're thinking of using:

Wordtracker Keyword Tool: http://freekeywords.wordtracker.com
Google Tools: www.google.com/trends and https://adwords
.google.com/select/KeywordToolExternal
Hoskinson.net's Keyword Analysis Tool: http://
seokeywordanalysis.com/seotools/
Overture Keyword Selector Tool: www.vretoolbar.com/keywords/

This leads to the idea that there can be many ways to refer to the same thing. How do you know which way is the best way? The answer is usually use them both or all.

Sometimes terms change in order to dodge some societal connotation baggage. An example is the shift from the term *nursing home* to more politically correct terms. The problem is that search statistics show that nonindustry people still search far more for *nursing homes* than the other terms. The wise strategy is to use them all. Include *long-term care facilities* in one place, *retirement homes* in another, and *assisted living communities* elsewhere. Before ditching a non-PC term, consider the advantages of creatively weaving it in, such as ". . . long-term care facilities (aka nursing homes). . . ."

Repurposing Your Content

It's always smart to leverage your work to the degree that you can. You saw several examples of maximizing exposure in the integrated marketing case studies in Chapter 7. There is no reason to reinvent content for every social media outpost.

Repurposing content doesn't usually mean exact duplication in every social media outpost you use. This is not a best practice. When you do share the same article in multiple places, provide an editorial comment so your different readers understand the context in which you're presenting the article. In Twitter, the available description space will be quite short; in LinkedIn and Facebook, it's much longer; and in a blog post, it can be as long as you wish. By changing up how you present the piece, you create variety for people who are connected to you in multiple places—and if they don't open it in one location, they might be inspired to in another. Also, you have the opportunity to see the way in which the content was framed most effectively based on the number of opens or forwards.

Disseminating your content in multiple ways, even if it is going to the same people, can achieve the proven benefits of message reinforcement and repetition. While you shouldn't emulate the old-style approach of the identical radio spot playing 30 times in 10 days, placing your messages strategically so that people stumble upon you in a variety of ways, across multiple channels, but related to the same area of expertise, that specialty is effectively reinforced.

Edelman's 2010 Edelman Trust Barometer research shows that it takes hearing something three to five times "about a specific company to believe that the information is likely to be true."[7] For your marketing, what this means is described beautifully by Paul Dunay[8]:

If you know this going into the launch plan—then it's [sic] just a matter of how you are going to sequence those messages (for example, do you send out the eBook first with a link to the video second and the press release third with the virtual event fourth and the blog/twitter buzz fifth?) And then what is the timing? How much time do you give each of them to "soak" in the market—like cooking, you start with the hardest vegetables first that take the longest to steep—so perhaps you start with more traditional channels first since they have longer lead times to get to market, and then start hammering the market later in the campaign to crank up the buzz. The choice is really yours but at least you know how to plan for the proper amount of content. And I would also argue that a single individual needs to hear your message 3 to 5 times but don't forget there is some "breakage" in the system—not every message you send hits every target every single time. So a good rule of thumb would be—double it and plan for breakage along the way.

Repurposing content is best accomplished with an integrated marketing plan. Review Chapter 6 for big-picture tactics and planning approaches. When you want to disseminate the same article or other content to multiple channels, it can be tempting to use cross-posting services to do so automatically, but I recommend against this (see the section "Cross-Posting with Third-Party Services" in Chapter 14). It's better to post manually so you can frame your shared content specific to each audience.

CHAPTER 13

Social Media Etiquette

When entering any unfamiliar society or culture, it's ideal to watch first to learn local rules and customs, before you jump in. Social networks have their own nuances. It's best to lurk at first, listening and monitoring the way people interact to learn these nuances before you enter the conversation. But if you do leap before you look, it's not the end of the world. Just bear one thing in mind to preserve your reputation: make your interactions about others, not about yourself. Then you'll be fine.

It Isn't All About You

As I've mentioned previously, with the exception of LinkedIn, social media were created as mechanisms for communication, not for marketing oneself. Unfortunately, lots of people don't realize this and they use social media very self-servingly, thinking that this is effective marketing. Aside from that behavior being unfitting in the social media space (see "How We Got Here" in Chapter 1) these people don't seem to realize: marketing is *not* about telling everyone how amazing you are. The majority of professionals and especially "firms" with corporate accounts in social media talk more about themselves than about anything else. Those who find it obnoxious "hide" or "unfollow" them. Don't be one of those who get tuned out.

Jordan Furlong, a consultant to law firms, has summarized the poor use of Twitter he's observed among law firms[1]:

I've reviewed dozens of law firm Twitter accounts, some owned by global giants and some by midsize or smaller operations, and in almost every instance I've come away shaking my head. Here's what a typical law firm Twitter account contains: copied-and-pasted headlines from the firm's press releases, with a link thereto; copied-and-pasted headlines from the firm's newsletters or blogs, with a link thereto; news that a lawyer at the firm has appeared in a media outlet, with a link thereto; news that a lawyer at the firm has received an award or designation, with a link thereto; news that the firm has successfully completed a client engagement, with a link thereto. . . . These Twitter feeds assume that you, the reader, care exclusively about what the law firm and its lawyers are doing or saying. Even the happiest and most satisfied law firm client, though, would probably not derive much value out of a channel that features exactly one program, 24/7. A good law firm Twitter feed keeps two things in mind: (1) it's all about the clients, and (2) it's not all about the firm.

Definitely don't write about and link only to your stuff. Instead, go out of your way to promote others liberally. Recommended "others:you" ratios are a minimum of 5:1 in LinkedIn, 7:1 in Facebook, and 10:1 in Twitter.

It's best to avoid a firm-centric feel in any of your writing. To create reader-centric content, take any firm-centric statements and flip them around. For instance, instead of "We helped a company accomplish x. . . ." write, "The company accomplished x with some guidance on these aspects. . . ." Make it about them, not you—your involvement is implied.

Take care not to begin sentences with, or overly use, *we* and *our*. Repetition of the firm's name should be avoided, too. Mentioning your firm name or using the word *we* from time to time is okay, but try to mention others first, as described above, thus indicating that *they* are your priority, not you.

A tool exists to help evaluate a site's self-centeredness. The "We We Calculator" is found at www.futurenowinc.com/wewe.htm.

Comment Etiquette

People like feedback. When you deliver a presentation, completed evaluation forms are always appreciated because people took time to share their thoughts with you, right? Comments on blog posts or other social media posts are much the same. When you receive comments, take them as a validation of your work. It reinforces that what you're doing is worthwhile and keeps you motivated to continue.

Even if you don't author your own blog, as you surf the Web, whenever you come across something on someone else's blog that makes you take pause—or even momentarily tempts you to bookmark the content, think how very much it will mean to the author to receive a comment, no matter how short, telling them you enjoyed it or simply that it made you stop and think. Comment exchanges often lead to deeper thinking, healthy debates and the launch of new friendships. Really!

"The thing to remember about people who comment on blogs, industry forums, and in response to e-zine articles is that they're likely to do it again," counsels Ardath Albee.[2] "How you treat them will play an influential role in determining how they interact with you in the future."

When other bloggers comment on your blog, always thank them and visit their blog, subscribing if it's remotely interesting to you. Try to reciprocate by finding something to comment about on their blogs and, better yet, look for content you might be able to write about and cite in a future blog post.

Locate the online communities discussing issues related to your specialties or blog topics. Contribute to the discussion either by posting on your blog and linking back to theirs, or by commenting directly on other blogs taking care to add value to the discussion (without pitching). Whenever you post comments, be sure to enter your blog URL where prompted (or your LinkedIn or Twitter URL if you don't have a blog) to create yet another reference point for people to find you and your content.

Blog TrackBacks

TrackBacks are a form of automated comment that link two or more separate blog posts together. It's created by an author citing someone else's post. Creating a "TrackBack" places an excerpt from your post, along with a link to it, on the other person's blog (see "Anatomy of a Blog Post" in Chapter 11). When you submit your post, a "ping" is sent to the receiving blog alerting them that they have received a TrackBack (very much like a comment notification) and they may need to approve your TrackBack before it shows up. You will find that you receive some traffic directly from the blogs where you've planted your TrackBack excerpts.

Other bloggers can do the same for your posts, and you'll be prompted to approve their TrackBack requests. Any time you cite another blog post, if they display a TrackBack URL, it is courteous to send a TrackBack and it is a great way to build readership and an acceptable way of associating yourself with other relevant and/or popular blogs.

Blog Feedback Expectations

Beginning bloggers worry about getting negative feedback, either as comments on the blog or finger wagging from licensing or regulatory boards or competitors. In reality, comments will be sparse, probably non-existent at first. You can also take comfort in knowing that nothing goes live on the blog until it's approved—comments queue up awaiting moderation by an authorized person such as an author or blog account administrator.

TIP: Approving Comments for Public Viewing

As a matter of course, it's best to approve all comments for public viewing unless they are offensive or bogus (i.e., spam). Most blog platforms have good spam filters to spare you the hassle of dealing with the bulk of incoming spam comments.

In the unlikely event someone would disagree with you outright, be gracious, approve the comment, and demonstrate maturity in your reply. First, try to use differences of opinion as opportunities to see things from a new perspective. I know of many bloggers whose minds have changed through good blog discussions. If the discussion remains respectful, it is healthy banter. If tension elevates, don't get into flame wars where you accuse people of being thickheaded or stubborn—you can simply write: "It looks like we'll need to agree to disagree on this one . . . thanks for the banter." The same guidelines apply when you are commenting on other people's blogs or social media sites.

If someone is especially rude in a comment, you don't have to post it, you can elect to reply privately or simply ignore it. If the feedback is extremely hostile or you're just not sure what to do, see the steps in Chapter 14 in the section "Crisis Response."

As a blog author, you are blogging to create a conversation so respond to comments, don't let them sit unrecognized. At a minimum, thank those who comment and let them know you appreciate their readership. You can post a comment after theirs, or you can send thanks privately, by email. It's best if you post it on your blog, though, so people can see you're accessible and responsive. People are more encouraged to contribute their thoughts when they perceive you'll notice and care.

Building a Reputation Through Others' Blogs and Sites

Even if you never blog, there are excellent ways to develop a name for yourself and gain some credibility in your practice area without a blog. Note, for example, the Freed Maxick case (Chapter 7) study how the firm's practioners, during their Tax Credit Locator campaign, posted comments on others' blogs that discussed tax credits, fielded related questions in LinkedIn groups and Twitter, and shared tips and information on the firm's Facebook page and Web site. They participated in existing discussions on topics that were important to their practice.

There are good ways to do this and not so good ways. When you post on other people's blogs, you have to be careful to not monopolize their blog. You don't want to be perceived as a jerk. There is a line that could be crossed where the blogger might think or say, "Hey, if you have so much to say, get your own blog . . ." so be aware of what you're doing in this regard. As long as your posts are adding value to the conversation, are never sales-y, and aren't overwhelming the bloggers' own posts or other comments, you should be okay.

To avoid being sales-y, don't list your contact information in the body of the comment and don't ever ask outright for people to contact you for more information. Your name and link will appear for others to click through if they are interested. For your greatest effectiveness, whatever link you're using in the comments that you post should contain your contact information. It would be wise, for instance, to link to your bio on your firm's Web site (if it's really good and has your contact information) or else link to your public LinkedIn profile page.

Other ways to get involved with social media and appear as an expert without creating your own content are through Twitter and bookmarking sites. Using Twitter, you can create "lists" of people who are relevant to the personas you are targeting, and retweet their content, always with the goal of being helpful and relevant. You can also use bookmarking sites like delic.io.us, digg.com, alltop.com, friendfeed.com, and stumbleupon. com to collect content relevant to your personas and their industries. Look in those forums for other content already tagged in ways meaningful to your personas and begin to read and filter that information into bookmarks of your own. Add new content as you find it.

"Hang out" at sites and blogs where the best content originates, posting ideas, and advice where fitting. Look for corresponding LinkedIn groups to join and participate in as well.

These activities can go a long way toward creating a solid online reputation. You don't have to do all of these things to achieve results—just one or two will help. Select the forums that you most enjoy. And as you make new contacts with similar interests, add them as new LinkedIn connections. I assure you, you'll be surprised where these relationships can lead you.

Posting Photos

Honor people's privacy by seeking permission before putting their photos on the Web—especially clients and employees. It's always a good idea to verify whether someone is comfortable with the photo, especially before the person is "tagged" by name in social media or wearing a nametag that is legible—and most especially if the photo shows the person drinking, doing something silly, or being very familiar with someone other than a significant other (e.g., with an arm around someone or in an embrace).

To ease the challenge this rule of etiquette presents, your firm should have a model release for all employees. It's a good idea to have people sign one upon joining the firm. It should cover all print and Web site usage. See "Sample Photography Release Form" for wording you might use in a very simple model release form. You should verify with your own legal counsel if it is sufficient for your needs.

Sample Photography Release Form

If you'll be using employee photos online, whether on a firm-hosted Web site or social media sites, you should have a signed model release form for each employee.

I hereby authorize INSERT COMPANY NAME ("Employer") and representatives, agents, employees, shareholders, officers, directors, partners, contractors, subcontractors, subsidiaries, heirs, and assignees ("Employer") to use my image, photograph, or other artwork ("Materials") in one or more of its products, Web sites, social media sites, and advertising. I give Employer permission to use, copy, or modify such materials for one or more of its products, websites, social media sites, and advertising.

I release Employer from any claims or actions of liability that may arise from the use or adaptation of the Materials for Employer products, Web sites, social media sites, and advertising.

Furthermore, I understand that by signing this contract, I am releasing Employer from any liability for compensation for such Materials.

Employee (print name):

Employee Signature:

Once permitted, after loading photos, you can tag people in them. Tagging is a tool that is used to tie a Facebook user and a photo together. Respect people's choices if they "untag" themselves and respect their desires if they request photos to be removed altogether. Individual privacy settings can be designated in Facebook to never show photos tagged of oneself to anyone or to certain people, but clients/friends of the firm may not be familiar with these settings.

CHAPTER 14

Best Practices

Effective social media use is more art than science. It shouldn't come as a surprise, then, that best practices include attitude, service, and responsiveness. This chapter also covers how to get the most from some third-party bookmarking and file-sharing sites—no matter what other tools you use—and what to do when your frequency or interest in social media changes. You'll also find a few miscellaneous tips that apply to *all* social media tools.

Attitude Is Everything

Anywhere you appear online, you are representing yourself in public. Be positive and caring. If you disagree with someone, do so respectfully, not aggressively. Approach your communications the way you would at an event. Your words and actions are permanent and can be overheard and rebroadcast by others. Your best policy is summarized with two words: be professional.

Negativity Is a Turnoff

If you're using social media for business development relationships, you may be doing yourself more harm than good if you've got "glass-half-empty" tendencies. Or maybe you know others who come across this way and don't realize it. This section of the book may help.

While descriptions of how the world mistreats you might elicit sympathy—some will surely rally round and empathize, thereby encouraging more of this posting behavior—humans are, overall, more attracted to optimists than pessimists. This carries over to business: people don't like to hire or refer others to Negative Nellys and Donny Downers.

It may not be such a big deal to air your daily woes in Facebook if contacts are limited to family and friends, though I suggest even family and friends can become annoyed by Eeyore behavior. If you have business contacts or possible referrers as "friends," and when using Twitter, LinkedIn, and blogs, think twice about your words. Being negative definitely undermines business development.

Everyone has the occasional bad day. Crummy traffic, bad service somewhere, kids out of control, or the occasional cold or flu. A random post now and again about such human things is no big deal if you usually compensate with a more positive outlook on life. But when downers are the trend, it's something you'll want to recognize and improve. Below are some ways to determine if you're being a "turnoff" and how to avoid it going forward.

Consider Your Demeanor

Most of us fall into one of two categories: those who believe "stuff happens" to us, and those who believe we make stuff happen. If you're a member of the former group, you probably have to work a little harder than the other group to avoid sounding like a victim of circumstance. By looking back at your postings, and especially other people's responses to them, you may find clues that suggest pessimism if you frequently solicit "hang in there" and commiseration feedback.

Another factor could be that you're in a funk and are feeling too stressed out or overwhelmed. If this is the case, consider taking a break from social media. It's also possible that the cause is stress from feeling obligated to be using social media. Maybe the social Web isn't something you enjoy in the first place. You aren't obligated to be there—you can take a pass. See "Retiring Your Social Media Accounts" later in this chapter.

Review Your Status Updates

In Twitter, look through your profile to see the mood or tenor of what you've been posting. In LinkedIn, from your home page, click on "Network Updates" over the status input field. Then choose the "My Updates" tab. In Facebook, the quickest, easiest way to get a big-picture recap is to use an app like "My Year in Status" which will auto-generate a random selection of your status updates. Go thru steps 1 and 2. On step 3, you'll see an option that says "Choose Different Statuses" that opens a chronological list of every status update you've posted over the last year (to find this app, type "My Year in Status" in Facebook's search box).

Pretend you don't know yourself, and read your posts as objectively as possible. Are you a complainer? What proportion are rants or whines versus neutral observations or upbeat messages.

You may also want to look at feedback trends. Do fewer people comment on your postings than on postings by other friends in your circle? Has your post feedback decreased as negativity increased?

Another way to gauge the temper of your status trends is to ask people who know you—trusted friends or family members. Preface asking this favor with "I'm trying to be more aware of how I come across to others. I really need frank feedback. I trust that you'll be honest with me." Then ask: "Would you mind looking at my postings and tell me if you think I'm coming across as more negative than positive?" Be open-minded to their feedback and thank them for their frankness. It's really hard to tell people you care about that they don't come across well, and most will try to soft-pedal any criticism.

How Negative Is Negative?

If you find more than 25 percent your postings are downers, it might not be a deep problem, just that "dilemmas" are an easy source of things to write about—and they are. Jerry Seinfeld has built a career out of talking about these things, but he obviously presents them with humor. Now that your awareness is heightened, perhaps you can simply inject some observational humor into your posts, rather than avoid posting about the "bummers." See the tips below for more ideas.

If more than 50 percent of your posts are downers, perhaps you are significantly unhappy with your job or the way things are going in life. This happens to all of us at times. It might wise to take a break from social media posts and redirect your energy toward working through the sources of your unhappiness. By no means be tempted to post a play-by-play of your personal therapy—a number of people seem unselfconscious about airing their personal struggles in social media, and it's very awkward for readers, whether or not they know the person well.

If you do discover you've been less than pleasant to listen to, and you aren't exactly an optimist by nature, I'm not suggesting you have to go through life feigning insincere joy—Pollyannas can be pretty annoying, too, you're just looking for balance. Try the ideas below.

Improve Your Image

Assessing and improving your image is marketing 101 stuff. It might be that the attitudes you've been conveying through social media reflect impressions you've created in "real-life" social situations, too. If so, no worries; just be glad you've become aware of it, and change it. Going forward, think twice before saying those words or pressing that post button.

Is your post a complaint or wish that something was different? If so, what's your purpose behind posting this? Looking for a shoulder? Hoping people will ask you to elaborate on the problem to show they care? If so, skip the post. The social Web is not the best place for this—it's permanent. Pick up the phone and call a good friend or loved one.

If what you've written is victim oriented (stuff happens), can you turn it to a positive projection (I'm gonna make stuff happen)? For instance, "Tomorrow is going to be a good day" instead of "Today was the worst day ever," or "Sure hope tomorrow is better than today," both of which solicit "What's wrong?" or "What happened?" questions which, when answered, invite sympathy or commiseration.

It may help to shift from posting about your feelings or life's events to less personal posts that share news, links, songs, anecdotes, tips, quotes, and that sort of thing. Or broadcast about other people and their merits—be a promoter of others.

Greater self-awareness often improves negative behavior. Many of us simply don't think about how we come across until someone brings it to our attention. Perhaps this helps you or someone you know self-assess and modify word choices.

Complaints, Customer Service, and Crisis

The openness and availability of social media is making companies, world-wide, pay a lot more attention when it looks like a customer service issue might be brewing. Being "more awesome" every day is a good strategy, but service flaws will still occur. Heading off problems before they escalate is the best thing you can do. This is difficult in firms with a historic culture of confrontation avoidance, hoping that problems will just go away. We really can't afford to put off proactive involvement with an increasingly unhappy client (or employee).

Blame Avoidance Is a Fatal Error

Mistakes happen—they are part of life and business. What matters to your customers is not whether you make mistakes, but how you handle them when they occur. When someone airs a problem or complaint, it's often our first instinct to explain why it happened. Don't do it. The person doesn't really care *why* it happened. They just want acknowledgment of the problem, and then they want amends. Two things to remember when dealing with complaints are: resist the urge to explain, and own the problem.

Never, ever explain who dropped the ball or offer any excuses about why. Here are the reasons to skip the explanation:

- Your explanation cannot help but demonstrate the client areas in which your systems and processes are weak—they will think less of you.
- Blaming others (or processes over which you should have some control or authority) reduces the impression of your personal integrity and effectiveness—they will think less of you.
- The explanation does not serve to correct the problem in any way, it only diverts attention from the resolution—they will think less of you.

Worse, these three things will almost certainly further aggravate clients because it makes them question, and doubt, their judgment in hiring you.

Second, own the problem even if it is not your fault. The first thing the client should hear is a sincere apology. It's actually quite liberating to apologize on behalf of yourself, others, or the organization. Just say, "I am so sorry this has occurred."

Immediately following the apology, state directly that it is your intention to either solve the problem or make up for it. Say something like, "I will do everything in my power to correct this and take steps to ensure that it does not happen again." If possible, add, "and to make it up to you for your inconvenience."

Almost always, these two statements will defuse a client's anger and frustration. Validate the concern or complaint, and apologize on behalf of the firm. You can then either propose a solution or ask what the client would like as a remedy. This approach, instead of causing clients to doubt their judgment in hiring you, reassures them that they hired someone of integrity and honor.

Nonhesitant ownership and resolution of issues reflects your firm in the best possible light and goes a long way toward establishing your firm as fair, reasonable, and authentic—this actually *builds* loyalty. See "Credibility through Fallibility" in Chapter 4. A public airing isn't always a bad thing. If handled well, your firm could be publicly recognized for its grace and exceptional handling of an issue.

Crisis Planning and Prevention

Social media crisis *planning* should be much the same as your past crisis media planning wherein companies have an established chain of communication and approved spokespersons who have had some media training. The main difference now, with the proliferation of social media, is that the people who are involved in the community aren't usually trained spokespersons—they are everybody—from interns to owners, and *everybody* needs to understand how to operate in social media, as well as how to spot problems early and not behave in a way that escalates them.

It's the *management* of crisis that is so much different now. Even if you have no presence in social media, this change affects you. Spin is not an option anymore, and time is not on the company's side the way it perhaps used to be. Truth and transparency are essential, as are speed and sincere commitment to resolving issues. All this while sitting directly under an "information" spotlight: company representatives with bad attitudes and those who say really stupid things—things that may not have seemed stupid at the time—are potentially broadcast within seconds. Every word spoken, emailed, or tweeted to clients now matters more than it ever did. Crisis management means being on our best behavior before, during, and after problems occur.

Now every company has a need to watch what's being said (see "Monitoring Online Mentions" in Chapter 6), but I suggest that's almost too late (though it is undoubtedly a necessity). For my company, I'd much rather make sure that service is primo; expectations are set, managed, and met; and employees and representatives realize the deleterious effects of poorly handled customer interactions.

Planning for the Worst

Your firm should have a community strategy that is carefully thought through. The odds are slim that you will ever have a problem, but if one should occur, what will you do?

Try to envision every type of crisis that could occur and determine what you will do if that event unfolds. The problems related to social media foibles are relatively minor, such as "What if our Twitter account is hacked?" or "What if former employees post offensive material on our Facebook page?" The possible airing of client engagements gone awry is what firms should be most concerned about. If your firm has a strong, positive presence in social media already, you have a better chance of overcoming any negative backlash quickly and with grace than if you have no social media presence when things hit the fan.

Jeremiah Owyang,[1] in his Web strategy blog, says the following:

Don't [start] without a clear set of policies, roles, and experienced staff. . . . Start by developing a social media crises plan and developing internal fire drills to anticipate what would happen. This doesn't mean you should live your social efforts in fear, but instead, forge key relationships with members now that will defend your brand in the long run.

By members, Jeremiah means members of the online community. Companies with an established social media presence find that loyal followers and fans often step in to defend the company when something uncharacteristic happens.

Crisis Response

In the face of a crisis being spread across social media, there are a handful of "must-dos" and no real alternatives that are appealing. Not doing these things will lead to worse problems. Every company needs to:

1. **Listen closely:** Monitor effectively and continuously.
2. **Respond quickly and appropriately:** Do the right thing.
3. **Be professional, responsible, and actionable:** Don't engage in flame wars; do own up and take care of it. Think of your long-term image versus "making a point."

In the event of negative comments, Hubspot advises[2]:

If it's helpful, rational feedback: address the comments; respond thoroughly, openly and honestly; follow up with action; don't extend the discussion. If the feedback is irrational or designed to draw you into an extended, [unconstructive] dialogue, don't respond; do make sure everybody at your company knows you've decided to ignore the comment.

A very interesting example of a comment response policy is that of the U.S. Air Force posted on David Meerman Scott's blog. The USAF has a solid social media presence and empowers all 330,000 of their airmen to communicate online. As you would expect, they have some good infrastructure in place. On David's blog (www.webinknow.com/2009/01/us-air-force-web-posting-response-assessment.html), you can download a full-sized version of the Air Force Web Posting Assessment, a tool that is used to evaluate social media comments and formulate an appropriate response.

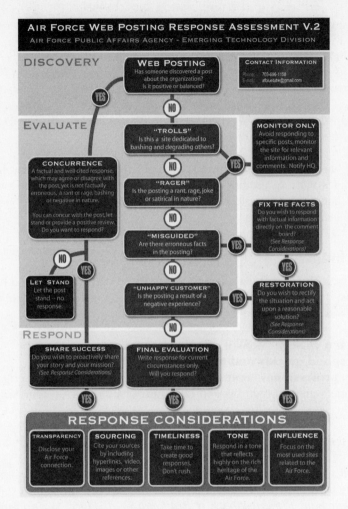

FIGURE 14.1 Air Force Blog Assessment Diagram Thumbnail

There are a number of lessons to be learned from various recent crises, including United Airlines ("United Breaks Guitars"), Southwest Airlines (Kevin Smith refused as a passenger due to weight), Nestlé (under attack by environmentalists), and Dominos (employee misbehavior—don't ask).

In the face of their unhappy client's increasing visibility, United stayed too quiet, too long—the "payback" YouTube video now has almost 9 million views. Dominos responded quickly and with a video from the CEO announcing that employees had been fired and warrants for their arrest were written. Because they didn't have a plan, or good communicators on the front line, Nestlé's "community manager" responded poorly and caused the situation to escalate. Then Nestlé exacerbated the problem by removing comments, among other things.

Lessons? Move fast. Don't shirk it off or expect it to blow over. Don't be rude or sneaky. Do be calm, honest, apologetic, and likable.

In reaction to unflattering posts on your public profiles, such as your Facebook company page or even your blog, don't disable the comments feature in a knee-jerk reaction the way Nestlé did. You cannot hide, and doing so implies guilt. If you force the conversation away from your site, it will simply move elsewhere and will probably get louder for your rejection. Stay part of the conversation to have more power than you will if you avoid it. If things get really tough, in Facebook, you can set the default wall view to display "Just Company" for awhile instead of "Company + Fans."

Before a crisis occurs, have clear comment policies for blogs and Facebook walls that describe circumstances under which you will or will not filter or edit comments. Do not otherwise hide or delete posts.

Crisis Creates Opportunity

It's been shown that when a company handles a crisis well, they are even better off than before, even if they had been guilty of making a mistake (see "Advantages of an Effective Online Presence" in Chapter 1). Again, it's not *if* we make mistakes, but how we handle them when they occur that really matters. Perception of "an honest mistake" is a lot better than denial or a cover-up.

In 2007, TurboTax had an unfortunate problem. Before midnight on the personal income tax filing deadline, their e-filing service was down; 200,000 customers were unable to file their tax returns on time. I was one. I have to say, they handled it beautifully. I blogged about it at the time: http://goldenmarketing.typepad.com/weblog/2007/04/stellar_apology .html and saw my post circulated through Intuit.

When I discovered the problem, I checked their Web site, where a notice read, "Keep trying . . . you might get through," and, most impressively, it said that their biggest priority is to protect taxpayers so they were "working with the IRS to assure returns would be considered filed timely."

Sure enough, the next morning, an email was in my inbox that read:

Dear TurboTax Customer,

We want to let you know that Intuit will be refunding any TurboTax credit card charges that were charged to your credit or debit card between 3 P.M. PDT Tuesday, April 17 and 4 A.M. PDT Wednesday, April 18.

We deeply regret the frustration and anxiety you may have experienced trying to e-file your return on April 17.

We worked closely with the IRS to allow taxpayers who were affected by the delay to file their returns until midnight tonight, Thursday, April 19, without penalty. Intuit will also pay any other penalties that customers incur as a result of the delay, although none are anticipated. We will be contacting you early next week with additional details about this refund. We value your business and appreciate your patience.

Sincerely,

Bob Meighan, Vice President, TurboTax Customer Advocacy Intuit, Inc.

Intuit did so many things well. They had information posted on their Web site immediately. Reassurance. Then they *made it right!* Not only did they protect their customers, they refunded the filing fee. This cost Intuit more than $15 million. Was their reputation worth it? Did they seal client loyalty? You betcha. And they built a lot of trust. Plus, people like me had said very nice things about them in public.

Conversely, I experienced an outage of my Voice over Internet Protocol (VOiP) service, but the company's Web site had no information about the issue. I resorted to searching Twitter to see if other customers were experiencing problems. Lo and behold, they were—which confirmed that the outage wasn't just my line. Unfortunately, while the company did have Twitter accounts, they only contained sales-related tweets. There were scores of tweets flying around from frustrated customers like me (see Figure 14.2).

At a time of customer need, they absolutely should have used the communication vehicle (especially since they couldn't call us) to tell us about the outage and reassure us about repair status. Yet they were absent the day of the incident. Other VOiP companies, by the way, were quick to chime in about the steps they take to assure stability of their services so such outages won't happen to their customers. Intuit's problem happened before Twitter was around, but I have no doubt they would have covered that base and used Twitter as a mechanism to communicate with customers during the crisis. The lessons here are to be forward thinking, highly communicative, and always listening.

Companies like Comcast, the cable giant, have used Twitter to conduct major brand repair. Yes, service woes are still aired, but customers constantly remark that they can tweet a cable service problem while they are on hold with the company's phone repair line, and get resolution through the Twitter account. As long as there is good to offset the bad, brands have a fighting chance.

FIGURE 14.2 Twitter Fail by VOiP Company

Part of crisis prevention is to not say things online that might come back to haunt you. When professional firms write for the Web, the content issues aren't any different from other written or electronic content (i.e., newsletters, memos, emails, and texts); it's just that it will have broader readership, which is exactly what you want. See the feature box for some tips on watching what you say in blog posts.

TIP: Watching What You Say (or CYA) in Blog Posts

Firms often worry about their blog authors providing advice that could get them into hot water. Here are some guidelines and ideas about how to minimize risk of incomplete advice or implying certain results. Start with these tips:

Continued

- Give "outs": If you're worried about leaving something out, then frame your advice with "some important considerations are . . ." and "don't forget to factor in . . ." (these also suggest you are sharing real nuggets).
- Avoid absolutes (e.g., always, never, will, must): Instead of "10 steps to assure . . ." try "10 steps for better . . ."
- The Federal Trade Commission says bloggers *must* disclose if they are being paid to promote or review a product.
- Whenever you are talking about something in which you hold an interest or could benefit, be real about it and say, "In the interest of full disclosure. . . ." Doing so promotes trust; failing to do so destroys it.
- Only use images that are legal for you to use (Creative Commons licensing or purchased). Don't just search Google Images and use whatever you want—you could get in a lot of trouble.
- Always cite and link to original sources. Always.

Leveraging Bookmarking Sites

A type of social media is the bookmarking site. Different bookmarking sites have different purposes. Some aggregate content and allow you to customize your own aggregation page (e.g., Alltop.com) plus easily find other content you might like based on topic areas. Others are more rating oriented, where users submit news stories, blog posts, Web sites, and other Web content they find, also tagging or rating it. Some sites (e.g., digg.com) are known for comments that are interesting (if not brutally honest) and reviews. Two very popular social bookmarking sites are del.icio.us and stumbleupon.com—both are easy to use and produce good-quality site referrals. There are a dozen or so others, including furl.com, reddit.com, newsvine.com, and mixx.com. Through content they've posted, users identify like-minded users or related topics to find even more content they might like.

By creating a profile and submitting, say, industry-related content, you could become relied upon as a good resource for that topic. You'll definitely achieve being associated with that subject matter. Moreover, you'll be directed to a stream of like information that makes it easy to stay abreast of things impacting the industries you serve or the services you provide. These sites also make it very easy for you to collect links you might want to find again and access them from any computer as well as share with friends or colleagues.

Housing Content on File-Sharing Sites

File-sharing sites such as YouTube.com, SlideShare.net, and Flickr.com are social sites that are instrumental for firms to leverage in storing and sharing graphical content, but a full-fledged "presence" (i.e., one that needs to be actively managed) on these by a professional firm is not essential, nor would it require the level of effort that a LinkedIn, Twitter, Facebook, or blog presence needs in order to be successful.

YouTube is the most popular video-sharing tool on the Web. It and Facebook are the two most searched databases aside from Google. Firms that create videos should load them to YouTube, then embed them on the firm's Web site, blog, or Facebook. The video probably will draw more search traffic on YouTube that can funnel back to the firm. Plus, the firm can save precious bandwidth and storage space by letting the video reside there.

SlideShare is an excellent tool used by credible companies—even the U.S. military—willing to widely share their PowerPoint presentations or PDF files (most uploads are PowerPoint). Tagging your content in SlideShare helps people find it and you, and Creative Commons licensing is assignable, so you can control people's access to your work. A fairly new user of SlideShare with only a handful of presentations uploaded thus far, I've been impressed with viewership. First, after you upload a file, you can embed a preview window on any Web site or blog. Second, as your presentation becomes popular with viewers who tweet it or share it on Facebook, SlideShare bumps your presentation up to its home page as "Hot on Twitter" or "Hot on Facebook." You receive a notification such as:

> *Congrats, "[presentation name]" is hot on Twitter this hour. [Presentation name] is being tweeted more than any other document on SlideShare right now. So we've put it on the home page of SlideShare.net (in the "Hot on Twitter" section). Well done, you!—SlideShare Team*

SlideShare also integrates with LinkedIn, so your presentations can be automatically embedded in your LinkedIn profile and new upload notifications automatically go to your contacts. SlideShare isn't the only provider of this service, you may wish to evaluate others, as well.

Flickr is one of several available photo-sharing sites. You can use it much the same way as YouTube and SlideShare. It's a nice way to share firm event photos and more. It also incorporates Creative Commons licensing. Be sure to honor privacy preferences of clients and employees before uploading, though. See "Posting Photos" in Chapter 13.

No matter what social media tools you're using, use these or similar sites liberally to house your content for quick and easy distribution to any channel. The built-in tracking will inform you, and the searchability will draw new visitors to you.

Cross-Posting with Third-Party Services

For those using social media for business reasons, I strongly recommend against using a service like Twitterfeed or ping.fm that "update all your social networks at once." This automated approach is problematic because we do tend to have many of the same contacts across our networks and because the generally accepted frequency of posts in some forums is much less than in others. For instance, Twitter users post far more frequently than Facebook users, who post more frequently than LinkedIn users.

Nothing will break if you post "too often," but you can become very annoying to Facebook and LinkedIn users if you funnel every tweet to them, flooding their wall. In Facebook, users may "hide" your personal or company pages so they don't have to deal with your too-frequent posts. If they hide you, they won't ever see any of your updates unless they go out of their way to visit your page. This defeats your purpose if your intent is to interact with people and have them interact with you.

If people want to see all of your postings across the Web, you can use a site like Friendfeed.com that aggregates users' postings into a single stream. This is another reason it's good to "mix it up" with regard to how you present information in different locations—if you don't, Friendfeed and others may see the very same post multiple times, which doesn't make you look very creative.

When it comes to cross-posting services—it's kind of like having a million fonts and graphics available to you in PowerPoint—just because you *can* do something doesn't mean you *should*. Manual or selective cross-posting is usually best.

Keeping Things Short When Space Is Tight

As a professional, you may be uncomfortable with abbreviations that resemble "text lingo." At just 140 characters per tweet, Twitter definitely teaches brevity. LinkedIn status updates are only a smidgen longer. A key to people understanding what you are trying to say in these forums is to view your posts as writing great "headlines." The more compelling your headline—think newspaper—the more likely you are to be read regularly as a valued content provider. And the more likely you are to be retweeted or forwarded. Some people pass stories and posts along based on title alone.

As you type your tweet, a countdown of remaining characters displays. Type what you want to say even if you exceed the character limit, then whittle down your words as needed.

Sometimes you'll find a need to abbreviate, whether it's your own post or shortening something that another person has written and that you are retweeting. It really is acceptable for you to occasionally resort to "U2" and "B4," but avoid writing every tweet in this manner if you want to convey an overall professional image.

When you shorten, it's best to avoid creating new, weird abbreviations. But there are some fairly common shortcuts. You'll see "mktg" for marketing, "preso" and "convo" for presentation and conversation, respectively, "yest" for yesterday, and so forth. Try to become comfortable with some abbreviations. If you'd like help shortening your tweets, you can try www.twonvert.com, a free service that automatically generates suggestions for conserving characters in your post. See "Common Terms Used in Social Media" for some frequently used shortcuts.

Common Terms Used in Social Media

Social media has popularized a set of new abbreviations and acronyms that allow conversations to fly even faster. Brush up your know-how with this quick list.

AFAIK: as far as I know
B/C, bcz, or cuz: because
BFN: bye for now
BTW: by the way
EM: email
fav/fave: favorite
FB: Facebook
FTF or F2F: face to face
FWD: forward
HT: hat tip
HTH: hope that helps
IIRC: if I remember correctly
IMHO: in my humble opinion
IRL: in real life
J/K: just kidding
LI: LinkedIn
NP: no problem
OH: overheard

Continued

OTOH: on the other hand
SM: social media
TMB: tweet me back
TY: thank you
TYVM: thank you very much
YW: you're welcome

Link Shorteners

You will quickly find that you want to share links and they consume a lot of characters—precious space you cannot afford to waste when you are using Twitter and LinkedIn. Most social media users rely on link-shortening services to convert their very long links into nice, short ones. Additionally, whether used in Web sites, blogs, or other social media sites, using link shorteners can give you powerful tracking capabilities to see which links interest people and which links don't.

A popular link-shortening tool is www.bit.ly.com because, while you can use bit.ly without signing up for an account, if you do create a (free) account, you can revisit bit.ly anytime to see click-through statistics for your links. Also, bit.ly will convert your long link to a link with a short string of letters and numbers, but if you have a bit.ly account, you can choose a custom (or vanity) name for your link, such as www.bit.ly/mybio instead of the random letter/number combo.

Other link-shortening services are http://tinyurl.com and http://ow.ly, but there are many, many more and new ones are added all the time. Some third-party Twitter reader applications (such as Tweetdeck) have built-in URL shorteners—a nice feature, indeed. A chart (updated August 2009) listing link shorteners and comparing their benefits, is found at http://searchengineland.com/analysis-which-url-shortening-service-should-you-use-17204.

Do be sure to test your shortened link before posting it. Sometimes they break, especially if they contained a search result (i.e., if the long URL had a question mark in it, sometimes characters following the "?" are dropped).

When Your Use Wanes

Even the best-laid plans sometimes go askew and people fall off the social media wagon. Perhaps you started out strong but stalled out. It's okay. Don't decide this means you should quit, even if you feel like you aren't meeting your own expectations for frequency.

Throughout this book, I've set some very high expectations for social media participation because I've described how to get the most out of involvement in social media—how to do it "best." And though I've tried to give reasonable "minimums" for activities and frequency, they might not be sustainable for everyone.

Give yourself permission to ebb and flow with your use patterns. If you've outwardly promised to do something such as "post daily" or stated "this is the first in a series of posts" and you don't follow through, just write something acknowledging it, forgive yourself, and avoid promising similarly in the future. The key is managing expectations—they can be changed once they are set. As blogger and tweeter Debra Helwig said to me recently, "We can't use perfectionism as a tool for failure. We need to find our personal 'happy' line and stay true to it."

Find a rhythm that works for you—especially with blogging, but also in other forums—and then set expectations for readers or contacts if your frequency is going to be low or sporadic.

Retiring Your Social Media Accounts

If you get involved in social media and decide it isn't for you, it's perfectly acceptable to stop. Some people detest Facebook. Others feel that Twitter sucks the life out of them. And others find that blogging doesn't suit their personal communication style or that they just don't have the time to dedicate to it. People understand if you want to stop, although some will probably be sad and will miss you when you leave, whichever community you decide to depart. Exiting is a highly personal decision, and it's possible to exit with grace.

If you enjoy Twitter or Facebook, but feel they are overwhelming and lure you to spend too much time using them, you might try taking a hiatus (a month or two) rather than canceling your account outright. Some people even ask a trusted friend or family member to change the password and keep it secret during this time. Because the novelty of these forums can draw you in more than you'd like, taking some time away can remind you that moderation will improve your enjoyment of them. If time away convinces you that a permanent break is what will ultimately make you happy, that's okay, too.

Even if you suspect you will quit entirely, start by simply notifying people that you are going to take a break. It's not uncommon for bloggers to announce they'll be taking a month off. If you do come back, you won't feel embarrassed about it. No matter what, though, don't just disappear.

When you notify people you're taking a break or quitting, it's best if you don't go into "why" if the "why" might sound like a judgment against others who use the platform. Posting "Twitter is nothing but useless drivel" or "Facebook is stupid" isn't a graceful exit. Neither is deleting your account or your blog without any explanation. In Facebook, it's usually better to just "deactivate" rather than permanently delete your account so your account remains stored on Facebook's servers and can be restored in the event you decide to return later. You can deactivate anytime, but extra steps are necessary to have Facebook permanently delete you. I don't recommend that you "deactivate" if you are just taking a break and intend to come back. Deactivating makes you and your posts disappear, which may be alarming to some people.

Similarly, if you have a blog and decide to discontinue writing for it, unless you have fewer than 20 or so posts, it's a good idea to leave the blog "live" on the Web. Leaving the blog up allows it to continue to draw traffic for you and allows others and you to continue to refer to, or forward, your past writing to others. If your last posting explains, much the way prominent consultant David Maister's "Suspension of Blog" post does, that you are wrapping it up, then you've managed expectations of readers, but they can still find your past writings to be a valuable resource.[3] Like David, do be sure to thank your loyal readers.

Though the history of social media is hardly more than a decade long, we've seen social platforms come and go. It's probable that the platforms discussed in this book will also go away. This doesn't mean it's unwise to build your presence in them. When new social platforms are introduced, social Web communities have been known to simply migrate to the new platform. It's very easy and very informal, usually just a matter of posting a message that says, "Hey, we've moved the conversation over here: [link]." Your Web presence continuously evolves and is very portable.

Quick Tips for Using Social Media

Every chapter in this book includes tips and ideas for using LinkedIn, Twitter, Facebook, and blogs, especially the detailed chapters in the HOW section. But here are some tips that apply to all social media tools:

Engaging Your Readers

- Find creative ways to engage your audiences: run opinion polls, host regular quizzes. There are dozens, if not hundreds, of contest and polling applications. If you do run a contest, you need to be aware of contest legalities—you know, those "no purchase required" terms you always hear at the end of sweepstakes advertisements? See this blog post for information about contest rules that may apply to you: www.blogher.com/scoop-facebook-contests.

- Learn everything you can about your target audience so that you can share information and ideas that are most meaningful to them. See what information seems to resonate based on what people respond to, forward, or retweet, or what gets the most "views," and seek to learn more about the individuals who are doing these things.
- Cultivate relationships with your readers. Ask them questions and act on their feedback. Retweet their information and promote them. Get involved.
- Lace your content with people's names and company names, especially in Twitter—reference their @names so they will know you are mentioning them.
- Hat tip others who inspire your posts or point you to news that you discuss.

Building Readership

- List your social media sites in your email signatures, on your Web site's bio page, and on your business card, and cross-reference them on all your online profiles.
- Interact often with sites and users who have authority and influence in the circles you should be in.

Being Authentic

- Always be real about who the voice is behind your social media interactions. If you use a freelancer or an agency to manage your social media accounts, determine how you'll handle transparency about this—don't hide it, advises Toby Bloomberg in her e-book.[4]
- Be personal in the way that you respond to people. Don't sound like you are parroting company rhetoric. Be friendly, helpful, and natural. Not scripted. Ever.
- Resist the urge to use auto-responses such as auto DMs in Twitter. People can tell the difference, and it is very impersonal—it gives a bad impression of you and your company. Better to send no message than to send an automated one.
- Don't abuse the forum with self-promotion. A dozen posts without puffery may excuse a puff piece, but still be up front about it. "Forgive me for this shameless self-promotion today. . ."

Formatting Text

- For ease of reading, avoid italics, using them for emphasis or foreign words only.

- Don't use all capitals in body text because it is the equivalent of a shout. For emphasis, it may be okay to capitalize a word here or there, but only do it intentionally, for effect.
- Left justify text in a blog or Web site. Don't center it or use full justification because it's very hard to read online.
- Don't underline text or use bright blue text unless the text is actually a link; it causes confusion to online readers.
- Link text should be more than just "click here." Anchor text (the clickable text in the link) should be as descriptive as possible.
- Don't use / between words unless you put spaces on both sides. While this looks funny, there's a good reason. Search engines may not be able to recognize the words on each side of the slash as independent words.

Recruiting via Social Media

- Encourage your employees to distribute job opening information throughout their online social networks.
- Maximize presence with career-oriented pages (it's best to have these separate from your customer-oriented page).
- Consider advertising in social media—particularly Facebook and LinkedIn—to snag the attention of passive job seekers (those who are not actively looking but may be intrigued).

Not Doing it Halfway

- Make sure people have something to see if they find you. Don't bother setting up an account if you are going to limit the view of your LinkedIn profile or protect your Twitter account so others cannot see your tweets or follow you back.
- In Facebook, if you use privacy settings in order to carefully mix business and personal contacts (see Chapter 10 for details on privacy settings) be sure that your profile isn't just a photo and a city. If you let someone in, and that is all they can see, they know they aren't really "in." What message does that send?
- In any of the third-party social media forums, when you post status updates, be sure you share some of your personal self even with your business contacts. If you are "all" business to the point that no one has insights to your personality, you miss much of the opportunity to deepen relationships through social media.

Summary of Part IV

Social media are an important extension of today's business communications. The same "rules" that hold true across business ethics and communications apply, but we have many more methods, each with their own nuances, than ever before. It's hard not to feel a little overwhelmed with all the shiny new toys. Just remember, social media are the next "phone." And just about as fun.

We still have to be very good at talking *and listening* to get the most out of the phone for business purposes. A little extra care is merited as we learn to make the most of these new communications tools and weave them into our marketing and daily business practices.

Social media tools make it extremely easy to stay in touch with people who are important to us personally and influential in our business success. Debra Helwig wrote, "When you lose regular contact with the people you do business with, even people who like and care about you, you very well may drop out of their scope."[5] When professionals tell me, "I'm too busy to use social media," I suspect they are then *far* too busy to stay in touch with people the "old" ways: one human at a time. The fact is, the busier we get, the more advantageous it is for us to leverage the power of social media to nurture multiple relationships in the same few minutes of any given day.

Here's wishing you tremendous success and fun new discoveries as you get to know, and benefit from, these interesting and powerful tools. But don't get too attached to them because it's certain they'll be replaced with something new and different in no time. In fact, the term *social media* is starting to mean less and less as the tools continue to change the way people view and use the Internet. As they become more ubiquitous, they simply become the Web.

Notes

Introduction

1. *Bates v. State Bar of Arizona*, 433 U.S. 350 (1977).
2. Bruce W. Marcus, "Marketing an Accounting Firm," *The Virginia Accountant*, September, 1980.
3. Sally Schmidt, "Law Firm Brochures: They're Here to Stay." *Minnesota Lawyer*, August 21 1987.

Chapter 1: Defining and Understanding "Social Media"

1. *http://dictionary.bnet.com/definition/Strategy.html.*
2. Stephen W. Brown, "Practicing Best-In-Class Service Recovery," *Marketing Management Magazine* (AMA: Summer 2000: 9).
3. *Levine, R., et al., The Cluetrain Manifesto* (Cambridge, MA: Perseus Books, 2000), 174.
4. David Meerman Scott, blog post, "The Gobbledygook Manifesto—Cutting Edge! Mission Critical! An Analysis of Gobbledygook in Over 388,000 Press Releases Sent in 2006," Web Ink Now, October 12, 2006. www.webinknow .com/2006/10/the_gobbledygoo.html.
5. David Meerman Scott, e-book, *The Gobbledygook Manifesto*, August 8, 2007. http://changethis.com/manifesto/show/37.03.Gobbledygook.
6. Stephen Baker and Heather Green, "Social Media Will Change Your Business," *BusinessWeek* online, February 2008. Modified from original article, "Blogs Will Change Your Business," May 2005. www.businessweek.com/bwdaily/dnflash/ content/feb2008/db20080219_908252.htm.
7. Robert Scoble, blog post, "The Corporate Weblog Manifesto," Scobleizer, February 26, 2003. http://radio-weblogs.com/0001011/2003/02/26.html.
8. Bob Ambrogi, blog post, "Who Was the First Legal Blogger?," Law.com, July 16, 2007. http://legalblogwatch.typepad.com/legal_blog_watch/2007/07/who -was-the-fir.html.

9. Ian Best, blog post, "Cases Citing Legal Blogs—Updated List," 3L Ephiphany Blog, August 6, 2006. http://3lepiphany.typepad.com/3l_epiphany/2006/08/cases_citing_le.html.

10. Kevin O'Keefe, blog post, "What Is the Worst Legal Ethics or Liability Issue LexBlog Has Seen in Lawyer Blogging?," Real Lawyers Have Blogs, October 11, 2009. http://kevin.lexblog.com/2009/10/articles/lexblog/what-is-the-worst-legal-ethics-or-liability-issue-lexblog-has-seen-in-lawyer-blogging/.

11. Kevin O'Keefe, blog post, "State of the AmLaw 200 Blogosphere: March, 2010," Real Lawyers Have Blogs, March 11, 2010. http://kevin.lexblog.com/2010/03/articles/large-law/state-of-the-amlaw-200-blogosphere-march-2010/.

12. Molly McDonough and Sarah Randag, blog post, "ABA Journal Blawg 100," ABA Journal Law News Now, December 1, 2007. www.abajournal.com/magazine/article/aba_journal_blawg_100.

Chapter 2: Social Media Policies and Guidelines: Rules of Engagement

1. "Proactively Implementing Social Media Policies: No Exceptions, No Excuses, No Delays," *Inside Public Accounting,* March 2010: 4–7.

2. Michelle Golden, "Charting a Firm's Social Media & Communications Policy," *Practical Accountant,* June 2009: 22–24.

3. Electronic Frontier Foundation, Bloggers' Legal Guide. www.eff.org/issues/bloggers/legal.

4. Hollis Templeton, blog post, "Social Media Benefits Trump Security Fears," Medill Reports Washington, June 10, 2009. http://news.medill.northwestern.edu/washington/news.aspx?id=133987.

5. Lawrence Savell, blog post, "Is Your Blog Exposing You to Legal Liability?," Law.com, December 22, 2006. www.law.com/jsp/llf/PubArticleLLF.jsp?id=1166695602960.

6. Kevin O'Keefe, blog post "What Is the Worst Legal Ethics or Liability Issue LexBlog Has Seen in Lawyer Blogging?," Real Lawyers Have Blogs, October 11, 2009. http://kevin.lexblog.com/2009/10/articles/lexblog/what-is-the-worst-legal-ethics-or-liability-issue-lexblog-has-seen-in-lawyer-blogging/.

7. Kevin O'Keefe, blog post, "NY Times Misses Boat on Legal Ethics Versus Lawyers Online Activity," Real Lawyers Have Blogs, September 16, 2009. http://kevin.lexblog.com/2009/09/articles/social-networking-1/ny-times-misses-boat-on-legal-ethics-versus-lawyers-online-activity/.

8. John Schwartz, blog post, "A Legal Battle: Online Attitude vs. Rules of the Bar," *New York Times* online, September 12, 2009. www.nytimes.com/2009/09/13/us/13lawyers.html?_r=2.

9. Jonathan Bailey, blog post, "20 Law-Related Questions Every Blogger Should Know," The Blog Herald, April 20, 2009. www.blogherald.com/2009/04/20/20-law-related-questions-every-blogger-should-know/.

10. Ibid.

11. www.kaspersky.com/news?id=207575817.
12. Jay Shepherd, blog post, "A Two-Word Corporate Blogging Policy," Gruntled Employees, February 26, 2007. www.gruntledemployees.com/gruntled _employees/2007/02/a_twoword_corpo.html.
13. Susan Heathfield, About.com Guide, "Blogging and Social Media Policy Sample," undated.   http://humanresources.about.com/od/policysamplesb/a/blogging _policy.htm.

Chapter 4: Finding Business Purpose in Social Media

1. Erik Qualman, *Socialnomics: How Social Media Transforms the Way We Live and Do Business* (Hoboken, NJ: John Wiley & Sons, 2009): Kindle Location 1600-01.
2. Ibid.
3. www.youtube.com/watch?v=5YGc4zOqozo.
4. Joe Marchese, blog post, "10 Things Changing Marketing in 2010," Media Post: Online Spin, December 22, 2009. www.mediapost.com/publications/?fa=Articles .showArticle&art_aid=119566.
5. Charles Feltman, *The Thin Book of Trust: An Essential Primer for Building Trust at Work* (Bend, OR: Thin Book Publishing Company, 2009).
6. Callan Green, blog post, "Killer Facebook Fan Pages: 5 Inspiring Case Studies," Mashable, June 16, 2009. http://mashable.com/2009/06/16/killer-facebook-fan -pages/.
7. Toby Bloomberg, ebook. *Social Media Marketing GPS,* May 17, 2010. http:// bloombergmarketing.blogs.com/bloomberg_marketing/2010/05/a-new-media -roadmap-for-creating-a-social-media-strategy-.html.
8. Tom Peters, "The Brand Called You," *Fast Company* online, August 31, 1997. http://www.fastcompany.com/magazine/10/brandyou.html.
9. Jennifer Beese, blog post, "Humanizing Your Brand," April 22, 2010. www .borderstylo.com/posts/136-humanizing-your-brand.
10. Francis Fukuyama, *Trust: The Social Virtues and the Creation of Prosperity* (New York: Free Press, 1995), 10.
11. Ronald Baker, *Mind Over Matter* (Hoboken, NJ: John Wiley & Sons, 2008), 50.
12. Ibid., p. 121.
13. www.socialcapitalresearch.com/measurement.html.
14. Stephanie Tilton, blog post, "How Web 2.0 Impacts B2B Marketing: An Interview with C. Edward Brice of Lumension," Savvy B2B Marketing, July 20, 2009. www .savvyb2bmarketing.com/blog/entry/176401/how-web-20-impacts-b2b -marketing-an-interview-with-c-edward-brice-of-lumension.
15. www.pewinternet.org/Presentations/2010/Mar/Boomers.aspx.
16. Paul Neiffer, interview with the author, December 7, 2009.
17. Tom Pick, blog post, "11 Myths of Social Media Marketing," May 24, 2010. http://myventurepad.com/MVP/107256.

18. Toby Bloomberg, ebook. *Social Media Marketing GPS,* May 17, 2010. http://bloombergmarketing.blogs.com/bloomberg_marketing/2010/05/a-new-media-roadmap-for-creating-a-social-media-strategy-.html.
19. Ardath Albee, *eMarketing Strategies for the Complex Sale* (New York: McGraw Hill), 56.

Chapter 5: Strategy Begins with "Who"

1. David Maister, *True Professionalism* (New York: Free Press, Simon & Shuster, 1997), 23–24.
2. David Meerman Scott, *The New Rules of Marketing and PR* (Hoboken, NJ: John Wiley & Sons, 2007), 32.
3. Jordan Furlong, blog post, "Figuring out Twitter," Law21.ca blog, April 27, 2009. www.law21.ca/2009/04/27/figuring-out-twitter/.
4. Erik Qualman, *Socialnomics: How Social Media Transforms the Way We Live and Do Business* (Hoboken, NJ: John Wiley & Sons, 2009), Kindle Location 2007-8.
5. August Acquila and Bruce Marcus. *Client at the Core* (Hoboken, NJ: Wiley, 2004).

Chapter 6: Integrated Marketing Tactics

1. Toby Bloomberg, ebook. *Social Media Marketing GPS,* May 17, 2010. http://bloombergmarketing.blogs.com/bloomberg_marketing/2010/05/a-new-media-roadmap-for-creating-a-social-media-strategy-.html.
2. Russell Lawson, blog post comment, Feburary 18, 2010. http://goldenmarketing.typepad.com/weblog/2010/02/whats-the-roi-of-social-media-is-the-wrong-question.html?cid=6a00d83451dc2e69e2012877b10534970c#comment-6a00d83451dc2e69e2012877b10534970c).
3. Stephanie Tilton, blog post, "How Web 2.0 Impacts B2B Marketing: An Interview with C. Edward Brice of Lumension," Savvy B2B Marketing, July 20, 2009. www.savvyb2bmarketing.com/blog/entry/176401/how-web-20-impacts-b2b-marketing-an-interview-with-c-edward-brice-of-lumension.
4. Nate Elliott, blog post, "Why Are Marketers So Bad at Measuring Social Media? (And How Can They Get Better?)," November 2, 2009. http://blogs.forrester.com/marketing/2009/11/why-are-marketers-so-bad-at-measuring-social-media.html.
5. Chris Cree, blog post, "How to Game Twitter to Add Thousands of Followers Every Day and Why You Really Don't Want to Do It," SuccessCREEations, March 19, 2009. http://successcreeations.com/1071/how-to-game-twitter-to-add-thousands-of-followers-every-day/.
6. Erik Qualman, *Socialnomics: How Social Media Transforms the Way We Live and Do Business* (Hoboken, NJ: John Wiley & Sons, 2009): Kindle Location 1740-46.

7. Stephanie Tilton, blog post, "How Web 2.0 Impacts B2B Marketing: An Interview with C. Edward Brice of Lumension," Savvy B2B Marketing, July 20, 2009. www .savvyb2bmarketing.com/blog/entry/176401/how-web-20-impacts-b2b -marketing-an-interview-with-c-edward-brice-of-lumension.
8. Stephen Baker, blog post, "Beware Social Media Snake Oil," *Bloomberg BusinessWeek,* December 3, 2009. www.businessweek.com/magazine/content/ 09_50/b4159048693735.htm.

Chapter 7: Case Studies and Examples

1. Rob La Gotta, blog post, "English Accountants Make Their Way to the Blogosphere," June 26, 2007. http://kevin.lexblog.com/2007/06/articles/cool -stuff/english-accountants-make-their-way-to-the-blogosphere/.
2. Peter Renton, "Accounting blogs.(THE BLOGSMITH)," Entrepreneur Magazine Online, May–June 2009. www.entrepreneur.com/tradejournals/article/201105202. html.
3. Tracy Coenen, telephone interview with the author, August 2006.
4. www.whataboutclients.com/archives/2005/08/about_dan_hull_1.html.
5. Peter Lattman, "Bubba, Hull & McGuire," Wall Street Journal Law Blog, February 2, 2006. http://blogs.wsj.com/law/2006/02/02/bubba-hull-mcguire/.
6. http://www.abajournal.com/magazine/article/blawg_100_2008/.
7. http://dick-price.blogspot.com/2008/03/divorce-no-nos-dont-drag-kids-into .html.
8. Kelliann Blazek, blog post, "Ernest Svenson aka 'Ernie the Attorney': LexBlog Interviews," March 26, 2010. www.lexconference.com/2010/03/articles/aba -techshow-2010/ernest-svenson-aka-ernie-the-attorney-lexblog-interviews/.
9. Reed Tinsley, email with the author, February 2007.
10. http://goldenmarketing.typepad.com/weblog/2007/05/a_running_list_.html.
11. Rob La Gatta, blog post, "Accounting Blog Success Also Visible at Domestic Firm," June 27, 2007. http://kevin.lexblog.com/2007/06/articles/cool-stuff/ accounting-blog-success-also-visible-at-domestic-firm/.
12. Jen Lemanski, email correspondence with the author, June 2010.
13. www.ethanolproducer.com/article.jsp?article_id=6293.
14. www.onlinecollegedegrees.org/2009/07/30/100-amazingly-insightful-people -you-can-learn-from-on-twitter/.
15. Rick Telberg, blog post, "CPAs Get Serious about Twitter," CPA2Biz.com, May 26, 2009. www.cpa2biz.com/Content/media/PRODUCER_CONTENT/Newsletters/ Articles_2009/CPA/May/Twitter.jsp.
16. www.journalofaccountancy.com/Web/CPAsEmbraceTwitter.htm.
17. Ibid.
18. Kevin O'Keefe, "Twitter Client Development Success Stories—Lawyers and Legal Professionals Chime In," Real Lawyers Have Blogs, June 25, 2009. http:// kevin.lexblog.com/2009/06/articles/success-stories/twitter-client-development -success-stories-lawyers-and-legal-professionals-chime-in/.

19. Ford Richardson Bryan and Sarah Evans, *Henry's Attic: Some Fascinating Gifts to Henry Ford and His Museum* (Detroit, MI: Wayne State University Press: 1996), 372.

Chapter 8: LinkedIn

1. Michael Finer, LinkedIn Profile, www.linkedin.com/in/michaelfiner.
2. Joel Ungar, telephone interview with the author, Feburary 21, 2010.
3. Steve Strauss, blog post, "Ten Terrific LinkedIn Tricks to Grow Your Business!" April 19, 2010. www.openforum.com/idea-hub/topics/managing/article/ten -terrific-linkedin-tricks-to-grow-your-business-steve-strauss.
4. Gale Crosley, conversation with the author, March 2, 2010.

Chapter 10: Facebook

1. The Kbuzz, blog post, "The Top 40 Facebook Pages as Voted by the Kbuzz," June 22, 2009. www.thekbuzz.com/casestudies/top40.aspx.
2. www.jdsupra.com.
3. Jenna Lebel, blog post, "Facebook's News Feed: What Makes the Cut," Buzz Marketing Daily, April 30, 2010. http://blog.thekbuzz.com/2010/04/facebook's -news-feed-what-makes-the-cut.html.
4. See note 1.
5. "Baby Boomers Get Connected with Social Media," eMarketer, January 28, 2010. www.emarketer.com/Article.aspx?R=1007484.
6. Paul Dunay, blog post, "Generating a Buyer Persona with Facebook Advertising," Buzz Marketing for Technology, March 30, 2010. http://pauldunay.com/ generating-a-buyer-persona-with-facebook-advertising/.

Chapter 11: Self-Publishing with Blogs

1. Brian Halligan, *Inbound Marketing: Get Found Using Google, Social Media and Blogs* (Hoboken, NJ: Wiley, 2010), Kindle Location764-65.
2. Robert Scoble, blog post, "The Corporate Weblog Manifesto," Scobleizer, February 26, 2003. http://radio-weblogs.com/0001011/2003/02/26.html.
3. Joe Pulizzi, Facebook conversation with the author, March 3, 2010.
4. Steven Covey, *The 8th Habit* (New York: Simon & Schuster, 2004), 32.
5. Paul Neiffer, interview with the author, December 7, 2009.
6. www.newyorkpersonalinjuryattorneyblog.com/2009/11/martindale- hubbell-now-sending-comment-spam-how-does-that-rate-updated.html ?showComment=1259674896146.
7. Bill Kennedy, email with author, June 3, 2010.
8. Erik Qualman, *Socialnomics: How Social Media Transforms the Way We Live and Do Business* (Hoboken, NJ: John Wiley & Sons, 2009), Kindle Location 2240-41.

Chapter 12: Writing for the Web

1. David Meerman Scott, Web Ink Now blog, "How Well Do You Know Your Buyer Personas?," March 23, 2010. www.webinknow.com/2008/07/how-well-do-you.html.
2. Ardath Albee, *eMarketing Strategies for the Complex Sale* (New York: McGraw Hill), 53.
3. www.dhcommunications.com/2009/04/pruning-deadwood-from-your-copy/.
4. Newt Barrett and Joe Pulizzi, *Get Content Get Customers* (New York: McGraw Hill, 2009), 38–39.
5. David Meerman Scott, ebook, "The New Rules of Viral Marketing: How word-of-mouse spreads your ideas for free" (2008), 13. www.davidmeermanscott.com/documents/Viral_Marketing.pdf.
6. www.google.com/support/webmasters/bin/answer.py?hl=en&answer=70897.
7. www.edelman.com/trust/2010/.
8. Paul Dunay, blog post, "Using Content to Build Trust in B2B Marketing," April 1, 2010. http://pauldunay.com/using-content-to-build-trust-in-b2b-marketing/.

Chapter 13: Social Media Etiquette

1. Jordan Furlong, "Twitter for Law Firms," Stem Law Firm Web Strategy blog, April 6, 2010. www.stemlegal.com/strategyblog/2010/twitter-for-law-firms/.
2. Ardath Albee, *eMarketing Strategies for the Complex Sale* (New York: McGraw Hill), 60.

Chapter 14: Best Practices

1. Jeremiah Owyang, Web Strategy blog, March 22, 2010. www.web-strategist.com/blog/2010/03/22/prepare-your-company-now-for-social-attacks/.
2. Rick Burnes, presentation on SlideShare, "Social Media Monitoring in 10 Minutes a Day," March 2010. www.hubspot.com/archive/monitor-social-media-presence-daily.
3. http://davidmaister.com/blog/603/Suspension-of-Blog.
4. Toby Bloomberg, ebook. *Social Media Marketing GPS,* May 17, 2010. http://bloombergmarketing.blogs.com/bloomberg_marketing/2010/05/a-new-media-roadmap-for-creating-a-social-media-strategy-.html.
5. Debra Helwig, blog post, "Out of Sight, Out of Mind," January 13, 2010. http://debrahelwig.wordpress.com/2010/01/13/out-of-sight-out-of-mind/.

Glossary

1. Ronald Baker, *Mind Over Matter* (Hoboken, NJ: John Wiley & Sons, 2008), 104.

Glossary

@

The symbol that precedes a user's Twitter "handle" for instant linking within Twitter to the other user's profile, and which alerts the user that he or she has been mentioned in a Twitter message or reply. It is also increasingly used outside of Twitter, such as in blog or Facebook comments, preceding someone's name when responding to a comment he or she made (e.g., "@ tim, yes that was funny").

Algorithms

Complex programming to weigh values.

Anchor text

The actual text comprising a hyperlink (e.g., "See Bill's article on …" where the words "Bill's article" are clickable to visit the article itself).

Autofill, autocomplete

Text that is suggested to a user as he or she begins typing letters into a form field, and can be selected to automatically complete the text being entered.

Back-end

A web or blog author's behind-the-scenes interface with the software platform that houses and manages the content.

Bio

A professional biography or curriculum vitae.

Block

To prohibit a social media site user from seeing or interacting with all or part of your profile.

Blog
Common name and abbreviated term for "web log," a type of Web site invented in the early 1990s consisting of time-stamped entries and search-engine-friendly programming. "Blog" refers to the whole site (all pages together, comparable to "Web site"). Blogs contain short articles (called "posts"), each housed on a separate URL, that can be commented on by readers.

Blogging
The act of writing and publishing posts for a blog.

Blogroll
On a blog, the list of links to other relevant blogs that a reader would find of interest.

Bot, bots
Automated programs that "crawl" the Internet to index Web page content.

Chat
See IM or Instant messaging.

Comments
Reader participation in social media, allows for wide-open and robust debates on blogs.

Connection
The people associated with your LinkedIn account.

Content
Written text or other material (videos, podcasts, illustrations) that, done well, convey qualifications and credibility through demonstrating knowledge and critical thinking skills.

Content, dynamic
Content that changes or is added to on a frequent basis.

Content, static
Content that is rarely, if ever, changed or added to.

Content management system
Software that facilitates the addition and editing of Web-based content.

Conversion
The movement of a person or company from a status of prospect to buyer.

DM
Direct message; in Twitter, a private messaging capability between individual users.

Domain mapping
When you designate a hosted blog account to refer to all blog content within your owned Web domain (that you or your business owns the rights to) versus referring to it on the domain of the hosted platform (e.g., www.yourblog.yourdomain.com/blogpost instead of www.yourblog .othercompanyhostingyourblog.com/blogpost).

Facebook
A social networking platform initially established by a Harvard student for students and opened to the public in 2006.

Fans
People who "like" or follow your company Facebook page.

Favorite
To mark or designate (by clicking a button) content such as a "tweet," a post in social media, or messages in Gmail, so it can be easily found again or noted by others.

Feed
See RSS.

Flame war, flaming
Web-based interaction rife with insults and hostility—often provocative.

Follower, following
A social media user who "follows" or subscribes to your Twitter, blog, or other social media account to receive your updates. Also called "friend," "fan," or someone who "likes" your company in Facebook.

Friend request
When a user (usually in Facebook) initiates a connection with another user.

Friend suggestion
When a user (usually in Facebook) suggests that you connect to a third person.

Geotagging
Inclusion of location-based metadata (usually GPS coordinates) to users and their postings, photographs, and other content in order to document, reference, and search for location-specific information and Web users.

Hashtag (#)
A user-generated "tag," often an acronym, always preceded by # (hash mark) to designate a themed discussion so it is easier to follow by clicking the hashtag or searching the hashtag either within Twitter or in a third-party site such as hashtags.org.

IM
Instant messaging; real-time, text-based communication by computer or smartphone between two or more people using freestanding software (e.g., Skype) or certain social media platforms (e.g., Facebook, Google Buzz) with built-in chat or IM features.

Interface
Means of interacting with the Web.

IC
Intellectual capital; defined as "knowledge that can be converted into profits" in 1995 at the Intellectual Capital Management Gathering Best Practices conference according to Ron Baker[1]. Also according to Ron, there are three types of IC: human capital, structural capital, and social capital.

Integrated marketing
Incorporation of multiple marketing channels—or communication vehicles—online or offline (e.g., print, direct mail, telephone, podcast, blog) within a marketing campaign.

Initiative
One or more elements in a strategy (course of action) to achieve a specific objective.

ISP
Internet service provider; the service through which Internet is received.

Jargon
Terminology specific to a given culture or field.

Keywords, key phrases
The criteria that people enter into search engines to find relevant Web sites referenced in search engine results.

Like
To click, almost as a brief comment in Facebook, to show appreciation, support, or recognition for someone's posting. Alternately, a user can "Like"

a company, which replaced Facebook's previous "Fan" feature; this means the user will receive updates from the company in his or her news feed.

LinkedIn
A user profile–based database that houses users' professional background information, their contacts, and their affiliated groups and associations.

Link shorteners
Services that convert long URLs or Web site addresses to much shorter Web site addresses. These are valuable for social media users because of character limitations in postings, and because link-shortening services often include a feature that counts click-throughs and can indicate others who share the link.

Live-tweet
Posting to Twitter in real time from an event, usually with a hashtag in each post for cross-reference with others live-tweeting at the event.

Lurk, lurking
To observe in a Web community without participating. As defined at http://bit.ly/definelurk: "Lurking is the very common practice of reading an online or email discussion without taking part in the discussion. ... What this term seems to imply in its usage is that some people benefit a great deal from a discussion without ever offering to enrich it with their own information or ideas. It is well understood and accepted, however, that there will always be lurkers in any discussion. And people who are new to a discussion are sometimes advised to lurk until they become familiar with the discussion."

Meme
A concept that spreads rapidly across the Internet (e.g., everyone posting a list about "x").

Mentions
References made about a company or person online.

Messaging
The intentional or unintentional perceptions created by a company or person through actions and words.

NAICS
North American Industry Classification System; a system of labeling and classifying companies by industry created in 1997 by the U.S., Canadian,

and Mexican governments to replace the Standard Industrial Classification (SIC) code system.

NFO
News feed optimization; a term created by the developers of Facebook to describe company page users' acts or behaviors that improve the chances of the company page activity showing up in its followers' news feeds.

Organic search
Search engine results attained through nonpaid means—usually accomplished through content containing terms known to be of interest to desired readers.

Phishing
Schemes executed through tricking Web users to share their login credentials so their accounts can be taken over and used by the hacker for malicious purposes.

Ping
To notify a Web site or a user of something, often of new content or information. An RSS feed reader is notified (aka "pinged") whenever an author posts something to a subscribed site. Some people refer to the sending of an email or text message as a "ping."

Platform
The hardware and software framework on which a computer application is run.

Plug-in
Software that enhances another application or program by increasing or customizing its functionality, usually created by third-party developers.

Podcast
A Web-based audio recording in a format that can be distributed or subscribed to by RSS feed.

Post
To submit content to the Web. In a blog, each individual single entry is called a "post" (comparable to a single "Web page").

Professionals
Lawyers, accountants, wealth managers, consultants, and others whose "services" consist largely of the delivery of their knowledge or intellectual capital.

Profile
The user-controlled informational page or listing within a Web site or social media application.

Referring site
The source of inbound Web traffic, could be a search engine or any other Web site, bookmarking site, or social media mention with a link.

Retweet
Reposting a tweet posted by another, giving credit to the original author (e.g., "RT @michellegolden [text here]") and posting the message verbatim or shortening it as necessary for space without changing the context.

RIA
Registered investment advisor; an individual who is registered with the U.S. Securities and Exchange Commission to manage others' investments.

ROI
Return on investment; a ratio, usually shown as a percentage, reflecting money gained on something relative to the money invested in it over a defined period of time.

RSS, RSS feed
Really Simple Syndication; the technology through which Web-published content (blogs, video, audio, etc.) is delivered to sites or "feed readers" (also called "aggregators") programmed to display the content "feeds." Web users may subscribe to RSS content to be informed whenever Web content is added to the subscribed sites.

RT
Retweet; Twitter term indicating that the text following "RT" is originated by whoever is named after the @.

SEO
Search engine optimization; the act of consciously writing and designing to be found online. Involves the strategic use and placement of keywords and phrases to improve the volume of traffic delivered to your site or blog from searches.

Sharepoint
A Microsoft product that supports online collaboration and Web publishing.

SIC
Standard Industry Classification; a system to code and label industries, created in 1937 by the U.S. government. It was replaced in 1997 by the North American Industry Classification System (NAICS).

Site
Location on the Web, reached through its address, or URL.

SM
Social media; a continually changing set of tools (and their users) that facilitate online relationships and information sharing; social media tools are built on a foundation of openness, authenticity, sharing, and spontaneity.

Spam, spammy, to spam
Unsolicited or inappropriate means of promoting yourself or your services online.

Static FBML
Facebook Markup Language; an application made to create customized elements on your Facebook company page.

Sticky
A Web page that holds readers' attention.

Strategy
A course of action, including the specification of resources required through one or more initiatives involving tactical steps using specific resources (such as social media tools), to achieve a specific objective.

Stream
Flow of data, typically aggregated from other sources or users.

Subscribe
The act of initiating an RSS feed to flow into the user's preferred destination, which could be a Web page, feed aggregator, e-reader (e.g., Kindle), or email. Most feeds are free, but some require paid subscriptions.

Tactics
The use of a specific tool or step within a marketing initiative comprises a tactical approach.

Tag, tags, tagging
Keywords used online to categorize content. In social media, users can tag content in accordance with their perception of relevance, so tags can be quite diverse. Tagging is also a tool that is used to link a photo or a posting with a particular user in Facebook or other applications.

Timeline
The main page view in Twitter in which posts are displayed chronologically. Each user has his or her own timeline, and then there is a main real-time view of postings made by the people one follows.

Tools
The social media tools that are featured in this book: LinkedIn, Twitter, Facebook, and blogs.

TrackBack
A method for one blog post to link to another blog post by automatically placing a link to, and an excerpt of, the second blog post at the end of the original blog post it references.

Trojan
A computer program (code) that people download believing it is harmless when in fact it contains malicious code that can harm a computer, a system, or its data.

Tweeps
People who use Twitter (tweet + peeps).

Tweet
Tweet (n.) is a post or message sent on Twitter, and tweet (v.) is the act of posting to Twitter.

Tweet-chat
Online gatherings of Twitter users to discuss an agreed-upon topic using a specified hashtag (e.g., #blogchat) to group tweets into an easy-to-find streaming conversation.

Tweetup
In-person gatherings of Twitter users.

Twitter
A forum that consists of a running thread of 140-character or less postings called "tweets." Users "follow" people of their choice and are followed by others interested in their posts.

Unfollow
To discontinue following someone in social media. Sometimes referred to as "unfriending" someone.

URL
A unique Web address.

URL shorteners
See Link shortener.

Vanity URL
A personalized or customized Web address for a specific page.

Videocast
Recorded video presentation posted to the Web to be viewed by others during or after its original play.

Virtual
Electronic, rather than physical, interaction.

Virus
A computer program (code), usually a malicious one, that infect a computer and copies itself to perpetuate the infection of more computers.

Wall
In Facebook, it's the location where you and friends post content that includes various personal messages, status updates, notifications related to activities, and photos. *Also see* Timeline.

Widget
Portable computer code that is pasted onto a Web site to perform a function without any additional programming. Functions include referring to another Web or social media site such as with a dynamic graphic (aka "badge") that includes a count or other changing information, or the display of information through RSS feeds or through simple queries.

Webinar
Seminar presented and "attended" online.

WordPress
A free blog software product with open source code.

About the Author

Social media enables professionals to illustrate their capabilities in ways never before possible, and beyond what we imagined even ten years ago. In public speeches and private groups, when professionals hear even part of what's included in this book, they are intrigued and inspired—and they say they wish they had known about this sooner. I don't profess to be a social media "guru"—in fact, I shudder when I hear that term. But I'm told that few have the passion for this topic that I do. And they say that the explanations and practical approaches I offer help bring clarity to them on the sometimes daunting and controversial subject of social media as I illustrate how these media are appropriate in the practices of accountants, lawyers, and other professional advisors.

I wrote this book because I want more professionals than I can possibly ever talk with personally to understand what new opportunities are theirs for the taking.

My career role is that of practice management advisor and marketing strategist. In growing my own practice, I stumbled into blogging in 2005 and quickly realized that it held the potential to be a holy grail among marketing tools for professional firms. In my quest to communicate this potential among the professions I love, I've been able to inspire or assist at least a third of today's accounting bloggers, and many legal bloggers, to get started: some with amazing success for them. Because it can lead to such dramatic results, I want to see much more growth in professionals' online presences. Now I get an increasing number of questions about the business application and effective use of other tools that are growing in popular use, such as LinkedIn, Twitter, and Facebook. That's how I came into the topic for this book. In fact, John Wiley & Sons contacted me out of the blue about writing the book having found me through—you guessed it—my blog.

I hope you enjoyed the book as much as I enjoyed creating it.

Professional Biography

Michelle Golden is a seasoned advisor to professional service firms with unique perspective, unmatched passion, and a frank demeanor. She has worked in-house both in public accounting and law firms. In her consulting, she applies her deep knowledge of firm operations and her excellent observation skills.

On the forefront of innovative practice management strategies, she is a senior fellow of VeraSage Institute (www.verasage.com), the think tank for advancing the professions. For her thought leadership, particularly in social media, she's listed as one of ten "Most Powerful Women in Accounting" in *Accounting Today* (Oct 19–Nov 1, 2009 Issue) and is named among the "Top 100 Most Influential People in Accounting" in *Accounting Today* in September, 2010.

She's been a longtime respected participant in the legal blog community and is the catalyst behind blogging in the accounting profession. Of the first 20 CPA blogs, she built or trained the authors of 12. Of the 180+ current CPA blogs, she consulted on or influenced at least one-third of them. She won a Marketing Achievement Award from the Association for Accounting Marketing (AAM) in 2007 for results generated with the very first multiauthor CPA firm blog.

Providing practice management counsel, Michelle leads strategic planning processes and marketing (firm, niche, and individual) planning, conducts and delivers 360-degree evaluations, facilitates problem solving, and recommends organizational improvements. Michelle is a skilled facilitator of meetings and retreats and holds the International Association of Facilitators Certified Professional Facilitator (CPF) designation.

Since 1999, she's helped more than 100 firms achieve results such as doubling revenue, attracting top talent, aligning operations with long-term objectives, creating an effective online presence, substantially increasing sales and proposal results, strategizing new product development and launch, and strengthening firms' relationships with their clients.

She is a frequent speaker and is published regularly in publications including *Accounting Today, AccountingWEB, BlawgWorld, CPA Practice Management Forum, CCH Journal of Tax Practice Management, Fortune's Business Innovation Blog, Inside Public Accounting, Journal of Accountancy, Law.com, Lawyer Marketing, Managing Partner, MarkeTrends, National Law Journal, Practical Accountant, WebCPA,* and various local *AmCity Business Journals.*

In 2010, she developed a Social Media Toolkit commissioned by the AICPA for members of its Private Companies Practice Section, and created Pocket Guides to various social media for the AICPA. She authored, "Guide to an Effective CPA Firm Website," a chapter of *Bull's Eye! The Ultimate*

How-To Marketing & Sales Guide, published by the American Institute of Certified Public Accountants (2010).

Michelle, a long-time member of AAM, founded its Member Discussion List in 1998, served multiple terms on its board, and was honored as 2001 AAM Volunteer of the Year. She is also a sustaining member of International Association of Facilitators (IAF) and served the organization as its U.S. Regional Representative and a member of its global board of directors.

Contact Michelle by email at michelle@goldenpractices.com, or find her on Twitter (@michellegolden), Facebook (www.facebook.com/ GoldenPractices) and LinkedIn (www.linkedin.com/in/michellegolden).

Index